MW01204780

DEVOTIONS
★ *for* ★
WARRIORS

DEVOTIONS
★ *for* ★
WARRIORS

A Christian Perspective of the Civil War

Mike Fisher and Joe Jared

TATE PUBLISHING *& Enterprises*

Devotions for Warriors
Copyright © 2009 by Mike Fisher and Joe Jared. All rights reserved.

No part of this publication may be reproduced, stored in a retrieval system or transmitted in any way by any means, electronic, mechanical, photocopy, recording or otherwise without the prior permission of the author except as provided by USA copyright law.

All scripture quotations are taken from the *Holy Bible, King James Version*, Cambridge, 1769. Used by permission. All rights reserved.

This book is designed to provide accurate and authoritative information with regard to the subject matter covered. This information is given with the understanding that neither the author nor Tate Publishing, LLC is engaged in rendering legal, professional advice. Since the details of your situation are fact dependent, you should additionally seek the services of a competent professional.

The opinions expressed by the author are not necessarily those of Tate Publishing, LLC.

Published by Tate Publishing & Enterprises, LLC
127 E. Trade Center Terrace | Mustang, Oklahoma 73064 USA
1.888.361.9473 | www.tatepublishing.com

Tate Publishing is committed to excellence in the publishing industry. The company reflects the philosophy established by the founders, based on Psalm 68:11,
"The Lord gave the word and great was the company of those who published it."

Book design copyright © 2008 by Tate Publishing, LLC. All rights reserved.
Cover design by Janae J. Glass
Interior design by Amber Gulilat

Published in the United States of America

ISBN: 978-1-60604-900-6
1. Religion: Christian Life: Devotional
09.01.28

*These devotions are dedicated to
America's brave military people and
veterans whose sacrifice has kept us free.*

Photographs of Civil War sites are by Mrs. Mike Fisher.

FOREWARD

BY J. V. D. HOUGH, M.D.

The American Civil War was the turning point in world history. God shook the world. This was an earthquake that caused man's freedom and independence to break open into the mind of man. The purpose and significance of each individual person would be indelibly printed on the minds and hearts of humanity since that time. It opened the door to see the value and independence of every human being individually, and yet it compelled man to unify for mutual safety, security, and respect. Perhaps in no better way can the tremendous change in world history be presented than to see the scenes from the lives of the men who were dirctly involved as they came to God in deepest devotion. They did indeed change the world politically, socially, and spiritually. This was the effect on the world, but its effect can be no less on you as your read these devotions and meet these godly men celebrating this reconciling and redemptive love. This book has tremendous appeal to me because of the incredible number of special occasions and notable people on every page and the view into their thoughts and actions as they faced death and destruction of all they loved and would die for.

I have known the two authors, Mike Fisher and Joe Jared, for over twenty-five years. I have seen them live their lives exemplifying the heart of a Christian warrior. Both are experts in the history of the Civil War and are collectors of artifacts and historical evidence from that great war. Academically and personally they know this story and sense the whispers of these great warriors that tell us the amazing intercession of God in their minds and hearts at this important time in history. Mike and Joe understand and reflect this intercession as they walk with Him daily and have written this book for our benefit. Because of them, I have seen the power of God's Spirit work victory after victory in the church, in the community, and with their families. I believe God has blessed us in their very unusual knowledge for the Civil War and their talents to express it. It is incredible that they were inspired to accumulate these three hundred sixty-five stories from the lives of these great warriors of the Civil War. In them you will gain wonderful devotional thoughts for your pleasure during your devotional times.

The authors have defined the amazing result of not only devotions to God but also of men giving a time for instinctive fellowship with God. The time of devotion is God's gift to man, a gift of divine intimacy. During times of war, extreme danger, the loss of physical comforts, and enemy destruction of life and its future, the body cries for supernatural protection. In devotions, our deepest instinct cries for God's holy presence. My own personal experience with this instinctive and compelling need for the realization of God's presence during war was during the Battle of Iwo Jima. His love and protection was a reality for me during that time, and I joined the Civil War veterans in the same wonderful Presence during a terrible time.

What we learn from war can be of lasting benefit. War is man's greatest sin, his greatest failure. It is insane! In mankind's attempt to find what he perceives to be a better life, he attempts to control evil by causing death! War is the result of the depravity of the mind of man producing a depraved society deliberately creating death in an attempt to find good. Oftentimes during its events, men are drawn to peace in heart and soul as the warriors find the Prince of Peace. Mingled with destruction is God's interaction into the minds of men.

Today, over one hundred years later, we find God's continual blessing of truth and light. Mike and Joe capture the scenes from these great moments in the lives of individual warriors. This becomes our heritage, and we join with thanks not only for the world order in which we live, but the gift of intimacy with Him.

The eternal gift of devotion and presence with God is priceless. Finally, the Eternal Safety conquers death and His love brings joy, peace, and eternal security. The redeemed demonstrate their declaration "that nothing can separate us from the love of God." During the Civil War the hearts of thousands of men on both sides had, during their time of devotion, pledged their love and allegiance to God and His Kingdom. Emerging from the carnage of that war was the divine victory as the thousands of warriors on both sides took time for devotions with God during which love and peace prevailed. This spiritual power fueled a new unity of government and peace among men and a compassion for the world as a new United States of America was reborn.

INTRODUCTION

There is a parallel between shooting wars and the spiritual conflicts of the Christian walk. II Corinthians 10:45 tells us, "For the weapons of our warfare are not carnal, but mighty through God to the pulling down of strongholds; casting down imaginations, and every high thing that exalteth itself against the knowledge of God, and bringing into captivity every thought to the obedience of Christ." (We used the King James translation of the Bible, since this is the version used by the soldiers in the War Between the States.) God uses the metaphor of war to characterize the Christian life. The victories, defeats, wounds, and healing of the spiritual conflict are usually less visible, but they are no less real.

Each of the following daily devotions consists in an anecdote about something that happened in the Civil War, a pertinent Bible verse, an application or insight, and a prayer. In both war and in spiritual life there is peril and adventure. It is helpful to see how those who went before us dealt with each. No one is exempt from this war. The authors hope that these devotions will encourage Christians in their pilgrimage and those who have not had the great privilege of being in a personal relationship with God to find Him.

This book should not be used in lieu of searching the Scriptures. God speaks through the Bible, and all the issues of life are addressed in it. The fear of the Lord is, as the Bible says, the beginning of wisdom. We hope that these devotions will augment (not replace) a daily time in God's Word.

To see flesh and blood men like Robert E. Lee, Stonewall Jackson, and Jeb Stuart live out their lives in the tumult of battle, in victory and defeat, is a strong encouragement toward duty and honor. We want to thank the men and women now in military service as well as the veterans for their sacrifice of time and sometimes of health and life. We salute you and pray that these words will strengthen you.

The authors are both Christians, veterans, and sons of the South. It is necessary, therefore, to say a few words about the twin issues of slavery and racism. The Scripture says that God "hath made of one blood all nations of men for to dwell on all the face of the earth ..." (Acts 17:26) No one can please the God who made of one blood all the nations and view himself as superior to someone of a different race. We do not defend slavery or racism. We do, however, seek a balanced view of history. The primary causes of the War Between the States were economic. Lincoln's Emancipation Proclamation did not come about until 1863, and the war began in 1861. The Emancipation Proclamation applied only to slaves in the southern states and not to those in Union states or in areas captured by the Union.

Of course, arguments about these things are legion. Slavery was undeniably a blot on the South. The North had its own sins. Abortion is a blot on the America of this present time. We do not approve of this evil practice, but we do not stop being Americans because of what some people do. The books listed in the bibliography, especially the history by Shelby Foote, can help in the process of finding the truth after passing through the minefields of historical revisionism.

JANUARY 1

On this day in 1863 Abraham Lincoln issued the Emancipation Proclamation freeing all slaves in the Confederate States or "in those states presently in rebellion against the United States." This did not apply to the border states of Kentucky, Missouri, and Maryland or the states loyal to the union.

There is a more terrible form of slavery than that which man can impose on man. It is slavery to sin. A greater Person than Abraham Lincoln brought about a greater emancipation. Jesus Christ bought us at the slave market of sin with His own blood and made us free.

"You shall know the truth, and the truth shall set you free" (John 8:32 KJV).

> Thank you, Father, that you have set free all people who have put their faith in Christ.

JANUARY 2

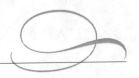

Benjamin Hollowell, an instructor of Robert E. Lee prior to his entrance to West Point, had this to say of young Lee: "He was a most exemplary pupil in every respect. He was never behind time at his studies; never failed in a single recitation; was perfectly observant of the rules and regulations of the institution; was gentlemanly, unobtrusive, and respectful in all his deportment to teacher and his fellow students. His specialty was finishing up. He imparted a finish and a neatness as he proceeded, to everything he undertook."

The Master teaches us that one who is not honest and diligent in carrying out small duties will not do well with great ones.

"Study to show thyself approved unto God, a workman that needeth not to be ashamed, rightly dividing the word of truth" (II Timothy 2:15 KJV).

> Father, help me to realize that no matter how
> much I think I know, there is much more to learn
> and even more to do. Help me, above all, to finish
> up well.

January 3

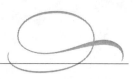

After the War for Southern Independence ended, Robert E. Lee was offered many positions of employment that would have been very lucrative. Instead he chose to be president of Washington College in Lexington, Virginia though his salary was very small. Through his leadership, little Washington College would become Washington and Lee University, one of the most distinguished centers of learning in the United States.

"I was thinking of my responsibility to Almighty God for these hundreds of young men. I shall be disappointed sir. I shall fail in the leading object that brought me here, unless these young men become real Christians. I dread the thought of any student going away from college without becoming a real Christian," said Lee. (Spoken to Dr. William White in 1865.)

A military man recognizes that a command given by a superior is not a trifle; it is a life and death matter. Our Commander in Chief has issued this command: "And Jesus came and spake to them, saying, All power is given unto me in heaven and earth. Go ye therefore, and teach all nations, baptizing them in the name of the Father, and of the Son, and of the Holy Ghost" (Matthew 28:19,20 KJV).

> Father, help us to be faithful and obedient disciples and loyal disciplemakers.

JANUARY 4

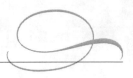

After the War Between the States ended, Robert E. Lee was offered many well-paying jobs, some for just using his name. One provided a home in New York City and a salary of $50,000, an enormous figure at that time. He refused saying, "I am grateful, but I have a self-imposed task which I must accomplish. I have led the young men of the South in battle. I have seen many of them die in the field; I shall devote my remaining energies to training young men to do their duty in life."

A true shepherd sacrifices personal comforts for duty—the welfare of his flock. This is what the Good Shepherd said: "Feed My lambs!...Take care of My sheep!...Feed My lambs!" (John 20:15b, 16b, 17b KJV).

> Father, help us to be shepherds, devoted to the
> Master Shepherd and the sheep He has given us.

JANUARY 5

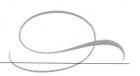

After the War Between the States was concluded, Robert E. Lee was indicted for treason and rebellion. He was never brought to trial because of the effect it would have on the South to rise up again in his defense. A pastor friend of Lee expressed great indignation over this action by the Federal Government when the indictments first surfaced. This was General Lee's response to him: "I have fought against the people of the North because I believed they were seeking to wrest from the South dearest rights. But I have never cherished toward them bitter or vindictive feelings and have never seen the day when I did not pray for them."

What moved General Lee to have a charitable heart, contrary to all natural inclinations, toward those who had invaded his homeland and caused devastation?

"But I say unto you, 'Love your enemies, bless them that curse you, do good to them that hate you, and pray for them which despitefully use you'" (Matthew 5:44 KJV).

> Father, do I have enemies? Are there those who mean to retaliate for harm I have done to them? I pray that may never be the case. And help me to forgive those who have offended me just as God in Christ forgave me.

JANUARY 6

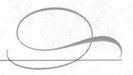

After a long council of war prior to a major battle, the officers under General Stonewall Jackson left to prepare their troops for the upcoming battle. General Richard Ewell, long a skeptic of the Christian faith, returned to Jackson's tent to retrieve something he had left behind. There he saw Jackson on his knees by his cot in fervent prayer. Ewell was so moved that he said, "If that is religion, I must have it." He soon put his faith and trust in Christ as his savior and Lord.

General Jackson did not compartmentalize his faith; instead, it permeated every domain of his life, public and private. He was the same man alone in his tent as he was in front of thousands of men. This is integrity.

"Let your light shine before men in such a way that they may see your good works and glorify your Father who is in heaven" (Matthew 5:16 KJV).

> Father, never let Your light shining through me grow dim. Instead may it shine ever brighter to show people the way to Jesus, just as the star guided the wise men to that stable long ago.

JANUARY 7

One day in 1875 in Memphis Tennessee, two men knelt in prayer in a parlor of a bank. One was Reverend Raleigh White, a minister of the Gospel. The other was Nathan Bedford Forrest, former trader of slaves, one of the originators of the Ku Klux Klan. But Forrest is better known as one of the greatest and most brilliant generals in the army of the Confederate States of America. Courageous in battle, he killed thirty-one Federal combatants in single combat. He was severely wounded four times and had thirty horses shot out from under him. Time after time he routed Federal forces much greater in number than his own. He was known as the "Wizard of the Saddle." Also known for his profanity and toughness, he gave his heart to Christ that day, receiving God's forgiveness and salvation.

No one is wicked enough to be beyond God's salvation; no one is great enough to deserve it.

"And if so be that he find it, verily I say unto you, he rejoiceth more of that sheep than of the ninety and nine which went not astray" (Matthew 18:13 KJV).

> Father, thank You that Jesus came to seek and save those who were lost—people of the past, of this present time, and of the future.

JANUARY 8

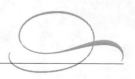

Section III of General Order No. 15, dated 7 February 1864, Army of Northern Virginia, Robert E. Lee Commanding: "Commanding officers will require the usual inspections on Sunday to be held at such time as not to interfere with the attendance of the men on divine service at the customary hour in the morning. They will also give attention to the maintenance of order and quiet around the place of worship and prohibit anything that may tend to disturb or interrupt religious services."

The true worship of the Maker of heaven and earth is no trifle, no casual event. It is to be addressed with reverence and awe.

"And let us consider one another; to provoke unto love and good works, not forsaking the assembling of ourselves as is the manner of some, but exhorting one another, and so much the more as you see the day approaching" (Hebrews 10:24,25 KJV).

> Father, thank You for the church of Jesus Christ and
> the freedom to worship Him in spirit and truth.

January 9

"I have never on the field of battle sent you where I was unwilling to go myself, nor would I now advise you to a course which I felt myself unwilling to pursue. You have been good soldiers, you can be good citizens. Obey the laws, preserve your honor, and the government to which you have surrendered can afford to be and will be magnanimous." (From General Nathan Bedford Forrest's farewell message to the Confederate troops under his command after their surrender to Federal forces, May 9, 1865)

"And He said to them, 'Render therefore unto Caesar the things which be Caesar's, and unto God the things which be God's" (Matthew 22:21 KJV).

An informed believer recognizes the obligation to be submissive to the government, knowing the sovereignty of God in the lives of individuals and nations. He applies God's precepts to every aspect of life in this world.

> Father, I realize that as a Christian I must be the very best citizen I can be. Help me to obey the laws, understand the times and events which You are bringing about, and pray for those in leadership positions.

JANUARY 10

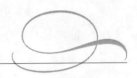

On May 10, 1863, General Stonewall Jackson lay on his deathbed after being wounded by friendly fire when he and his escort were mistaken for Union cavalry by the 18th North Carolina Regiment. These were his last words: "Let us cross over the river and rest under the shade of the trees."

"To every man upon this earth death cometh soon or late." Whether late or soon, we hope to live a significant life and leave behind a true legacy.

"For I am ready to be offered,

"Let us cross over the river and rest under the shade of the trees."

and the time of my departure is at hand. I have fought the good fight, I have finished my course, I have kept the faith" (II Timothy 4:6-7 KJV).

> Father, help me to live each day that I might have a conscience void of offense toward You and others so that when it is my time to "cross over the river," there will be no regrets.

JANUARY 11

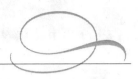

"It is your duty and mine to lay down our arms, submit to the 'powers that be,' and to aid in restoring peace and establishing law and order throughout the land." (Taken from General Nathan Bedford Forrest's farewell message to the Confederate troops under his command on May 9, 1865. This was the last Confederate army east of the Mississippi River to surrender).

The bitter pill of temporal defeat can be swallowed if one has hope of eternal victory in Jesus Christ.

"Blessed are the peacemakers: for they shall be called the children of God" (Matthew 5:9 KJV).

> Father, in a fallen world full of conflict, help me
> to be one who reconciles, a faithful peacemaker.

JANUARY 12

"Surrender means that the history of this heroic struggle will be written by the enemy; that our youth will be trained by Northern school teachers; will learn from Northern school books their version of the war; will be impressed by all the influences of history and education to regard our gallant dead as traitors and our maimed veterans as fit subjects for derision," said Confederate General Patrick Cleburne (killed at the battle of Franklin, Tennessee, 1864).

The only perfectly true and impartial history of nations will be that kept in the books of Heaven.

"And thou shalt teach them diligently unto thy children, and shalt talk of them when thou sittest in thy house, and when thou walkest by the way, and when thou liest down, and when thou risest up" (Deuteronomy 6:7 KJV).

> Father, help me to pass on with a sense of urgency the pure truth of Your Gospel. Let me not be deceived by revisions of history. Also help me not to be a party to revising history, but to teach others the truth of His Story (of what Christ is doing in His gracious interventions in human events) so that they may learn and that Christ may be glorified.

JANUARY 13

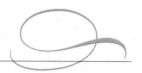

On September 17, 1862, at the Battle of Sharpsburg, Maryland, there were more American casualties in one day in a single battle than in any other in our nation's history—twenty-three thousand.

What if the person I was so bitter about suddenly dropped dead? Would my conscience be at rest? Or would I have huge regret that I had not tried to bury the hatchet?

"And all the country wept with a loud voice" (II Samuel 15:23a KJV).

> Father, what a terrible day that must have been with so much bloodshed and carnage brother killing brother, friend slaying friend. And at the end of the day the battle was considered a "draw." What a waste! Help me to see the true value of every human being that I may be a reconciler and not a sower of discord.

JANUARY 14

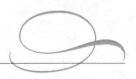

As he fell mortally wounded while trying to rally his men against Union forces that were breaking his lines, General Bernard Bee of

Where Jackson stood as a stone wall at I Manassas, Virginia, 1861.

South Carolina commanded his men, "Look, men, there stands Jackson like a stone wall. Rally behind the Virginians!" Jackson's stand and attack began the victory that won the battle of First Manassas, Virginia, the first large scale battle of the War on July 21, 1861.

The believer's struggle requires physical courage occasionally; more often it calls for moral courage to swim against the tide of this dying world's values and culture.

"Therefore, my beloved brethren, be ye steadfast, unmovable, always abounding in the work of the Lord, forasmuch as ye know that your labor is not in vain in the Lord" (I Corinthians 15:58 KJV).

> Father, strengthen me to stand firm for righteousness. Grant me the courage, not just to withstand temptation, but also to go on the offensive against evil wherever I encounter it. And help me to do this only for the glory of Christ.

JANUARY 15

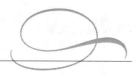

The last words General Robert E. Lee spoke from his deathbed were, "Strike the tent!" During the war this command was given when the army was moving from one place to another. Perhaps General Lee was remembering times gone by and was in the process of moving from one place to a much better place.

"Henceforth there is laid up for me a crown of righteousness, which the Lord, the righteous Judge, shall give me at that day: and not to me only, but unto all them also that love His appearing" (II Timothy 4:8 KJV).

All of us who will be overjoyed at the appearing of Jesus Christ (either when we die and go to Him, or when He comes to us) will have at least this crown to cast at His feet in worship: the crown of righteousness.

> Father, when it is time for me to "strike the tent,"
> may I enter Your rest with the joy and excitement
> of a child opening a Christmas gift. What we
> hope for is "exceeding abundantly above all that
> we ask or think."

JANUARY 16

"It is well that war is so terrible lest we should grow too fond of it." Robert E. Lee, Battle of Fredericksburg, Virginia, December 13, 1862. General Lee spoke these words after witnessing his army repulse eleven different attacks from the Federal Army, costing them casualties numbering 12,535 killed, wounded, or missing.

Is your heart basically good? Or do you agree with God's assessment, that the human heart, even yours, is deceitful above all else and desperately wicked?

"From whence come wars and fightings among you? Come they not hence even of your lusts, that war in your members? Ye lust, and have not; ye kill and desire to have, and cannot obtain; ye fight and war, yet ye have not because ye ask not" (James 4:12 KJV).

> Father, what is this evil and devious thing within me that enjoys killing and destruction? Is it not a wicked sin nature with which I was born and of which I will be forever free on that day? Until then, help me to live in the new nature that loves life and abhors death and killing.

JANUARY 17

One Confederate soldier was heard to remark about his commanding officer, Robert E. Lee: "I would attack the very gates of Hell if that old man would give the order."

"Loyal—faithful in allegiance to one's lawful sovereign" (Merriam Webster's Collegiate Dictionary.)

"And I sought for a man among them that should make up the hedge and stand in the gap before Me for the land, that I should not destroy it; but I found none" (Ezekiel 22:30 KJV).

> Father, help me to build up a wall of righteous-
> ness and stand in the gap where Your judgment
> and wrath come against sinful people. Help me to
> pray fervently for them and warn them. Help me
> to be as loyal and loving to You as that Confederate
> soldier was to his commanding officer.

JANUARY 18

After the failed attempt to finish the War for Southern Independence ended in a defeat at Gettysburg, Pennsylvania, Robert E. Lee desired to bear the blame alone: "No blame can be attached to the army for its failure to accomplish what was projected by me, nor should it be censured for the expectations of the public. I am alone to blame in perhaps expecting too much of its prowess and valor." After a brief study it is to be noted that the timidity and tardiness of some of Lee's subordinates, more than anything, led to the Confederate defeat.

In his magnanimity, Lee did not seek to defend himself for failure. Perhaps he was entrusting himself to the gracious judgment of Christ rather than the vain judgment (or approval) of men.

"Jesus answered, 'I have told you that I am He; if therefore ye seek me, let these go their way'" (John 18:8 KJV).

> Father, I confess I spend too much time in defense of myself. I try to rally support for positions I take rather than leaving all of it in Your hands. Please remind me to devote myself to furthering the Gospel instead of my own designs.

JANUARY 19

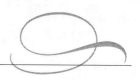

On the third and last day of the Battle of Gettysburg, July 3, 1863, twelve thousand five hundred Confederate soldiers prepared to charge across a 3/4 mile field and throw themselves against strong Federal positions to try and break their lines. Long since had passed thoughts of causes and states' rights. This attack, if successful, could end the war and give them a new nation and the liberty they desired. But the heart of each man beat with devotion to the one who had ordered the attack: Robert E. Lee. For him they would attempt the impossible.

Real love leads to real sacrifice.

"Greater love hath no man than this, that a man lay down his life for his friends" (John 15:13 KJV).

> Father, may I always be grateful and enjoy the liberty that I have in Christ. May I be as devoted to Christ as Lee's men were to Lee, obeying Him with fervor and loyalty.

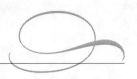

After taking over command of the Union Army of the Potomac in Virginia in the spring of 1863, General Joseph Hooker said, "May God have mercy on Bobby Lee, for I will have none." In May of that year the Union Army was soundly routed at the battle of Chancelorville, Virginia with casualties of seventeen thousand. The Army of Northern Virginia, commanded by Robert E. Lee, accomplished this. General Hooker was removed from command some months later.

Even our greatest abilities are not the result of our own doing; God gave us our abilities when He made us, and the glory should be attributed to Him.

"Pride goeth before destruction, and a haughty spirit before a fall" (Proverbs 16:18 KJV).

> Father, what is there in which I can be prideful?
> What can I boast about except that I know You
> and, more importantly, that You know me?

JANUARY 21

By 1864 hunger was rampant throughout the South. The Confederacy was literally starving. Union General Philip Sheridan was ordered to bring devastation to the Shenandoah Valley of Virginia which had been compared to Eden in its beauty, lushness, and produce. It had been the breadbasket of foodstuffs for the Confederate Army in the east, as well as for the civilians and noncombatants in the area. General Sheridan said, "If a crow flies across the Shenandoah, he will have to carry his own rations." He carried out his threat.

Circumstances sometimes lead us to justify cruelty, but on the day of reckoning, cruelty will be taken into account by the God of all mercy.

"He that oppresseth the poor reproacheth his Maker; but he that honoreth him hath mercy on the poor" (Proverbs 14:31 KJV).

> Father, You have said, "Blessed are the merciful, for they shall obtain mercy" (Matthew 5:7). Whenever You bring the opportunity, help me to render mercy to others, for I have received great mercy from You.

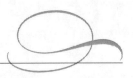

"I am of the opinion that all who can should vote for the most intelligent, honest, and conscientious man eligible for office," said Robert E. Lee

Although he was the most powerful and popular man in the Southern Confederacy, Robert E. Lee always placed himself under the authority of those who had been elected to political office. He had no desire for his country to be ruled by the military, but was quite content with the civilian leadership. America's founders recognized that few men are as honorable as General Lee and that none can be trusted with absolute power. They built into the government "checks and balances" including the separation of powers into executive, legislative, and judicial. To protect us from tyranny, the Constitution must be preserved. An informed public is essential.

"...but find some capable, honest men who fear God and hate bribes" (Exodus 18:21a KJV).

> Father, I confess I am remiss by not keeping up with the issues and events. Thank You for the gift of free elections in the U. S. May You guide Your people to choose wisely, and may those who have sacrificed to bring about and protect my right to vote always be in my heart and my prayers.

JANUARY 23

"Do your duty in all things. You cannot do more. You should never wish to do less." (Robert E. Lee)

Robert E. Lee, when given the choice of defending the Union or his state of Virginia, chose the latter. He could not raise his sword against his family, his friends, his country—Virginia. To do so would be a dereliction of duty, a dishonor.

"He that is faithful in that which is least is faithful also in much" (John 16:10a KJV).

> Father, help me to be faithful in performing my duties as a soldier in the army of Christ. Help me to remember I bear the name, honor, and reputation of the One who enlisted me.

January 24

Grenville L. Gage wrote a letter to his wife just before the battle of Sharpsburg, Maryland, September 17, 1862. Gage served in the Palmer Guards, 1st Texas Brigade, Army of Northern Virginia. The first phase of the battle raged in the Miller Farm cornfield. The 1st Texas Brigade lost nine color bearers and suffered 82.3% casualties, the largest of any regiment, North or South, in any engagement of the war. Among those who fell in the cornfield was Grenville L. Gage.

"Dear Wife, little children, Uncle, and Grandmother, you cannot imagine how glad I would be to see you all. While I write, tears run down my cheeks. But I thank God I have one consolation, and that God is with me in this far off distant land."

God draws nearest in our times of direst need.

"For He has said, 'I will never leave thee, nor forsake thee'" (Hebrews 13:5b KJV).

> Father, no matter where I go, wherever I am,
> You are with me and live in me. This You have
> promised.

January 25

Another part of Grenville Gage's letter to his wife: "I thank God that I often feel His presence in my poor heart. I want you all to pray for me. Pray that I may live to a consistent life that I may live in the discharge of every known duty. Oh pray that I may be permitted to return to family in peace."

In Jesus we can face all the adversities and tribulations of life with courage.

"Yea, though I walk through the valley of the shadow of death, I will fear no evil: for Thou art with me; Thy rod and Thy staff they comfort me" (Psalm 23:4 KJV).

> Father, apart from You I am overcome by the smallest adversity. With You I am an overcomer and a victor.

Another part of Grenville Gage's letter: "Dear Wife, I want you to raise your little children up in the fear of the Lord. Teach them the way in which they should go, and I hope they will not depart from it."

Children learn by seeing faith in action. What a solemn duty for parents to live in integrity, for their actions to be consistent with their words!

"Train up a child in the way he should go; and when he is old, he will not depart from it" (Proverbs 22:6 KJV).

> Father, help me to impart to my descendants and all who come after me the truth of the Gospel. May they fear You and never lose sight of Your holiness.

JANUARY 27

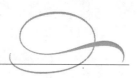

Grenville Gage's letter continues: "Tell Virilla, John, James, Wilson, Asborn, and little Ann that their Papa wants them to mind their mother and be good little children and that I will be home to see them as soon as I can."

Respect for parents predisposes a child to respect God. Disrespect for parents has the opposite effect.

"Children, obey your parents in the Lord for this is right. Honor thy father and mother; which is the first commandment with promise" (Ephesians 6:12 KJV).

> Father, I confess that I often failed to obey my parents—with dire consequences. Also I confess that I have often failed to obey You—with even worse consequences. Help me to obey You from my heart's desire. How much better everything is when I do.

JANUARY 28

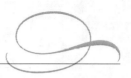

At the battle of Gettysburg, Pennsylvania, Lieutenant Thomas C. Holland commanded Company G, 28th Virginia, Army of Northern Virginia. On July 3rd, 1863, being a part of Pickett's Charge, Lieutenant Holland and a part of his company broke through Union lines on Cemetery Ridge. As he scrambled over a low rock wall, a bullet pierced his cheek and exited the back of his head. Of the eighty-eight men of Holland's company who took part in Pickett's charge, eighty-one were listed as killed, wounded, or missing that evening. Lieutenant Holland recovered in a Federal hospital. Fifty years after the battle, Holland returned to the spot where he was wounded at Gettysburg and shook the hand of the Union soldier who had shot him.

For some Christians, forgiveness is very difficult. It becomes much less so when we see our sin in the light of God's holiness. What enormities we have committed against Him! By comparison, what small harms others have done to us.

"And be ye kind, one to another, tender hearted, forgiving one another even as God for Christ's sake hath forgiven you" (Ephesians 4:32 KJV).

> Father, Thomas Holland forgave the man who shot him and tried to kill him. Is there anything that another could do to me that I could not forgive? How could I fail to forgive, considering Your forgiveness of me?

JANUARY 29

Upon being told that the chaplains and men of his army were praying for him, Robert E. Lee tearfully responded: "Please thank them. I deeply appreciate it. I can only say that I am nothing but a poor sinner, trusting in Christ alone for salvation and need all the prayer they can offer me."

A poet said, "More things are wrought by prayer than this world dreams of." Prayer is often the most practical thing one can do; it should be our first resort, not our last.

"We give thanks to God the Father of our Lord Jesus Christ, praying always for you" (Colossians 1:3 KJV).

> Father, help me to remember that there are many
> ways to help others, but the greatest good that I
> can do is to pray for them.

JANUARY 30

On June 2, 1864, Federal General U.S. Grant ordered an attack for the next day on Confederate lines. Many, especially the common infantrymen who would make the attack, thought the lines were impregnable. The evening before many were seen sewing or pinning their names and addresses on the backs of their uniforms. One soldier added, "Kilt at Cold Harbor, Virginia, June 3, 1864." Forty-five minutes into the attack, seven thousand Union soldiers lay dead or wounded.

There was once a statue at Fort Dix, New Jersey, called, "The Ultimate Weapon." It was the statue of an infantryman. How profound is the privilege of being an infantryman of Jesus Christ!

"Deal courageously, and the Lord shall be with the good" (II Chronicles 19:11b KJV).

> Father, thank You that Your commandments are
> not confusing, burdensome, or wrong. Help me
> to be joyful and quick to carry them out, thankful
> that You consider me worthy of serving You.

JANUARY 31

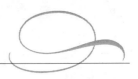

Confederate General Cleburne looked long and steadily through a telescope at the fortifications of the Federal Army prior to the attack on their lines at the Battle of Franklin, Tennessee. He had been ordered by his superior, General Hood, to make this attack. He remarked, "They have three lines of works." After a last look he added, almost to himself, "And they are all completed." General Cleburne and five other generals, along with thousands of soldiers, were killed in the attack.

In eternity's perspective, how precious will zeal for the cause of Christ appear? Won't it be seen as worth every danger and sacrifice?

"How are the mighty fallen, and the weapons of war perished" (II Samuel 1:27 KJV).

> Father, General Cleburne obeyed this order at the cost of his own life and the lives of thousands. There at Franklin, Tennessee, in 1864 the Confederate Army was destroyed. I serve a Commander who is wise and whose orders are always perfect. Help me to be as courageous and obedient as General Cleburne was in carrying them out.

FEBRUARY 1

Due to some amazing events, Union General George McClellan obtained Confederate General Robert E. Lee's battle plans (along with the disposition of his divided army) just days before the battle of Sharpsburg, Maryland. He wired President Lincoln: "I think Lee has made a gross mistake, and he will be severely punished for it. I have all the plans of the rebels, and will catch them in their own trap. Will send you trophies."

General Lee's army was not destroyed at Sharpsburg. A few months after the battle McClellan was removed from command for the second and last time. The war continued another two and a half years. Wouldn't it have been wiser to make no presumptions on the future?

"Though the Lord be high, yet He hath respect unto the lowly; but the proud He knoweth afar off" (Psalm 138:6 KJV).

> Father, I want to be near to You at all times. May the sin of pride never raise a wall or drive a wedge between our sweet fellowship.

FEBRUARY 2

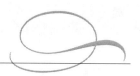

After General Joseph Johnston was wounded, the command of the Confederate army was given to Robert E. Lee. Some of his troops privately called him, "Old Granny Lee" for his appearance, and the "King of Spades" for all the fortifications that were dug on the Atlantic Coast under his supervision. Yet he is regarded now as one of history's great military geniuses.

Few of us will be counted among the great and mighty, but each of us has a hidden treasure, a gift from God Almighty, that can be used for His glory.

"For the Lord seeth not as a man seeth; for man looketh on the outward appearance, but the Lord looketh on the heart" (I Samuel 16:13 KJV).

> Father, I am not to judge anyone, and especially
> not for his appearance. Help me to understand
> that You love every person. Each one is of great
> value because of that.

FEBRUARY 3

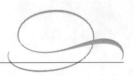

At the battle of Fredericksburg, Virginia, eighteen thousand Federal soldiers were massed to attack the Confederate Army across the Rappahannock River. The attack was stalled and thrown into disorder because of the artillery fire of two cannon commanded by twenty-four-year-old Major John Pelham of Alabama. Drawing return fire from Federal cannon, and with one of his cannons disabled, Major Pelham refused to withdraw even after being ordered three times. Manning one of the cannons himself, he finally ran out of ammunition. Only then did he retreat. Seeing this, General Lee said, "It is glorious to see such courage in one so young." He would thereafter be called, "That gallant Pelham." Pelham was killed in action three months later at the battle of Kelley's Ford, Virginia.

How can we, young or old, ever hope to demonstrate the kind of courage that Pelham displayed?

"Wait on the Lord; be of good courage, and He shall strengthen thine heart" (Psalm 27:14 KJV).

> Father, when I meditate on Your precious Son
> and all He did for so many, I can only rejoice in
> my gallant Jesus.

FEBRUARY 4

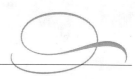

General Stonewall Jackson was seriously wounded at the battle of Chancelorsville, Virginia. This resulted in the amputation of his left arm. The battle was a great victory for the Confederate army, mostly due to the brilliant leadership of Jackson who maneuvered Lee's divided army to the rear of the Federal army and forced it back across the Rappahannock River. General Lee observed that Jackson had lost his left arm, but Lee had lost his right. Upon waking from his surgery and finding the amputation, Jackson said, "I believe it was according to God's will, and I can wait until He makes His object known to me." One week later Jackson was dead of pneumonia.

"Nevertheless, not My will, but Thine be done" (Luke 22:42b KJV).

The strength to accept God's will when it seems adverse is in knowing that it is for the best. And to know God intimately is to know that His will is truly the best thing for us. Some day, in the perspective of eternity, we will fully understand.

> Father, strengthen me that I may accept that
> everything works for good in concert with Your
> will, Your plans, and Your purpose.

FEBRUARY 5

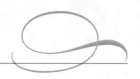

Upon learning of General Stonewall Jackson's wounds caused by "friendly fire" at the battle of Chancelorsville, Virginia, Robert E. Lee said to Jackson, "Could I have directed events, I would have chosen for the good of the country to be disabled in your stead. I congratulate you upon the victory, which is due to your skill and energy." Jackson replied, "General Lee is very kind, but he should give the praise to God."

God created all things; because of His will alone they were brought into being. To Him alone belongs the glory.

"Fear God and give glory to Him" (Revelation 14:7a KJV).

> Father, help me to hasten to give praise and glory where it is due—to You. I understand as General Jackson did that in me, that is in my flesh, "dwelleth no good thing."

FEBRUARY 6

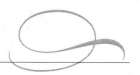

At the battle of Fredericksburg, Virginia, General Thomas Cobb of Georgia was in command of the Confederate troops behind a stone wall at the base of a hill called Marye's Heights. This would be the position that thousands of Federal troops would try to overcome. Given permission to fall back if outflanked or enfiladed, General Cobb responded, "Well, if they wait for me to fall back, they will wait a long time." General Cobb's Georgians reinforced by several regiments of North Carolinians repulsed eleven different Federal attacks and inflicted tremendous casualties on Union ranks. General Cobb was shot by a Union sniper during the action and died.

"How the mighty are fallen in the midst of the battle" (II Samuel 1:25a KJV).

How rare is a zealous heart, and how precious in God's sight.

> Father, as a general Thomas Cobb could have chosen a place of safety during the battle, but he chose to die leading men that he loved in a cause he believed in with all his heart. Help me to be as committed to loving and serving Christ and His people.

FEBRUARY 7

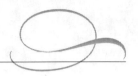

On Christmas Day, 1862, twelve days after a great victory over Union forces at the battle of Fredericksburg, Virginia, General Robert E. Lee wrote Mrs Lee: "My heart is filled with gratitude to Almighty God for His unspeakable mercies with which He has blessed us in this day, for those He has vouchsafed us from the beginning of life, and particularly for those He has vouchsafed us during the past year."

"Every good gift and every perfect gift is from above, and cometh down from the Father of lights..." (James 1:17a KJV). We have no good thing that was not given by Him alone.

"Praise God from whom all blessings flow. Praise Him all creatures here below. Praise Him above ye heavenly host. Praise Father, Son, and Holy Ghost."(Doxology.)

> Father, help me to be thankful in all situations,
> in wins or losses, in joy or sorrow, in good or bad,
> for You are at work bringing glory to Yourself and
> good to those who love You.

FEBRUARY 8

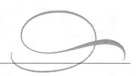

General Lee continues in his Christmas letter to Mrs. Lee: "What would have become of us without His crowning help and protection? Oh, if our people would only realize it and cease from vain selfboasting and adulation, how strong would be my belief in final success and happiness to our country!"

"Blessed is the nation whose God is the Lord, and the people whom He hath chosen for His own inheritance" (Psalm 33:12 KJV).

Jesus had twelve apostles; three of them were closer to Him than the others. Only one, John, was called "the disciple whom Jesus loved." Do you want to be closer to Him? You may.

> Father, few people in either the Confederate States or the United States were aware of what You were doing during that time. The same problem plagues us today. It takes someone who is very close to Christ to see His hand in history. Help us to be so close to You that our eyes are enlightened by Your Word.

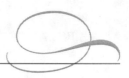

General Lee continues his Christmas Day letter to Mrs. Lee, 1862, Fredericksburg, Virginia: "But what a cruel thing is war; to separate and destroy families and friends, to mar the purest joys and happiness God has granted us in this world; to fill our hearts with hatred instead of love for our neighbors and to devastate the fair face of this beautiful world."

"For this is the message that we have heard from the beginning, that we should love one another" (I John 3:11 KJV).

All wars begin in a dark and secret place: in men's hearts.

> Father, those who know the cruelty of war best are those who have to fight in them. There are no good wars, but some wars are necessary in this fallen world to defend one's freedom, family, and homeland. Grant that we may fight only when it is necessary.

FEBRUARY 10

General Lee concludes his letter to Mrs. Lee, December 25, 1862, Fredericksburg, Virginia: "I pray that, on this day when only peace and good will are preached to mankind, better thoughts may fill the hearts of our enemies and turn them to peace."

"And they shall beat their swords into plowshares, and their spears into pruning hooks: nation shall not lift up sword against nation, neither shall they learn war any more" (Isaiah 2:4b KJV).

Peace will settle upon all nations in that day Isaiah spoke of because peace with God through Jesus Christ will swallow up every heart.

> Father, one day when all of Your enemies are destroyed, mankind will not know of war or learn of it. The peace that your people have prayed for through all of the centuries will at last come forever! Thanks for giving us this hope.

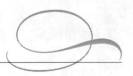

As the food supply began to dwindle in the South, and the necessities became more scarce, President Jefferson Davis had this to say about the women: "I never see a woman dressed in homespun that I do not feel like taking off my hat to her, and although our women never lose their good looks, I cannot help thinking that they are improved by this garb."

"In like manner also, that women adorn themselves in modest apparel, with shamefacedness and sobriety; not with braided hair, or gold, or pearls, or costly array" (I Timothy 2:9 KJV).

Over time inward beauty works its way outward.

> Father, thank you that the godly woman never fades; her love for Christ keeps her forever young and vibrant.

FEBRUARY 12

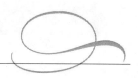

As the war progressed and it became more clear that the Confederacy would receive no help from the European countries that had received the South's exports, Jefferson Davis made these remarks in Jackson, Mississippi: "In the course of this war our eyes have often turned abroad. We have expected sometimes recognition, and sometimes intervention at the hands of foreign nations and we had a right to expect it. This has not happened and I know not why this has been so, but this I say: Put not your trust in princes and rest not your hopes in foreign nations. This war is ours; we must fight it out ourselves."

"Woe to them that go down to Egypt for help; and stay on horses, and trust in chariots, because they are many; and in horsemen because they are very strong; but they look not unto the Holy One of Israel, neither seek the Lord" (Isaiah 31:1 KJV).

To those who earnestly seek Him the Lord gives His secret counsel in times of intimate prayer. In the hour of need, isn't it wiser to seek Him before considering other sources of help?

> Father, forgive me for putting my confidence in princes and political leaders to do for me what only You can do.

FEBRUARY 13

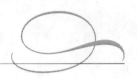

At the outbreak of the war many families were split in their allegiance, some to the Union and some to the Confederacy. This was the case with General J. E. B. Stuart, Lee's cavalry commander, and his father-in-law, General Phillip St. George Cooke, a brigadier general in the cavalry of the United States. General St. George Cooke commanded the troops that pursued Stuart and his cavalry as they completely circled the Union army while on a reconnaissance in 1862. General Stuart had this to say about his father-in-law's decision to serve the Union rather than his home state of Virginia: "He will regret it but once, and that will be continuously."

"And a man's foes shall be they of his own household" (Matthew 10:36 KJV).

To be for Christ is to make enemies. It is so sweet to know Him and so bitter to taste the enmity of some of your own dear kinsmen.

> Father, conflict is terrible, but so much more as it
> divides families. Teach us to pray for those who don't
> yet know You or your Son, even if they hate us.

FEBRUARY 14

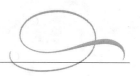

When he learned that command of the Confederate Army defending Richmond, Virginia in 1862 would pass from the wounded General Joseph Johnston to General Robert E. Lee, Union General George McClellan said, "I prefer Lee to Johnston the former is too cautious under grave responsibility. Personally brave and energetic to a fault, he yet is wanting in moral firmness when pressed by heavy responsibility, and is likely to be timid and irresolute in action." General McClellan had many occasions to regret he had ever said this.

"Answer a fool according to his folly, lest he be wise in his own conceit" (Proverbs 26:5 KJV).

The exercise of charity in our thoughts about others is a mark of God's grace upon us.

> Father, forgive me for making a rash and hurried opinion about anyone until I get all the facts and come to know the person. Help me to accept all those You bring into my life and not to reject them.

FEBRUARY 15

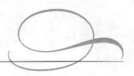

During the war many prominent people, both North and South, suffered the loss of loved ones—even wives and children—by diseases or accidents. This was an added burden to those already experiencing the terrible stress of a bloody war. Among those so afflicted were President Abraham Lincoln, President Jefferson B. Davis, and Generals Robert E. Lee, James Longstreet, and John B. Hood.

Where could these men find consolation after such sorrow? Where can we?

"For I will turn their mourning into joy, and will comfort them, and make them rejoice from their suffering" (Jeremiah 31:13b KJV).

> Father, thank You that You comfort us exactly as
> we need. You turn our mourning into joy, our suf-
> fering into rejoicing, our death into life.

FEBRUARY 16

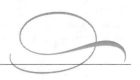

At the battle of New Market, Virginia, in 1864, Confederate General John Breckinridge was forced to move his last reserve force into line. These were the 257 cadets from the Virginia Military Institute. Breckinridge's force of four thousand five hundred was fighting an army of ten thousand under the command of Union General Franz Sigel. The cadets ranged in age from fifteen to seventeen years; they not only plugged a hole in the Confederate line but charged across a rainsoaked wheat field (later called the Field of Lost Shoes because the cadets ran out of their shoes), captured an enemy cannon and greatly helped the Confederate victory. Ten of them were killed, forty-seven wounded. One of those killed was Thomas G. Jefferson, a descendant of Thomas Jefferson.

Union cannon overlooking New Market Battlefield, Virginia, 1864.

From what spring did these young men drink such courage?

"For Thou art my hope, O Lord God. Thou art my trust from my youth" (Psalm 71:5 KJV).

> Father, there are some who live to old age, and their lives are empty. There are others who die young but have lived life fully. Fullness and contentment are not found in the length of life, but in having the peace and purpose that come from Christ. Please let me have a life of peace and purpose.

FEBRUARY 17

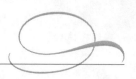

Hetty Cary was regarded as one of the most beautiful girls in the South and seemed to symbolize the southern belle to perfection. Handsome and dashing Brigadier General John Pegram won her heart and they were married in the winter of 1865. Their marriage in Richmond, Virginia was the social event of the year in a war-weary South that had not much to celebrate at the time. Three weeks later the wedding guests and the pastor who had officiated at the wedding gathered again. This time it was to attend General Pegram's funeral and to comfort the young widow. John Pegram at age twenty-three had been killed in action at the battle of Hatcher's Run, Virginia. Less than two months later John's older brother, Brigadier General William Pegram was also killed in action at the battle of Five Forks, Virginia, a week before the Confederates surrendered at Appomattox.

"Therefore shall the land mourn, and everyone that dwelleth therein shall languish" (Hosea 4:3a KJV).

How important it is to have perspective, to see life and death as God sees, not with temporal blinders, but with eternity in our hearts.

> Father, how terribly sad this must have been for everyone. Thank You that one day there will be a great reunion for all who have trusted Christ. Death will be gone forever. There will be nothing left to separate us from those we love.

FEBRUARY 18

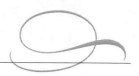

William R. Terrill and his younger brother by four years, James B. Terrill, were born in Virginia. Both attained the rank of brigadier general. Both were killed in action: William at the battle of Perryville, Kentucky and James at the battle of Bethesda Church, Virginia. The difference was that William wore blue and James, gray.

"He will swallow up death in victory, and the Lord God will wipe away tears from off all faces" (Isaiah 25:8a KJV).

God transcends our causes. His cause is to gather in His elect from the ends of the earth.

> Father, thank You that in this world of destruction, death and madness we find reason and purpose in the person of our Lord Jesus Christ.

FEBRUARY 19

At the battle of Yellow Tavern, Virginia, on May 11, 1864, General J. E. B. Stuart's Confederate Cavalry of four thousand five hundred fought against Union General Phillip Sheridan's cavalry of ten thousand six miles north of Richmond, Virginia. They turned them away from the Confederate Capitol, but not before General Stuart suffered a wound that would later prove fatal. As General Stuart was taken from the battle he saw some Southern troops leaving the field. He admonished them: "Go back! Go back! And do your duty as I have done mine, and our country will be safe. Go back! Go back! I had rather die than be whipped."

"So likewise ye, when ye shall have done all those things which are commanded you, say, 'We are unprofitable servants; we have done that which was our duty to do'" (Luke 17:10 KJV).

When those who ran from the fight were old, would they have remembered it with any peace of heart?

> Father, honor and duty meant so much to men I admire, past and present. May it mean as much to me. I expect no praise or acclamation for just doing my duty.

FEBRUARY 20

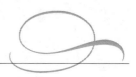

General Stuart suffered a terribly painful and mortal wound. As the time drew nearer to his death, these were his comments: "Well, I don't know how this will turn out; but if it is God's will that I shall die, I am ready...God grant our forces success, but I must be prepared for another world...I am resigned if it be God's will; but I would like to see my wife. But God's will be done...I am going fast now. I am resigned; God's will be done." At 7:00 p.m. May 12th, 1864, those around General Stuart's deathbed sang his favorite hymn: "Rock of Ages, cleft for me, let me hide myself in Thee; let the water and the blood, from Thy side a healing flood, be of sin the double cure, cleanse me from its guilt and power." He tried to sing with them, but he was too weak. At 7:38 p.m. he died.

"Father, into Thy hands I commend My Spirit': and having said this, He gave up the ghost" (Luke 23:46b KJV).

Every day and every hour, especially in the hour of death, we may hide ourselves in the Rock of Ages, cleft for us.

> Father, thank You for General Stuart's assurance
> of where his journey would take him. That same
> assurance is mine.

February 21

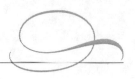

As this terrible conflict continued and the casualty count climbed and the food and resources declined, the North was fighting to win the war; the South was fighting to survive. Desolation and despair were quickly gripping the Confederacy. But while there was still a glimmer of hope; the fighting would continue. Did not the South have Robert E. Lee?

"And the whole land shall be a desolation and an astonishment" (Jeremiah 25:11a KJV).

In this world of astonishing desolation it is only in the invisible realm that we find hope. Yet, we have received a signal from the invisible realm. A Man was resurrected after death on a cross and three days and nights of burial in a sealed tomb.

> Father, hope is a wonderful gift You have given man. Some hope is merely a wish, but there is a hope that is assured. Thank You that because of the empty tomb I have the assured hope of Heaven. I have put my hope in Christ and in what He has done for me.

FEBRUARY 22

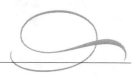

Legend has it that a sorely wounded rebel soldier, surrounded by a host of Union soldiers, yet still defiant, was asked by them why he was still fighting so hard. His reply through bloody lips was, "Cause you all are down here. This is our land and you're on it." Life decisions are not always complicated to the one who tries to do what he thinks is right.

"For Thy lovingkindness is before mine eyes, and I have walked in Thy truth" (Psalm 26:3 KJV).

To walk in the truth is to take a step toward it. Then the next step becomes clear, and the next. At last the darkness gives way to dawn, and dawn to noontide radiance.

> Father, truth is not too complicated for those willing to follow it. Help me to resist the flesh and to walk in the truth.

FEBRUARY 23

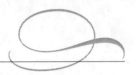

There had been widespread burning, pillaging, and destruction by Federal troops in Virginia and throughout the South. When the Confederate Army advanced through Maryland and Pennsylvania prior to the battle of Gettysburg, General Robert E. Lee issued this order: "I cannot hope that Heaven will prosper our cause when we are violating its laws. I shall therefore carry on the war in Pennsylvania without offending the sanctions of a high civilization and of Christianity."

We live mostly unaware of our own inner depravity. Given the right circumstances, what enormities are we not capable of?

"Whether therefore ye eat, or drink, or whatever ye do, do all to the glory of God" (I Corinthians 10:31 KJV).

> Father, General Lee knew that the depravity of man in wartime, left unchecked, would lead to things much more terrible than battles or even wars lost. He would not allow it in his own command. Please help me to walk with You, not offending the high sanctions of the faith.

FEBRUARY 24

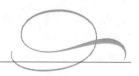

This is more of Robert E. Lee's orders to his army as they marched through Pennsylvania on their way to Gettysburg: "It must be remembered that we make war only upon armed men and that we cannot take vengeance for the wrongs our people have suffered without lowering ourselves in the eyes of all whose abhorrence has been excited by the atrocities of our enemies and offending against Him to whom vengeance belongeth, without whose favor and support our efforts must all prove in vain."

Remembering that we have been forgiven much, we must learn to extend grace to the undeserving.

"Dearly beloved, avenge not yourselves, but rather give place unto wrath for it is written, 'Vengeance is Mine; I will repay, saith the Lord'" (Romans 12:19 KJV).

> Father, a time is coming when Christ will make all things right. Rather than rejoice when You justly judge the wicked, help me to pray that they will realize their position before You, repent, and receive forgiveness along with new life in Christ.

FEBRUARY 25

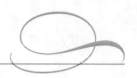

At the battle of Fredericksburg, Virginia, in 1862 one of Stonewall Jackson's junior officers voiced some concern about the vast number of Union soldiers coming at their lines and the vulnerability of their lowlying defensive position. General Jackson answered, "Major, my men have sometimes failed to take a position, but to defend one, never! I am glad the Yankees are coming."

We can receive a challenge gladly when we are anchored on the transcendent stability of God.

"I can do all things through Christ which strengtheneth me" (Philippians 4:13 KJV).

> Father, Stonewall Jackson believed the cause for Southern independence to be right. He had faith in You and confidence in his men to defend what they had gained. Help me to hold fast what You have fought for and won for me in the cause of Christ.

FEBRUARY 26

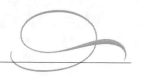

Lewis Armistead and Winfield Scott Hancock served together in the U. S. Army in California prior to the war. They were like brothers to each other; Armistead and Mrs. Hancock were like a brother and sister. As the cannons roared at Fort Sumter, South Carolina signaling the beginning of the war, the officers met for the last time at a military ball before going off to fight. Armistead would offer his services to the Confederacy, Hancock to the Union. As they parted, weeping, Armistead said, "Hancock, may God strike me dead if I ever lift my hand against you." They would meet again two years later in a small Pennsylvania town called Gettysburg.

"A man that hath friends must show himself friendly, and there is a friend that sticketh closer than a brother" (Proverbs 18:24 KJV).

True discipleship happens in the context of friendship; we influence each other for good.

> Father, thank you for the family of God, for brothers and sisters in Christ You have given us to love and to be loved by.

FEBRUARY 27

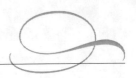

As General Armistead and approximately three hundred of his Virginians breached the Union lines on the afternoon of the third day of battle at Gettysburg, Pennsylvania, he would be struck by a Federal bullet and mortally wounded. He would be one of fifty-one thousand casualties suffered in that terrible battle. Forty-five minutes earlier twelve thousand five hundred Confederates had started toward the Union lines from less than a mile away. Only four thousand made it back to their own lines after that failed attack. Armistead's friend, Union General Hancock, was also wounded but would recover. As Armistead lay by a Union cannon, he gave some of his personal effects to a Union officer to give to Hancock's wife. It has been said that among the effects was his Bible.

"I am distressed for thee my brother Jonathan; very pleasant hast thou been unto me. Thy love to me was wonderful, passing the love of women" (II Samuel 1:26 KJV).

Perhaps by God's grace there is someone I can befriend as Jonathan did David and David, Jonathan.

> Father, thank You that in Christ there can be a relationship like that of David and Jonathan. We saw this lived out in the lives of two career soldiers, one wearing the blue, the other, the gray. Help me to be a friend and to have friends.

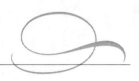

FEBRUARY 28

In General George Pickett's division at the battle of Gettysburg on that fateful July 3, 1863 attack were three brigades commanded by

Monument to Confederate General Lewis Armistead, Gettysburg, Pennsylvania.

Generals Lewis Armistead, Richard Garnett, and James Kemper. As Armistead and Garnett viewed the strong Federal fortifications, Garnett said, "This is a desperate thing to attempt." Armistead replied, "It is, but the issue is with the Almighty, and we must leave it in His hands." Richard Garnett was killed during the attack; his body was never recovered. Lewis Armistead died from his wounds after breaking through the Union lines, and James Kemper was seriously wounded and taken captive. After the attack failed General Lee ordered General Pickett to prepare for a Union counterattack with his division. General Pickett responded, "General Lee, I have no division now."

"The lot is cast into the lap, but the whole disposing thereof is of the Lord" (Proverbs 16:33 KJV).

God is not obliged to grant success, as we understand success, to His children. One of the great mysteries is that God allows us to suffer. Yet we know that He is noble. Therefore, we face adversity in faith.

> Father, often we may not understand the things
> You do or why You do them, but we have seen
> and know enough to trust You. We entrust our
> very souls into Your care.

FEBRUARY 29 (LEAP YEAR)

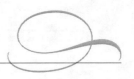

Much has been written about the fateful charge of June 3, 1864 by fifty thousand Union troops on entrenched Confederate lines defended by thirty thousand Southerners at the battle of Cold Harbor, Virginia. The men who participated never forgot. Confederate musket fire and cannister simply swept away line after line of Federal attackers. One Union captain recalled, "That dreadful storm of lead and iron seemed more like a volcanic blast than a battle." Another soldier said, "A boiling cauldron from the incessant pattering of shot which raised the dirt in geysers and spitting sounds." The ground in front of the Confederate lines was covered with dead and wounded Federals. Confederate General Evander Law said, "I had seen the carnage in front of Marye's Hill at Fredericksburg and on the old railroad cut which Jackson's men held at the 2nd Manassas, but I had seen nothing to exceed this. It was not war; it was murder." The attack was over in thirty minutes. Seven thousand Union soldiers never made it back to their lines.

"Thou makest us turn back from the enemy...Thou hast given us like sheep appointed for meat" (Psalm 44:10a & 11a KJV).

Adam and Eve no doubt had small awareness of what their rebellion would bring upon their descendants, the human race, until they held the limp, dead body of Abel in their sorrowing hands. God did not take away all the consequences of sin, but He did provide a plan of redemption that gives inner peace and the hope of a better day when war, and death, will be no more.

> Father, thank You for the coming day when there will be no more pain or crying, or suffering, or death.

MARCH 1

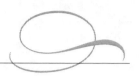

Confederate General Johnston Pettigrew of North Carolina was in command of what was left of his brigade after the battle of Gettysburg. As the Confederate Army retreated south and was crossing the Potomac River, General Pettigrew and his North Carolinians were serving as the rear guard. They were attacked in a foolhardy fashion by approximately forty Union cavalrymen who were all killed, but not before one shot General Pettigrew in the stomach. After three agonizing days of intense suffering, he died. At the time of his death ten general officers had died and eight had been wounded at Gettysburg badly enough to be put out of action. General Lee said this of General Pettigrew: "He was an officer of great merit and promise." The whole South mourned General Pettigrew, especially the people of North Carolina.

"Oh that my head were waters, and mine eyes a fountain of tears that I might weep day and night for the slain of the daughter of My people" (Jeremiah 9:1 KJV).

How slow we are to appreciate the heart of God as He beholds human suffering!

> Father, in homes of the North and South there was great mourning. In homes of the wealthy and homes of the poor there was weeping. Families of the gifted and families of the simple suffered. But You suffered and wept more than all because You loved them all. I love You because You first loved me.

MARCH 2

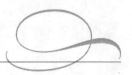

On the second day of battle at Gettysburg toward evening, General J. E. B. Stuart arrived at the battlefield. He had been missing for a week as the Union army had come between his cavalry and the main Confederate army. Since Stuart's cavalry served as eyes for General Lee, there had been no intelligence or reconnaissance. The Confederate army consequently had not known the location of the Union army. When Stuart arrived, Lee greeted him with a coldness that a witness found "painful beyond description." Then Lee softened as he remembered Stuart's service in the past; he considered Stuart as a son. The same witness said that Lee's manner became one of great tenderness as he said, "Let me ask your help now. We will not discuss this matter further. Help me fight these people."

"And be ye kind to one another, tenderhearted, forgiving one another, even as God for Christ's sake hath forgiven you" (Ephesians 4:32 KJV).

The great difference between the Christian faith and all others is in one thing: grace.

> Father, how can I fail to forgive another person,
> no matter what he does to me, when I consider
> what forgiveness for my sins cost Your Son?

MARCH 3

At Fort Towson in Indian Territory, which is now Oklahoma, General Stand Waite surrendered the last Confederate fighting force on June 23, 1865, nearly three months after Lee had surrendered to Grant. General Waite was a veteran of the battles of Wilson's Creek, Elk Horn, Prairie Grove, and many lesser fights. He had also taken part in the Trail of Tears from Georgia to Oklahoma. His force was made up of various men from the Cherokee (his own tribe), Creek, Seminole, and Osage tribes.

"Rejoice not when thine enemy falleth and let not thine heart be glad when he stumbleth" (Proverbs 24:17 KJV).

It does not glorify God to sneer at vanquished enemies.

> Father, remind us that we lose nothing when we glorify You by reflecting Your honor, courage, character, and integrity. These things will last forever.

MARCH 4

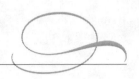

As the Confederate Army retreated back to Virginia after their defeat at Gettysburg, the wagon train of wounded stretched for seventeen miles. Very few of the wagons had a layer of straw, and none had springs. Many of the wounded had been without food for thirty-six hours and were suffering beyond description. A Confederate Cavalryman was heard to say, "I realized more of the horrors of war than I had in all the two preceding years."

"Like a father pitieth his children, so the Lord pitieth those that fear Him" (Psalm 103:13 KJV).

We don't fully know why we suffer so much in this life. We do know that in Jesus there is tribulation, a kingdom, and perseverance (Revelation 1:9). He is not obliged to tell us why we suffer, but He has been gracious to give us perseverance, and in the end a kingdom.

> Father, how that terrible scene must have grieved
> Your loving heart. The cries of the wounded were
> not lost on You as You rode in each wagon with
> each suffering warrior.

MARCH 5

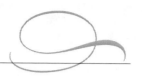

Brigadier General Dorsey Pender of North Carolina was wounded on the second day of the battle at Gettysburg. The wound was at first not thought to be fatal, but on the long wagon trip back to Virginia, the wounded leg became infected and was amputated. The infection spread and ran rampant through the rest of his body. Two weeks after his wound he lay dying. These were his last words: "I can confidently resign my soul to God, trusting in the atonement of our Lord Jesus Christ. Tell my wife I do not fear to die. My only regret is to leave her and my dear children. I have always tried to do my duty in every sphere of life in which Providence has placed me." Dorsey Pender was twenty-nine years old.

"For I know whom I have believed and am persuaded that he is able to keep that which I have committed unto Him against that day" (II Timothy 1:12b KJV).

Great clarity comes when the handwriting on the wall spells "death." We are relational beings. On General Pender's heart the primary concerns were God and family. We must keep this focus now, before the clock strikes midnight for us.

> Father, General Pender had no regrets as he was readying himself to see You face to face. Understandably he would miss his wife and children, but reunion would come. This very brief separation could not be compared to the eternal glories of heaven brought about by the grace of God and the cross of Christ.

MARCH 6

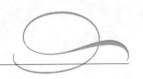

After Union General William Sherman and his powerful army captured Atlanta, Georgia from a much smaller Confederate Army, he set out on his infamous "March to the Sea." Beginning with Atlanta, the Union Army forged a path sixty miles wide and 300 miles long of pillage, burning, and destruction. What they could not use, they destroyed. Crops, homes, animals. Nothing was spared. Sherman said he would "make Georgia howl." "War is hell. It is of no further use to me; it shall be of no use to the enemy. Burn it!" One could mark the Union army's trek through Georgia by the ashes of homes with only chimneys standing. He reached Savannah in December of 1864 and presented the city as a Christmas present to President Lincoln. He then turned north into South Carolina. It was the first state to secede, and it suffered even worse than Georgia.

"And the children of Israel cried unto the Lord: for he had nine hundred chariots of iron; and twenty years he mightily oppressed the children of Israel" (Judges 4:3 KJV).

Our enemy, the devil, is not made of flesh and blood, but the destruction he wreaks makes a wider swath through the world than we realize.

> Father, we don't have King Jabin of Canaan or his army commander, Sisera, or even General Sherman oppressing us. But spiritual enemies much more powerful than they try to defeat us and steal our joy. Please show Yourself strong for us and give us the victory.

MARCH 7

Wilbur McLean lived in a beautiful home in Northern Virginia about twenty miles south of Washington, D.C. near the town of Manassas. The first major battle of the war was fought near his property on July 21, 1861. In fact Confederate General P. G. T. Beauregard may have used his home for his headquarters. Wanting to remove himself as far as he could from the war, McLean moved far south and west to the town of Appomattox, Virginia where he thought he and his family could be safely away from the fighting. Ironically it was in his sitting room on April 9, 1865 that Robert E. Lee surrendered his army to U. S. Grant. It has been said that the war started and ended in the home of Wilbur McLean.

To walk by faith is to walk with Christ wherever He leads. Sometimes He leads through the valley of the shadow of death.

"I would hasten my escape from the windy storm and tempest" (Psalm 55:8 KJV).

> Father, often in the tempests of life, You don't provide escape. But You are always with me, protecting me. The trials won't last, and when they pass I will be stronger and better for them.

MARCH 8

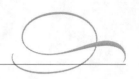

A Confederate soldier hugged the ground as the Union cannon answered the Confederate shelling with deadly accuracy. This was July 3, 1863, the third day of the battle at Gettysburg. There had already been six hundred casualties from the Federal shelling as the Southerners tried to find whatever cover they could in the trees on Seminary Ridge. Soon this soldier and twelve thousand five hundred others would move out across a field to attack the center of the Federal lines. As he prepared his heart for an almost impossible mission, he saw a jackrabbit scurrying away from the rumble of war. He remarked, "Run, Old Jack! If I didn't have a reputation to protect, I'd be running too."

"Be of good courage, and he shall strengthen your heart, all ye that hope in the Lord" (Psalm 31:24 KJV).

In God we can find strength to carry out frightening duties.

> Father, You have created man in Your image. The qualities of honor, duty, and courage are parts of that image which contribute to the makeup of the best parts of man. Please encourage us to carry out our duties.

MARCH 9

At the battle of Shiloh, Tennessee, April 6, 1862, Confederate Commanding General Albert Johnston led an attack on a portion of the Union line. The attack was successful, and upon strengthening his position on the field, he slumped in the saddle. His aides took him to a draw and laid him under a tree. One of his boots was full of blood. A bullet had nicked an artery, and he died before a tourniquet could be applied. Ironically General Johnston had sent his surgeon and other medical personnel to treat Union prisoners just before he was wounded.

"But I say to you, love your enemies, bless them that curse you, and do good to them that hate you" (Matthew 5:44A KJV).

Only one person has ever been able to obey this command perfectly—the one who gave it. But the Spirit of Jesus in us strengthens us to follow His example.

> Father, perhaps some of those Federal soldiers hated General Johnston. In saving some of their lives he gave up his own. Please show how to love our enemies.

MARCH 10

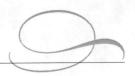

At the battle of the Wilderness in May of 1864, the Federal Army trampled the fence and garden of Mrs. Permelia Higgerson on their way to the battle. Mrs. Higgerson berated them for the damage to her property and predicted their quick repulse. A Union soldier from Pennsylvania said, "We didn't pay much attention to what she said, but the result proved she was right." After repeated bloody clashes in the woods, the Federals retreated back across this field. Mrs. Higgerson taunted them as they passed, "Ye shall not afflict any widows or fatherless child. If thou afflict them in any wise, and they cry at all unto Me, I will surely hear their cry" (Exodus 22:22, 23 KJV).

The sheer volume of human suffering, then and now, may cause a sense of futility. But God can use and magnify our feeble efforts to alleviate suffering. In so doing, we reflect His character.

> Father, we are not absolutely sure that Mrs. Higgerson was a widow. But we are sure that many widows and orphans suffered in this war, particularly in the South. Was victory worth the cost of surrendering Christian charity? Help me to be aware of the needy and helpless and be Your instrument to minister to their needs.

MARCH 11

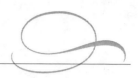

At the battle of Fredericksburg, Virginia in December, 1862, thousands of dead and wounded Union soldiers lay in front of the Confederate position at Marye's Heights. There had been one bloody repulse after another in a vain attempt to defeat the Confederates. Now the battle was over and the wounded were crying out for water. Unable to withstand their moans and cries for aid, nineteen year old Sergeant Richard Kirkland received permission from his commanding officer to grab as many canteens as he could carry, climb over the wall, and give drink to the enemy wounded. He did this at great peril because the Federal soldiers, seeing this, would not know his intentions. Indeed several shots were fired at him until they saw his acts of mercy. Then cheers rang out from both sides. He would become known as "The Angel of Marye's Heights." One year later he was killed at the battle of Chickamauga.

To show mercy is beautiful; to do so at great personal risk is Christlike.

"When the poor and needy seek water and there is none, and their tongue faileth for thirst, I the Lord will hear them. I the God of Israel will not forsake them" (Isaiah 41:17 KJV).

> Father, this act was one of the greatest exhibits of mercy, love, and Christlikeness that the war produced. Richard Kirkland will always be remembered, not for his military prowess, but for his Christian charity. Grant me courage to do likewise.

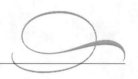

One of the reasons for the bloody carnage and high death count in this war was that the weapons far surpassed the military tactics. Attacks were made in formation as the military leaders had learned in the academies by studying Napoleon. Now there were .58 caliber rifledbore muskets, accurate up to a thousand yards, as opposed to the much less accurate smooth bore muskets. This new musket, that could fire three rounds a minute, caused eighty percent of all war wounds. Also introduced in this war were submarines, ironclad ships, trench warfare, mortars, Gatling guns, and repeating rifles.

"Hell and destruction are never full; so the eyes of man are never satisfied" (Proverbs 27:20 KJV).

A time is coming when men really will turn their swords into plowshares, their spears into pruning hooks. In the Bible it is called the Millenium.

> Father, we have quickly mastered the art of kill-ing. In those days a charge of cannister could wipe out a formation; now a single bomb can destroy a major city. We long for the time when righteousness will conquer evil, when war, killing, and death will not be even remembered.

MARCH 13

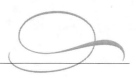

During the war the care for the wounded was primitive at best and deadly at worst. Fifteen percent of the wounded died of their wounds. In World War II the percentage was four percent and in Vietnam two percent. Nothing was known about boiling instruments and often bandages

Stonehouse used as a hospital at II Manassas, Virginia, 1862.

were removed from the dead and placed on the wounded. The most common treatment of the wounded was amputation. A skilled surgeon could amputate a limb in two and a half minutes. Neither side could have imagined the tremendous amount of wounded in those large battles. Some lay for days, untreated. Many times the troops advancing to the battle had to pass by a church or school or home that had been made into a field hospital. Outside a window would be a pile of amputated limbs in a stack as high as the opening.

"Woe is me for my hurt! My wound is grievous, but I said, 'Truly this is grief but I must bear it'" (Jeremiah 10:19 KJV).

Our griefs in this life are truly grievous, but they are temporary. We have set our hearts on pilgrimage. As we pass through the valley of Baca, we make it a place of springs.

> Father, how terrible must have been the suffering of the wounded, yet it could not compare to the agony of the One who was wounded for our transgressions and bruised for our iniquities.

MARCH 14

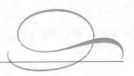

Disease ran rampant through both the Confederate and Union armies. It was the chief killer during the war, taking two men for every one who died of wounds. There were six million cases of disease in the Union armies alone; this meant that theoretically, on the average, every man was sick at least twice. Good, sanitary conditions were nonexistent and thousands upon thousands of men were crowded together in a relatively small area. This made disease spread easily. Malaria, dysentery, measles, and pneumonia were among the main culprits.

"Who forgiveth all thine iniquities; who healeth all thy diseases" (Psalm 103:3 KJV).

There is a vaccine for the most horrible disease of all—sin. It is the cross of Christ.

> Father, when I die it will probably be due to some disease. But I have been cured of the worst disease of all, the curse of sin. I die, yet I live! Thanks be to Christ for His cross and His shed blood.

MARCH 15

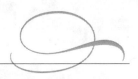

This war, although not a civil war, was fought as one as far as divisiveness was concerned. At the battle of Vicksburg, Mississippi, the State of Missouri furnished twenty-two regiments to the Union army and seventeen regiments to the Confederate. Four of Abraham Lincoln's brothers-in-law fought for the Confederacy, one of whom, Lieutenant A. L. Todd, was killed in action at the battle of Baton Rouge, Louisiana. John Crittendon had two sons and a nephew with the rank of general. One son, Thomas L. Crittendon and the nephew, Thomas T. Crittendon, served in the Federal army while the other son, George Crittendon, gave his services to the Confederate States. This was a war of blood against blood.

"Thou shalt not hate thy brother in thine heart. Thou shalt in any wise rebuke thy neighbor, and not suffer sin upon him" (Leviticus 19:17 KJV).

It is the believer's duty to be subject to the government, even to accept being drafted into the military in a time of national need, to discharge weapons toward the opposing lines, and to trust God with the outcome of great events. It is not a sin to kill in such a battle; it is a sin to kill or mistreat prisoners or civilians deliberately or to murder.

> Father, any man who has put his trust in Christ is my brother. How difficult it must have been for men to level and aim their muskets at other men who might have been their brothers. How sad and tragic is war, especially war involving Christian against Christian. Help us to be peacemakers.

MARCH 16

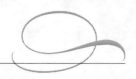

At the battle of Gettysburg, Pennsylvania, on the third day after Robert E. Lee's army failed to break the center of the Confederate lines, he was riding with his staff past a line of Union prisoners. One of the prisoners yelled out defiantly, "Hurrah for the Union!" General Lee dismounted and walked over to the prisoner, who was now frozen in fear, and said, "Young man, I hope all will be well with you." He remounted and rode away. Prior to his involvement in the war when he struggled with the decision to accept or reject President Lincoln's offer to command the Federal army in its invasion of the South, Lee said, "A Union that can only be maintained by swords and bayonets, and in which strife and civil war are to take the place of brotherly love and kindness, has no claim for me."

"Be kindly affectioned one to another with brotherly love; in honor preferring one another" (Romans 12:10 KJV).

By grace we must learn not to manipulate outcomes, but to walk in all the precepts of Scripture and trust God with outcomes.

> Father, how easy it is to rationalize that the end justifies the means, to set aside Your commands and precepts. Forgive me of putting my desires ahead of Your commands. Forgive me of failing to love my brothers. Guide me back to the truth, and help me to grip it firmly.

MARCH 17

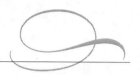

During the Shenandoah Valley Campaign of 1862, Confederate General Stonewall Jackson marched his force of sixteen thousand more than six hundred miles in thirty-nine days, fighting five major battles and defeating four separate Federal armies totaling sixty-three thousand men. This unbelievable military feat relieved the pressure that a huge Union army was putting on Richmond, Virginia, the Confederate capital. Jackson's strategy is being discussed in military circles to this day.

"A little one shall become a thousand, and a small one, a strong nation. I, the Lord, will hasten it in his time" (Isaiah 60:22 KJV).

The Church needs men who will obey Christ in faith no matter how great the opposition.

> Father, all things are possible for those who trust and obey You. Great odds mean nothing to You. The more impossible the task, the greater the glory to You.

MARCH 18

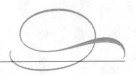

As he began his infamous March to the Sea from Atlanta to Savannah in 1864, Federal General William T. Sherman had this to say, "If the people raise a howl against my barbarity and cruelty, I will answer that war is war and not popularity seeking." Twenty-seven years later at Sherman's funeral, former Confederate General Joe Johnston, Sherman's main opponent as the two armies fought many a bloody contest, was a pall bearer. In a cold, wind-driven rain he refused to wear a hat, for he said Sherman would not have if the situation were reversed. Johnston, after becoming soaking wet, became ill and died of pneumonia a short time later.

The gentleness of Christ makes men great.

"Let him eschew evil and do good. Let him seek peace and ensue it" (I Peter 3:11 KJV).

> Father, Joe Johnston chose to forgive William Sherman for the devastation and cruel treatment done to his beloved South. He also showed great respect to the man who had been his chief antagonist. Please fill me with Your Spirit that I may be as magnanimous.

MARCH 19

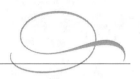

Lieutenant General Ambrose Powell (A. P.) Hill was one of the finest division commanders in the Army of Northern Virginia. Always spoiling for a fight and known for his fiery red shirt that he always wore in combat, Hill saved the day for the Confederates in a number of

Confederate cannon covering a field where Union troops broke through Confederate lines, Petersburg, Virginia, 1865.

major battles, particularly at Sharpsburg, Maryland. It is worth noting that his name was on the lips of both Stonewall Jackson and Robert E. Lee on their deathbeds. On April 2, 1865 after a nine and a half month siege, Federal forces broke through Confederate lines at Petersburg, Virginia. General Hill and his courier, Sergeant G. W. Tucker, galloped off to view the situation. As they rode, Hill remarked to Tucker, "Should anything happen to me, you must go back to General Lee and report it." Moments later they encountered two Union soldiers that Hill ordered to surrender. He was answered by musket fire; one of the balls struck Hill through the heart, killing him instantly. When Sergeant Tucker reported back to General Lee, Lee's eyes filled with tears as he said, "He is at rest now, and we who are left are the ones to suffer."

"Come unto Me, all ye that labor and are heavy laden, and I will give you rest" (Matthew 11:28 KJV).

It is the heart of faith that enters into Christ's Sabbath rest.

> Father, thank You for giving us rest in times of stress and suffering.

MARCH 20

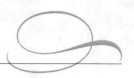

The 26th North Carolina Regiment of the Army of Northern Virginia has the tragic distinction of the most casualties in a single battle in the war. At the battle of Gettysburg, Pennsylvania it lost 708 of its men, 85 percent of its total strength. In one company eighty-four men, every man and officer, was hit. The sergeant who made the report had bullet wounds through both legs. In May of 1864 at the battle of Spotsylvania, Virginia, approximately twelve thousand casualties were counted within one square mile.

"My heart is sore pained within me, and the terrors of death are fallen upon me" (Psalm 55:4 KJV).

War and wandering are our heritage in Adam; peace and fulfilment, our heritage in Christ.

> Father, death and suffering are what mankind took on when it chose to ignore and disobey You and be a god in itself. Praise God the Father and Jesus Christ for providing the cross as the antidote for the venom of sin.

MARCH 21

Confederate cavalry officer and the famous Gray Ghost, John S. Mosby, had this to say about combat, "War loses a great deal of its romance after a soldier has seen his first combat. I have a more vivid recollection of the first than the last one I was in. It is a classical maxim that it is sweet and becoming to die for one's country; but whoever has seen the horrors of the battlefield feels that it is sweeter to live for it."

"For me to live is Christ and to die is gain" (Philippians 1:21 KJV).

As Hamlet said, "To be or not to be, that is the question." But to know Jesus Christ is to transcend this question because whether in the body or out of it, we are His.

> Father, it often seems easier to die for the cause of Christ, than to live daily in obedience while dying to self and denying the flesh. Help me to be willing to die for Christ, but also to live in union and harmony with Him.

MARCH 22

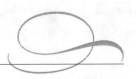

On Sunday morning, April 22, 1865, while President Jefferson Davis attended worship services, he received word from General Lee that Union forces had broken through his lines and that the Confederate government must be evacuated from Richmond as soon as possible. In May of that year President Davis was captured by Federal cavalry. He was charged with treason and complicity in the assassination of President Abraham Lincoln. Davis was imprisoned without a trial at Fort Monroe, Virginia in the harshest of conditions. Two years later in May, 1867 he was released on bail; in December, 1868, all charges were dropped.

"It is of the Lord's mercies that we are not consumed because His compassions fail not. They are new every morning; great is Thy faithfulness" (Lamentations 3:22,23 KJV).

Vindictiveness should find no harbor in the heart of a believer.

> Father, help me to be merciful to others whenever they offend me, remembering Your tender mercies to me. When I err, let it be on the side of compassion.

MARCH 23

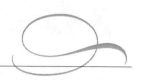

On April 12, 1865 General John B. Gordon of Georgia was selected to surrender officially the Army of Northern Virginia to Federal forces at Appomattox, Virginia. General Joshua Chamberlain, a hero of Gettysburg, was selected by General Grant to accept the surrender and the laying down of arms and Confederate flags. As General Gordon marched the ragged, bloody, but unbowed remnant of Lee's proud army down the road to surrender, only 28,231 men remained in the ranks. Only eight thousand were bearing arms. As they came in view, marching proudly, many without shoes, General Chamberlain called the Federal troops lining the road to attention and present arms. He paid tribute to a fallen foe who had fought so valiantly in so many battles. Upon seeing this General Gordon, on horseback, faced Chamberlain, raised his sword, and brought the tip down to his toe. He then shouted a command to the Confederate soldiers to come from a rigid right shoulder shift to shoulder arms, returning the salute. Honor answered honor! Reconciliation had begun.

"And all things are of God, who hath reconciled us to Himself by Jesus Christ, and hath given to us the ministry of reconciliation" (II Corinthians 5:18 KJV).

In heaven there will be no more enmity, but we are commanded to begin reconciliation here.

> Father, help me be a reconciler between You and people and between people and people that the Gospel might not be hindered. May this bring tangible help to people and glory to You.

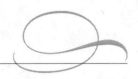

According to their beliefs, the people of the South and the North used different names to describe the War. This often takes place today. In the South the War is called "The War Between the States," "The War of Northern Aggression," and "Mr. Lincoln's War." The South would not accept the name, "The Civil War" as is commonly used today because a civil war is fought for the control of a nation by two or more parties. The Confederate States of America intended to be a sovereign nation, separate from the United States. The people of Virginia also called the conflict, "The War of Defense in Virginia." Northern sources, after the War, often referred to it as "The War of the Rebellion."

"Thus saith the Lord, ye shall not go up nor fight against your brethren the children of Israel. Return every man to his house, for this thing is from Me" (I Kings 12:24 KJV).

In this present age there is such a thing as a just war; it is a war to defend your people, your spouse or mother or father or son or daughter from foreign aggression. But we must pray for those in authority that, so far as it depends on us, there may be peace

> Father, only You know the right or wrong of this war, and whether it needed to be waged at all. What is known by all is that 620,077 men died fighting it. Help us to pray for the decision-makers in today's government for wisdom and grace.

MARCH 25

Prior to the battle of Shiloh, Tennessee, it was feared that the Union army had discovered how near the Confederates were; this made a surprise attack by the Confederates inauspicious. Commanding General Albert Sidney Johnston held council with his subordinates. One advised that the attack should be canceled because, "There is no chance for surprise. Now they will be entrenched to the ears." General Johnston knew that another Federal army was on the march from Nashville to link with the army he was facing. That would make the enemy force double his own. Should he make the attack or wait and face two combined Union armies? Albert Sidney Johnston gave the order, "Gentlemen, we shall attack at daylight tomorrow (April 6, 1862). I would fight them if they were a million." He did not survive the battle. President Jefferson Davis had this to say of his favorite general: "I hoped and expected that I had others who would prove generals, but I knew I had one, and that was Sidney Johnston."

"He teacheth my hands to war, so that a bow of steel is broken by my arms" (Psalm 18:34 KJV).

In Christ lie all the treasures of wisdom and knowledge. He is the wonderful counselor.

> Father, General Johnston was another man of noble character who made an important decision based on the facts as he viewed them. Help me to make important choices only after consulting You. And then let me be bold in deeds.

MARCH 26

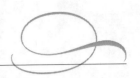

As the Confederates marched on their way to do battle with the Union army at Shiloh, Tennessee, a brief rest stop gave opportunity for a message from their commanding general, Albert Sidney Johnston, to be read to each unit. "Soldiers of the Army of the Mississippi: I have put you in motion to offer battle to the invaders of your country. With the resolution and disciplined valor becoming men fighting, as you are, for all worth living or dying for, you can but march to a decisive victory over the agrarian mercenaries sent to subjugate and despoil you of your liberties, property, and honor."

"Though I walk in the midst of trouble, Thou wilt revive me. Thou shalt stretch forth Thine hand against the wrath of mine enemies, and Thy right hand shall save me" (Psalm 138:7 KJV).

We followers of Jesus Christ have been set in motion to offer battle against the world, the flesh, and the devil with "the resolution and disciplined valor becoming men fighting." This battle is indeed for all that is worth living or dying for.

> Father, help me as my old sin nature tries to invade
> my thoughts to tempt me to sin against You. May
> the Holy Spirit aid me to set my mind to walk
> with You in obedience, trust, and service.

MARCH 27

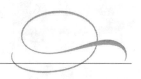

General Albert Sidney Johnston's message to his troops prior to the battle of Shiloh, Tennessee continues: "Remember the precious stake involved. Remember the dependence of your mothers, your wives, your sisters, and your children on the result; remember the fair, broad, abounding land, the happy homes and the ties that would be desolated by your defeat."

"O Lord, be gracious to us; we have waited for Thee. Be Thou their arm every morning, our salvation also in the time of trouble" (Isaiah 33:2 KJV).

Our lives have a powerful effect for good or for evil on those we love most. They may be blessed by our victories or hurt by our defeats.

> Father, help me to be as responsible to those who depend on me while I depend on You for everything.

MARCH 28

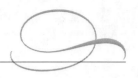

General Albert Sidney Johnston concludes his message to the Confederate soldiers at Shiloh: "The eyes and hopes of eight millions of people rest on you. You are expected to show yourself worthy; worthy of the women of the South, whose noble devotion in this war has never been exceeded in any time. With such incentives to brave deeds, and the trust that God is with us, your generals will lead you confidently to the combat, assured of success." At the end of the second day of battle, the Union army held the field. The uniting of the two Federal armies on the day before proved too much for the far smaller Confederate force.

"The Lord gave, and the Lord hath taken away. Blessed be the name of the Lord" (Job 1:21b KJV).

A mature faith realizes in times of distress that God is in control and that God is good regardless of the adversity of circumstance.

> Father, often things that You do are not to our preference because Your thoughts are higher than ours and Your ways higher than ours. May Your will be done.

MARCH 29

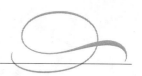

At the battle of the Wilderness in May of 1864, Union General John Sedgwick was berating the men of his staff for flinching and dodging bullets fired at them by Confederate sharpshooters eight hundred yards away. He felt that such behavior was detrimental to discipline and morale. He admonished them by saying, "What? Men dodging this way for single bullets? What will you do when they open fire along the whole line? I am ashamed of you, dodging that way." He laughed and repeated, "They couldn't hit an elephant at this distance." No sooner were the words out of his mouth than he was struck under the left eye by a fifty-eight caliber bullet fired by a Southern sniper. He died in the arms of one of his aides. There was much grieving over his death, for he was well known in both armies. But nowhere was his loss mourned any more than by his dear friend, Robert E. Lee.

"Blessed are ye that weep now, for ye shall laugh" (Luke 6:21b KJV).

Only in the perspective of eternity in Christ is there hope in the face of suffering and death.

> Father, again, war and death part friends in sorrow and weeping. Only in Christ can sorrow turn to joy and tears to laughter.

MARCH 30

In 1862 in the Shennandoah Valley of Virginia, successive victories in battle were enjoyed by General Stonewall Jackson and his Confederate army of sixteen thousand men over four different Federal armies numbering sixty-three thousand. In one such battle, due to his superb strategy, his men's toughness, and most of all, what Jackson believed to be the intervention of God, a victory was literally pulled from defeat. General Jackson touched the arm of a subordinate and pointed to the Federal troops as they fled the field, pursued by his ragged "Foot Cavalry." He remarked, "He who does not see the hand of God in this is blind, sir. Blind!"

"I called upon the Lord in distress: the Lord answered me and set me in a large place" (Psalm 118:5 KJV).

All of our victories in life have been due solely to the help of God.

> Father, how comforting it is to know that Your eye is always on me. How many times I have cried out to You, and You have rescued me! You have lifted me up out of a pit and have made my feet like the feet of a deer, and have set me upon high places. Thank You!

MARCH 31

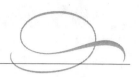

On the way to battle with a strong, intrenched Federal army at Franklin, Tennessee, Major General Patrick Cleburne rested his division in the town of Ashwood, Tennessee. As his eyes fell on Saint John's Churchyard, he remarked, "A beautiful spot. It would be worth dying for to be buried in such a beautiful spot." Two days later, Confederate General Cleburne would be buried in the place that he had admired so much and which gave him such peace and rest. Finally, years later, his body was brought back to Arkansas and buried on a ridge overlooking his home town of Helena.

"Look Thou upon me, and be merciful to me as Thou usest to do unto those that love Thy name" (Psalm 119:113 KJV).

More important than a beautiful cemetery is a beautiful reception on the other side.

> Father, for the believer there are many things worse than physical death. Patrick Cleburne committed his life into the care of his Savior. He was fully prepared for life or for death. So may I be.

APRIL 1

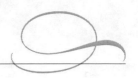

As the attack was about to launched on the Federal frontal positions of very strong fixed battlements at the battle of Franklin, Tennessee, Confederate General Daniel Govan remarked to Major General Patrick Cleburne, who was also from Arkansas, "Well General, there will not be many of us that will get back to Arkansas." Cleburne replied, "Well, Govan, if we are to die, let us die like men." Cleburne did die along with Brigadier Generals Otho Strahl, John Carter, Hiram Granbury, John Adams, States Rights Gist, and 1,744 other Southern soldiers. The casualty count was over seven thousand. The Confederate Army of Tennessee never fully recovered from the battle of Franklin and was destroyed as a fighting force less than one month later at the battle of Nashville, Tennessee.

"Precious in the sight of the Lord is the death of his saints" (Psalm 116:15 KJV).

Eventually none of us will "get back to Arkansas. " As the hymn says, "This world is not my home, I'm just a passing through."

> Father, every person has value, for Christ died for
> all, but especially precious are those who love You
> and are brought home to You.

APRIL 2

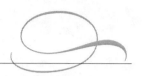

After the death of Confederate General Patrick Cleburn at the battle of Franklin, Tennessee on November 30, 1864, his old Corps Commander, William Hardee, pronounced his epitaph as well as that of his division. When he learned of Cleburne's death, he wrote, "Where this division defended, no odds broke its line; where it attacked, no numbers resisted its onslaught, save only once; and there is the grave of Cleburne."

"And they brought him to Jerusalem and he died, and was buried in one of the sepulchres of his fathers. And all Judah and Jerusalem mourned for Josiah" (II Chronicles 35:24b KJV).

The testimony of all the Scripture is that all who die in the Lord are blessed.

> Father, in every war that we have fought, good and godly men have died. What they have in common is that they are mourned and that a gracious God loves them. Thank You for this truth because it gives us hope.

APRIL 3

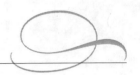

Of the six different Union generals that Robert E. Lee faced on seven different occasions, John Pope was the only one Lee had a great dislike for, even calling him a "miscreant that must be suppressed." Lee faced George McClellan at the Seven Days battle and again at Sharpsburg, Maryland. He fought Ambrose Burnside at Fredericksburg, Virginia, Joe Hooker at Chancelorsville, Virginia, and George Meade at Gettysburg, Pennsylvania. He faced U.S. Grant at the Wilderness, Spotsylvania, Cold Harbor, Petersburg, and Appomatox, Virginia. Those generals he respected, but he could not abide John Pope because of his cruel, harsh treatment of the civilians around the Virginia battlefields.

"Go from the presence of a foolish man when thou perceivest not in him the lips of knowledge" (Proverbs 14:7 KJV).

Aside from the gracious intervention of Providence, all of us would be harsh and cruel to others in one way or another. But God will intervene for us when we invite Him.

> Father, Your Holy Spirit makes the difference in a man's life, turning him from darkness to light, death to life, and self-love to love of God and others. Please make me such a man.

APRIL 4

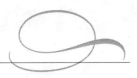

In the summer of 1862 the Union Army of the Potomac was in disarray. Fighting hard, but poorly led, they had been pushed back from the outskirts of the capital of the Confederacy by a much smaller force led by Robert E. Lee and Stonewall Jackson. Union General John Pope had enjoyed some minor success in the western theater of war. He was sent east to lead the Federal army to destroy the army of Lee and Jackson. He caused resentment in his new army with these words: "I have come to you from the west where we have always seen the backs of our enemies. I desire you to dismiss from your minds certain phrases which I am sorry to find so much in vogue amongst you such as 'holding positions,' and 'lines of retreat,' and 'base of supplies.' Let us discard such ideas. Let us look before us and not behind. Success and glory are in the advance, disaster and shame lurk in the rear." Thus he insinuated that his soldiers, unlike himself, were poor fighters and cowards. On August 28-30, 1862 at II Manassas one of the greatest Confederate victories happened along with one of the worst Union defeats. Pope was removed from command and sent to Minnesota to fight a Sioux uprising. He was never a part of the War Between the States again.

"For the wicked boasteth of his heart's desire" (Psalm 10:3A KJV).

Wisdom reveals that even the mighty did not make themselves so; God has given to each his abilities and the opportunities to use them.

> Father, I have nothing to boast of except that I know
> You and, more importantly, You know me. Thank
> You for this profound privilege.

APRIL 5

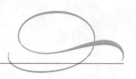

After a series of running skirmishes over six days across Alabama, the Confederate cavalry under the command of General Nathan Bedford Forrest demanded the surrender of Colonel Abel Streight. These battles had taken their toll on both sides. Without knowing it, the Union force had a better than two to one advantage in men and equipment. Then occurred one of the greatest ruses of the War when Forrest, by trickery and bluff, convinced Streight that he was hopelessly outnumbered and outgunned. Demanding immediate surrender, Forrest threatened to destroy the Union forces totally; Streight acquiesced and surrendered his command of 1,466 to the six hundred Confederates.

"For by wise counsel thou shalt make thy war: and in a multitude of counselors there is safety" (Proverbs 24:6 KJV).

A wise leader is not ashamed to ask for advice from men and from God.

> Father, a whole regiment of Union Cavalry was captured at Gaylesville, Alabama. I do not know whether Colonel Streight sought counsel from any subordinates, but I realize that for me it is essential. Please surround me with godly and wise people.

APRIL 6

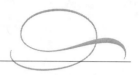

At the battle of II Manassas, August 28–30, the battle was fought on the same ground as I Manassas a year earlier. The Union Army was under the command of General John Pope. One of Pope's failings was that he refused to accept information that displeased him. While concentrating nearly his whole force to try to dislodge General Stonewall Jackson's II Corps from an abandoned railroad cut, he received intelligence that large numbers of Confederate troops were massing on his left flank where he had left a thousand men to guard. Refusing to believe this news he left the thousand unreinforced to face James Longstreet's I Corps of thirty thousand who would soon fill the air with the "Rebel Yell."

"The way of a fool is right in his own eyes, but he that hearkeneth unto counsel is wise" (Proverbs 12:15 KJV).

Pride and foolishness are different sides of the same coin.

> Father, John Pope refused to accept what he didn't want to hear; the result was 14,462 casualties and a battle lost. Oh the terrible price of stubborn pride! No one can really afford to pay it. Please keep me far from pride.

APRIL 7

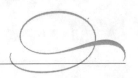

Jesse H. Hutchins from Alabama enlisted in the Confederate army just three days after the firing on Fort Sumter which began the war. He had survived 1,454 days of service only to die in the war's last twenty-four hours. He was killed battling Union cavalry just a few yards from the Appomattox, Virginia courthouse on the evening of April 8, 1865. General Lee would surrender his army to General Grant the next day in the McLean home at Appomatox.

"To everything there is a season, and a time to every purpose under the heaven: A time to be born and a time to die" (Ecclesiastes 3:1, 2a KJV).

Sometimes the events of our lives seem bitter and meaningless. They are not so from God's perspective if we are walking with Him.

> Father, our lives are in Your hands. All will die. But all will also exist somewhere, in either happiness or horror, for all eternity. This is a motivation to live as we should each day, yielded in obedience to the Holy Spirit. Please help us to do that.

APRIL 8

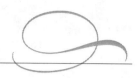

It is interesting, but sad, that outside of a few Southern prisoners of war who might have died of their wounds after they surrendered, and some unknown dead, there are no Confederate dead buried in the national military cemeteries. There are some Union soldiers buried in Confederate cemeteries such as the three Lufkin brothers from Maine buried in the Southern Cemetery at Spotsylvania, Virginia. One Federal soldier is buried in a small Confederate plot in Appomattox, Virginia. At the battle of Shiloh, Tennessee, dead from both sides were buried in mass graves, but the Union dead were exhumed and reburied in the National Cemetery there. Not so the Confederates. One thousand seven hundred twenty-eight lie in three mass graves; in one of those lie seven hundred, ten bodies deep.

"Though the Lord be high, yet hath He respect unto the lowly" (Psalm 138:6a KJV).

When God made us in His image, He gave us dignity; every one, great or small, who bears that noble image should be afforded dignity even in burial.

> Father, You know each rebel soldier, dropped one on top of another in a crude grave in a field in south Tennessee. Though they are not cared for by man, yet You care for them.

APRIL 9

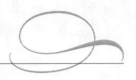

As Lee's surrender of the Army of Northern Virginia became inevitable (and in view of the harsh terms General Grant had demanded in some of his previous victories), some suggested to Lee that the Confederate Army should disperse and continue the fight as guerillas. This was General Lee's reply: "The homes of our men have been overrun by the enemy and their families need them badly. We have now simply to look the fact in the face that the Confederacy has failed. And as Christian men we have no right to think one moment of our personal feelings or affairs. We must consider only the effect which our action will have upon the country at large."

"And He said to them all, if any man will come after Me, let him deny himself, and take up his cross daily, and follow Me" (Luke 9:23 KJV).

The Christian life is not, in this world, health, wealth, and prosperity. It is a life of sacrifice by design of our Maker.

> Father, how very difficult it is to die to the selfish flesh when it struggles for supremacy in my life. Yet my whole being desires more than anything to walk closely with You in fellowship. Help me to do so.

General Lee continues: "The men have no rations and they would be under no discipline. They are already demoralized by four years of war. They would have to plunder and rob to provide subsistence. The country would be full of lawless bands in every part and a state of society would ensue from which it would take the country years to recover. The enemy's cavalry would pursue in the hopes of catching the principal officers and wherever they went there would be fresh rapine and destruction. But it is still early in the Spring, and if the men can be quietly and quickly returned to their homes there is time to plant crops and begin to repair the ravages of war. That is what I must try to bring about. General Grant will give us as honorable terms as we have the right to ask or expect. The men can go to their homes and will only be bound to not fight again until exchanged."

"Acquaint now thyself with Him and be at peace. Thereby good shall come unto thee" (Job 22:21 KJV).

The ability to discern God's precepts provides a means of knowing what to do in murky situations and hard decisions.

> Father, while it may have been difficult for General Lee to see good in his situation, it did not keep him from doing good. Help me to see things from Your perspective for Your glory.

APRIL 11

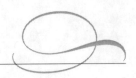

Confederate General J. E. B. Stuart was deeply loved for his dashing and brave deeds. Many a Southern belle's heart skipped a beat around him for he was as handsome as heroic. At military balls and suppers he was always surrounded by adoring women of all ages. But there was never a hint of scandal about him for he was deeply in love with his wife. He named their daughter after her. His daughter's name was on his lips as he died. General Stuart never cursed, gambled, or smoked, and he had promised his dying mother, at age 12, that he would never take a drink of alcohol. He kept his promise.

"When thou vowest a vow unto God, defer not to pay it; for He hath no pleasure in fools. Pay that which thou hast vowed" (Ecclesiastes 5:4 KJV).

People who do not do as they say have told a lie; when they do this habitually they become mere liars.

> Father, J. E. B. Stuart was faithful to keep his promise to his mother; he was also faithful to his wedding vows to his wife. Thank You for his example of Christlikeness.

APRIL 12

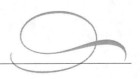

In a war there are often prolonged absences between soldiers and their loved ones. It was during one of those times that General J. E. B. Stuart, commander of General Robert E. Lee's cavalry, wrote this in a letter to his dear wife: "When I entered West Point I knew many and strong temptations would beset my path, but I relied on 'Him whom to know is life everlasting' to deliver me from temptation, and prayed God to guide me in the right way and teach me to walk as a Christian should; I have never for a moment hesitated to persevere; indeed, since coming to this far land I have been more than ever satisfied of the absolute importance of an acquaintance with Jesus our Lord."

"There hath no temptation taken you but such as is common to man, but God is faithful who will not suffer you to be tempted above that ye are able; but will with the temptation also make a way to escape, that ye may be able to bear it" (I Corinthians 10:13 KJV).

It is only in Christ that we have much desire to resist temptations; it is only in Him that we find the resources to do so.

> Father, temptation comes to all; it even came to
> Jesus. Thank You for the Holy Spirit who helps
> us to resist, overcome, and be victorious.

APRIL 13

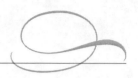

It had taken the Union army of thirty-five thousand men four and a half days to march the twenty miles from Washington, D.C. to Manassas, Virginia to battle the Confederates. This was the largest concentration of fighting men in one battle on the North American continent up to this time. It was thought that the war would be decided in this battle much like Napoleon and Wellington at Waterloo. At least that is what the elite from Washington thought as they came out in their buggies and carriages to see this grand army in colorful uniforms put the "ragged rabble" of a rebel army to flight. The bureaucrats and politicians and their ladies spread out their blankets and picnic baskets to watch the fight. Late on Sunday afternoon, July 21, 1861, over the picnic grounds streamed the Federal army in a rout. Many had thrown down their weapons and were running for their lives. There were riderless horses and wagons without drivers; some did not stop running until they reached Washington. This was called ever after "The Great Skedaddle."

"Whereas ye know not what shall be on the morrow... For that ye ought to say, If the Lord will, we shall live, and do this, or that" (James 4:14,15 KJV).

Only one thing about the future is certain: every word that God has said will surely come to pass.

> Father, there are few things that are certain. One is Your love for me. Help me to focus on doing Your will and not just making my own plans and expecting You to bless them.

APRIL 14

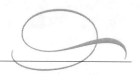

At 3:30 on the afternoon of July 21, 1861, at the battle of I Manassas, after standing "like a stone wall" on Henry House Hill, and blunting the Union army attack, Stonewall Jackson was readying his troops for a counterattack. These were his instructions: "Hold your fire until they're on you. Then fire and give them the bayonet. And when you charge, yell like furies!" They did and charged with the whole Confederate line of twenty-thousand. Thus the "rebel yell" was born.

"And they cried, 'The sword of the Lord and of Gideon'" (Judges 8:20b KJV).

As we Christians trust and obey our great leader, He enables us to stand like a stone wall.

> Father, there is a cry to strengthen men's resolve in battle, and there is a cry to celebrate a victory achieved and a war won. "It is finished," is that cry. Thank You, Lord Jesus, for Your victory at the cross.

APRIL 15

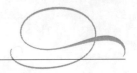

In the battle of Petersburg, Virginia, in 1864, General Lee and some of his staff were observing the fighting. The enemy fired on them. Lee ordered his men back out of harm's way, but remained where he was. After a short time he leisurely walked over and picked up something from the ground. Oblivious to the danger bursting around him, he placed the small object on a tree limb above his head. He then walked to safety where his staff stood amazed. He had risked his life for an unfledged sparrow that had fallen from its nest.

"Are not five sparrows sold for two farthings and not one of them is forgotten before God" (Luke 12:6 KJV).

Not a single atom in the universe has ever strayed outside of God's attention.

> Father, if You are mindful of every little sparrow, how much more is Your care for me whom You have created in Your image and for whom You sent Your Son to die?

APRIL 16

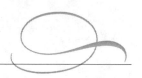

A tremendous Christian revival and renewal broke out throughout the South in 1863 and 1864. The genesis of this began in the Confederate military where many of the commanders were pious men of deep faith. Among them were Robert E. Lee, Stonewall Jackson, J. E. B. Stuart, John Gordon, D.H. Hill, Albert Sidney Johnston, Leonidas Polk, and Sterling Price. A host of other top Southern officers came to faith in Christ and were baptized after the war began. These included Joe Johnston, John Bell Hood, Braxton Bragg, Richard Ewell, Stephen D. Lee, and Jefferson Davis, President of the Confederate States of America.

"These are the chief of the mighty men whom David had, who strengthened themselves with him in his kingdom, and with all Israel, to make him king according to the Word of the Lord concerning Israel" (I Chronicles 11:10 KJV).

The amazing paradox of the life of faith is that only those who lament their weakness and failures may become mighty warriors for the Kingdom of God.

> Father, as David had mighty men who were great warriors and men he could trust, so the South had mighty men who were trustworthy and valiant warriors for You. Please help me to be as great a warrior as I can be for Your Kingdom.

APRIL 17

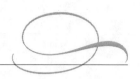

A grim future awaited any prisoner of war from either side during the war. The Confederacy was starving and not able to feed itself, much less the two hundred seventy thousand Union prisoners. At the beginning of the war prisoners were exchanged, but that was brought to a halt by Union General U.S. Grant by initiating a war of attrition. Eight percent of all the Union prisoners of war died of disease and hunger. The Confederate prisoners were no better off as they were ill clothed and ill prepared for the great cold of Northern prison camps. As a result weather-related disease and hunger claimed twelve percent of them. Confederate Captain Henry Wirz, Commandant of the Andersonville, Georgia Prison Camp was tried for war crimes after the war, convicted, and hanged.

"Beloved, if God so loved us, we ought also to love one another" (I John 4:11 KJV).

God's command of love extends even to our enemies, that we should love even them.

> Father, even in war there can be charity if men choose to obey You. Help me to love others with the same love that I receive from You. Help me to pray for my enemies.

APRIL 18

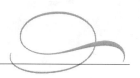

During the war, battle raged on the sea as well as on the land. Since the Confederacy had no navy, they refitted a few Union ships that had been abandoned at Southern ports. Among these were the first "iron clad" ships, the CSS Virginia and the USS Monitor that battled to a draw in the ocean off Hampton Roads, Virginia. The first submarine was also employed in this war, the CSS Hunley. It destroyed the Federal ship, Housatonic, only to sink itself with all eight hands off the coast of Charleston, South Carolina. The Federals hunted down and sunk the CSS Alabama off the coast of Cherbourg, France, after twenty-two months, but not before its sailors had boarded 447 vessels, including sixty-five Union ships, and had taken two thousand prisoners.

"They that go down to the seas in ships, that do business in great waters; these see the works of the Lord, and His wonders in the deep" (Psalm 102:23,24 KJV).

Those who lie dead in all the ocean bottoms of the earth are not hidden from the eyes of the Lord. Some day the sea will give up all its dead and they will stand before the Lord.

> Father, how majestic is Your name; You rule over land and sea. You know the weight of each wave that crashes on the rocks. You calm the wind and the seas. This reveals to us Your sovereignty over all.

APRIL 19

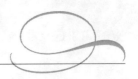

Leonidas Polk was the Episcopal Bishop of Louisiana. He was also a graduate of West Point and an Academy classmate of Jefferson Davis, President of the Confederacy. When he offered his services to his new nation, he was commissioned as a major general and given command of Southern troops in the Mississippi Valley. He was vilified in the North as a man of the cloth taking up the sword. People in the South rejoiced that he had transferred from the Army of the Lord to the Army of the Confederacy. He said he felt "like a man who has dropped his business when his house is on fire, to put it out; for as soon as the war is over I will return to my proper calling." Interspersed with his military duties, General Polk was actively involved in his first love, witnessing for Christ and encouraging men in the faith. He baptized General Joe Johnston and General John Bell Hood who had lost a leg at Chickamauga and the use of an arm at Gettysburg.

"Preach the Word; be instant in season, out of season; reprove, rebuke, exhort with all longsuffering and doctrine" (II Timothy 4:2 KJV).

We need to be praying for opportunities and boldness to share the Gospel.

> Father, all Christians are ministers of the Gospel
> and should be ready any time to give an answer
> to anyone who asks us for the reason of the hope
> that is in us. Thank You for this privilege.

April 20

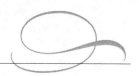

On June 14, 1864 at the battle of Atlanta, Georgia, Generals Polk, Johnston, and Hardee were reconnoitering the Federal position and drew the attention of the Union artillery. As the generals moved to a safer position General Polk, walking slower, was struck by a shell that passed through his body, killing him instantly. General Hardee cried out in grief, "My dear, dear friend." General Johnston placed his hand on the head of the dear Christian brother who had baptized him a short time before and said, "We have lost much. I would rather anything but this." When President Davis heard of Polk's death he said, "This is an irreparable loss and the country has sustained no heavier blow since the deaths of Sidney Johnston and Stonewall Jackson." Union General William Sherman had no use for the clergy in general and Leonidas Polk in particular because of his military service to the South. Sherman wrote in his dispatches to Washington, D.C.: "We killed Bishop Polk yesterday and made good progress today."

"For we which live are always delivered unto death for Jesus' sake, that the life of Jesus might be made manifest in our mortal flesh" (II Corinthians 4:11 KJV).

Every one who walks with Christ will have dear friends and bitter enemies in life and at the end of life.

> Father, whether through our lives as we live or through our deaths as we die, may Christ be glorified.

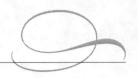

There are many who mistakenly believe that the single purpose of this war was over slavery. Robert E. Lee declared that the institution of slavery was a moral and political evil in any country. Long before the war he freed the slaves his wife had inherited. President Jefferson Davis said that even if the Confederacy was successful in winning the War for Independence, slavery was doomed, and the Southern states would sooner or later, by one means or another, set the slaves free. General Joe Johnston never owned a slave. Neither did General A. P. Hill or General Fitzhugh Lee, Robert E. Lee's nephew. Union General U. S. Grant had slaves and held them until the 13th Amendment set them free. Grant had said, "If I thought this war was to abolish slavery, I would resign my commission and offer my sword to the other side."

"He that answereth a matter before he heareth it, it is folly and shame unto him" (Proverbs 18:13 KJV).

Often conflicts, whether military or political, are more and complex than we realize and especially more complex than history textbook writers describe them.

> Father, help me to gather all the facts about a
> situation before I make a judgment.

APRIL 22

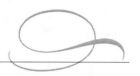

As General Sherman and his Federal army marched through Georgia and South Carolina, they soon took the city of Columbia, South Carolina. In that city stood an Ursuline Convent and Church. Sherman promised that the convent and church would not be harmed, but soon drunken Federal soldiers broke into the chapel, stealing the gold vessels and setting fires. The cross soon crashed down in flames. The soldiers laughed and said, "Now what do you think of God? Ain't Sherman greater?" Soon they advanced to the church and said, "All out! We're blowing up the church." It was soon reduced to ashes. When General Sherman arrived at the ruins, he said, "Oh there are times when one must practice patience and Christian endurance." The Mother Superior answered, "You have prepared us for one of these moments. This is how you keep your promises." The village church was set ablaze in Hardeeville, South Carolina; as it came crashing down, a Union sergeant said, "There goes your d___ old gospel shop."

"Have the workers of iniquity no knowledge, who eat up My people as they eat bread? They have not called upon God" (Psalm 53:4 KJV).

Our deeds are so transparent before God that we are like goldfish in a bowl with no place to hide.

> Father, the wicked have no idea of what a terrible enemy You can be. I pray that all who partici-pate in evil deeds, especially those that are overtly against You, will repent, call upon Your name and put their trust in Jesus Christ before it is too late.

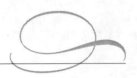

It has been stated that the United States has never treated a nation that it has defeated in war as harshly as the Confederate States of America. The Union waged total war on civilians during the war itself and even during the reconstruction afterwards. This compares ironically with how the United States treated our major enemies in World War II, making Germany and Japan two of the wealthiest and strongest nations in the world. Injustice was done, but the offended must respond with forgiveness.

"And be ye kind to one another, tenderhearted, forgiving one another, even as God for Christ's sake hath forgiven you" (Ephesians 4:32 KJV).

We must never ask God to give us what we deserve, for we deserve eternal judgment. Christ bore that judgment in our place. Shall we not then forgive those who hurt us as Christ forgave us who caused His hurt?

> Father, as a disciple of Christ I must forgive. No one could do anything as horrible to me as my sins have done to Jesus Christ. For His sake, You forgave me. I must do no less.

APRIL 24

In 1863 Union General Thomas Ewing issued the infamous "Order 11" which decreed that four pro-Confederate counties in Missouri be completely cleared of the entire population. After fifteen days, anyone still found in this area could be executed by Federal troops. Also any woman suspected of giving aid to Confederate irregulars, including the wives, mothers, and sisters of the irregulars, were to be arrested by Union troops and interned in a dilapidated building in Kansas City. General Ewing had been warned that the building was on the verge of collapse. It did, killing four women and seriously injuring many others. General Ewing then ordered all women and children of pro-Confederate guerrillas to leave the State of Missouri and not come back.

"O Lord God of my salvation, I have cried day and night before Thee. Let my prayer come before Thee. Incline Thine ear unto my cry. For my soul is full of troubles and my life draweth nigh unto the grave" (Psalm 88:13 KJV).

We are appalled into passivity at the massive suffering in the world, but we can at least help one person.

> Father, so often I focus on the small inconveniences in my life and ignore those who are suffering and sorrowful. Forgive me and point me to those whom I can help by Your grace.

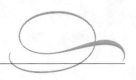

The role that some blacks and former slaves had in the struggle for the South's independence is little known. In 1990 Jerry May was memorialized by the Sons of Confederate Veterans and given a twenty-one gun salute. It was stated that he was honored, not because he was black and a former slave, but because he was a Confederate soldier. General Nathan Bedford Forrest said this of the black troopers that rode with him in the 7th Confederate Tennessee Cavalry: "Better Confederates did not live." An estimated five percent of Stonewall Jackson's force at Fredericksburg, Virginia in 1862 was black. Professor Walter Williams, a black man himself, said, "Black Confederate soldiers no more fought to preserve slavery than their successors fought in World War I and World War II to preserve Jim Crow and segregation."

"Surely he shall not be moved forever. The righteous shall be in everlasting remembrance" (Psalm 112:6 KJV).

God "made of one blood all nations of men." He remembers the righteous of all races.

> Father, thank You that You are not a "respecter of persons." Red and yellow, black and white, they are precious in Your sight.

APRIL 26

Former slave Robert Brown ignored emancipation and stayed as a friend and servant to Confederate President and Mrs. Davis after the war ended. While President Davis was jailed in a Federal prison, and Mrs. Davis ordered by Federal authorities to stay in Savannah, Georgia (a hotbed of lawlessness as were many cities in the South right after the War) Brown took the Davis children to Canada for safekeeping. On the ship a white abolitionist was insulting President Davis within the hearing of the Davis children. Brown walked over to the man and asked, "Do you believe I am your equal?" "Certainly," the man replied. "Then take this from an equal," Brown said as he knocked the man unconscious.

"A friend loveth at all times, and a brother is born for adversity" (Proverbs 17:17 KJV).

True friends become manifest when fair weather friends can not be found.

> Father, Robert Brown was a dear friend to the Davis family when they had very few. May I be a friend to the friendless as Christ has been a friend to me.

APRIL 27

Confederate Private Henry Stanley fought for the 6th Arkansas Regiment and was captured at the battle of Shiloh, Tennessee. This was the same Stanley that ventured to Africa to find Christian missionary, Dr. Livingston after the war. E. M. Bounds survived banishment from his home state of Missouri by Federal authorities and three different brutal imprisonments by the Union military to become one of the great expositors of the power of God through prayer. As the Holy Spirit worked through his life, a great Christian revival took place in the western theater of the war as it had in the east. Bounds' book, "Power Through Prayer," has never been out of print. Bounds understood the vital necessity of prayer; every day he spent the hours of 4:00 a.m. to 7:00 a. m. in prayer.

"For I know the thoughts that I think toward you, saith the Lord, thoughts of peace and not of evil to give you an expected end" (Jeremiah 29:11 KJV).

When we walk in dark places, we need perspective to see the dawn just over the horizon. Faith provides that perspective. Prayer and God's promises are the key to faith. A disciplined daily quiet time with Him is a vital essential.

> Father, I'm sure that as Stanley and Bounds suffered in prison camps they had no idea of the future and hope that would be coming to them in Your time. Help me to focus on You and Your promises in spite of my situation.

APRIL 28

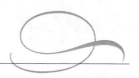

On May 10, 1864 Confederate soldier J. R. Montgomery of Mississippi was mortally wounded at the battle of Spotsylvania, Virginia. As he lay dying, he wrote a letter to his father. When the letter was discovered, it was stained with his blood. It said: "Dear Father, this is my last letter to you. I went into battle this evening as courier for General Heth. I have been struck by a piece of shell and my right shoulder is horribly mangled and I know death is inevitable. I am very weak, but I write to you because I know you would be delighted to read a word from your dying son. I know death is near and I will die far from home and friends of my early youth, but I have friends here too who are kind to me. My friend Fairfax will write you at my request and give you the particulars of my death."

"Wherefor as by one man sin entered into the world and death by sin, and so death passed upon all men, for that all have sinned" (Romans 5:12 KJV).

As we age, thoughts of the inevitable hour inevitably increase. But Christ was dead and came to life; because of Him, so may we who know Him expect to come to life again.

> Father, I know that some day death will overtake me. How thankful I am that Christ has removed its sting and conquered it at the cross and the empty tomb.

APRIL 29

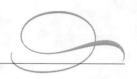

The letter of Confederate J. R. Montgomery to his father concludes: "My grave will be marked so that you may visit it if you desire to do so, but it is optionary with you whether you let my remains rest here or in Mississippi. I would like to rest in the graveyard with my dear Mother and Brothers but it is a matter of minor importance. Let us all try to reunite in heaven. I pray my God to forgive my sins and I feel that His promises are true, that He will forgive me and save me. Give my love to all my friends. My strength fails me. My horse and my equipment will be left for you. Again, a long farewell to you. May we meet in heaven. Your dying son, J. R. Montgomery."

"Precious in the sight of the Lord is the death of His saints" (Psalm 116:15 KJV).

J. R. Montgomery had supernatural calm in the face of death. And so may we.

> Father, this dear soul had placed his confidence in Your promises in the Bible. His salvation was secure as is mine, for we have trusted the same Savior, Jesus.

APRIL 30

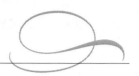

After the fall of New Orleans to Federal forces in 1862, the commander of the occupying troops was Union General Benjamin Butler. The women of the city were appalled at Butler's coarse, crude behavior; they rejected his advances toward them. Incensed, he issued Order Number 28: "As the officers and soldiers of the United States have been subject to repeated insults from the women calling themselves 'ladies' of New Orleans in return for the most scrupulous noninterference and courtesy on our part, it is ordered that hereafter when any female shall by word, gesture or movement insult or show contempt for any officer or soldier of the United States she shall be regarded and held liable to be treated as a woman of the town plying her avocation." This order gave license to all manner of depravity.

"I am weary with my groaning; all the night make I my bed to swim. I water my couch with my tears" (Psalm 6:6 KJV).

The wicked are always with us, and sometimes they make us groan. Nevertheless they are like the chaff that the wind drives away. Some day we will look, and they will be utterly gone. This is one of the aspects of the hope we have in God.

> Father, sometimes the night of suffering is long,
> but joy comes with the morning. It may be cloudy
> and dark, but the sun is shining above the clouds.
> Thank You for the gift of hope.

MAY 1

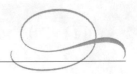

In the summer of 1862, the Confederate army under the command of Robert E. Lee drove a much larger Federal army (commanded by George McClellan) away from Richmond, Virginia to the James River where they retreated by boats. This involved a series of bloody battles known as the Seven Days' Battles. Southern General D. H. Hill, upon witnessing the slaughter of his men at Malvern Hill, the last of the battles, remarked, "It was not war, it was murder." Even though in retreat before Lee's brilliant tactics, the superior weapons of the North cost the South dearly. This was to be the tragic case for the whole war. The casualty count for the Seven Days' Battles was: Union, 15,849; Confederate, 20,614.

"And the country wept with a loud voice" (II Samuel 15:23a KJV).

In the pilgrimage of this life we all go through vales of weeping. But the fact is we do *go through*, and joy lies beyond.

> Father, Both the North and the South had hoped
> that I Manassas was as bad as the war would get.
> But then came Shiloh and the Seven Days' battles
> and even worse bloodshed later. The present time
> has its own griefs. Please help me to be a true
> comfort for those who grieve and mourn.

MAY 2

Very few estates in the South escaped desolation and destruction, especially those in the southeast. Before the war Mississippi was one of the wealthiest states in the Union; now it is one of the poorest. Some of the effects of the war continue today. Nearly the entire war was waged in the South with giant armies moving through the countryside and "total war" targeting even civilians. Winchester, Virginia changed hands seventy-two times before the end.

"O my God, incline Thine ear, and hear; open Thine eyes, and behold our desolations. We do not present our supplications before Thee for our righteousness, but for Thy great mercies" (Daniel 9:18 KJV).

We must not lay up our treasures here where moth and rust corrupt, and thieves steal, and wars destroy, but rather in Heaven where there is no moth, rust, thievery, or war.

> Father, thank You for not giving me what I deserve.
> I could not bear it. Instead, You have given me
> mercy and have extended amazing grace.

May 3

Part of the genius of Robert E. Lee was the ability to put himself in the place of the Union General that opposed him. This enabled him to anticipate the enemy's plans and movements. A host of Union commanding generals came against him: first George McClellan, then John Pope, McClellan again, Ambrose Burnside, Joe Hooker, George Meade, and finally U. S. Grant. Lee's military brilliance enabled him to win victory after victory in spite of overwhelming odds.

"I understand more than the ancients, because I keep thy precepts" (Psalm 119:100 KJV).

Meditating on God's Word has temporal and eternal benefits.

> Father, General Lee knew where his brilliance and military genius came from. He was always quick to give You the glory for any success, and he assumed blame for anything that could be regarded as failure. Please help me to emulate those qualities.

MAY 4

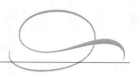

Prior to the war, poet Ralph Waldo Emerson said of the South: "If it costs ten years and ten to recover the general prosperity, the destruction of the South is worth so much." Massachusetts Congressman Wendell Phillips spoke these words: "I hold that the South is to be annihilated. I mean the intellectual, social, aristocratic South—the thing that represented itself by Slavery and the Bowie Knife, by bullying and lynch law, by ignorance and idleness. That South is to be annihilated." Reverend W. J. Sloane of New York said, "It is better that the six millions of white men, women, and children of the South should be slaughtered than that slavery should not be extinguished."

"A wrathful man stirreth up strife, but he that is slow to anger appeaseth strife" (Proverbs 15:18 KJV).

Slavery is clearly wrong, but is genocide the solution?

> Father, I have a choice: to stir up strife or be a peacemaker. I choose the latter because You disapprove the former.

MAY 5

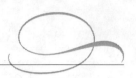

At the battle of Five Forks, Virginia in March of 1865, the Confederate army felt secure in their position opposite Union lines. The three senior officers, division commander George Pickett, cavalry commander Fitzhugh Lee, and Thomas Rosser, left their posts to partake of a "shadbake" at nearby Hatcher's Run, Virginia. They had not left any orders or told subordinates where they were. In the three hours of their absence, the Union army attacked in force. The Confederate army could have done likewise with a measure of success had they been so ordered. Upon hearing the noise of the Union attack, General Pickett raced back, but only in time to see half his division killed or captured.

"Watch therefore, for you know neither the day nor the hour wherein the Son of Man cometh" (Matthew 25:13 KJV).

Jesus' command to watch and pray is not an idle word. No doubt General Pickett was a more watchful man after this irreparable loss.

> Father, these senior officers should have been at their posts. Help me to be found faithful and at my post in serving my Supreme Commander now and upon His return.

MAY 6

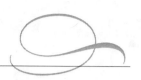

On September 17, 1862, the battle of Sharpsburg, Maryland was fought to a bloody draw. It was waged in three phases, the first being in a cornfield near Dunker Church, a house of worship used by a German-American pacifist group. The battle opened here at 6:00 a.m. and raged for three hours. After repeated charges and counterattacks. Union General Joe Hooker said of the field: "Every stalk of corn in the northern and greater part of the field was cut as closely as could have been done with a knife, and the slain lay in rows precisely as they had stood in their ranks a few moments before. It was never my fortune to witness a more dismal battlefield." After plugging a breakthrough of the Confederate lines and driving the Union forces back, General John Bell Hood was asked about his Texas division. He said, "My division lies dead on the field."

Dunker Church, Sharpsburg, Maryland, 1862.

"For the mighty man hath stumbled against the mighty, and they are fallen both together" (Jeremiah 46:12b KJV).

God will eventually bring about a just peace between all nations on that day when He rules the world with a rod of iron. Until then it is for us His followers to be peacemakers wherever we can.

> Father, man left to his own devices would self-destruct. Thank You for Your intervention in showing us the true way in Christ.

MAY 7

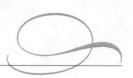

Union General Joseph Mansfield at age fifty-eight had served in the military for forty years, mostly in engineering and staff work. Two days prior to the battle of Sharpsburg, Maryland, after repeated requests, he was given command of XII Corps. This Corps was to be heavily involved in the first phase of the battle. Saying goodbye to a friend before the battle, he said, "We may never meet again." Less than one hour after leading his Corps into combat, Mansfield was mortally wounded; he died the next day. Confederate Brigadier General William Stark of Louisiana also died in the first phase. Killed in the second phase were Union General Israel Richardson and Confederate General George B. Anderson, age thirty-one. In the third phase of the battle of Sharpsburg Union General Isaac Rodman and Confederate General Lawrence O'Brian Branch died.

"The beauty of Israel is slain upon the high places. How are the mighty fallen!" (II Samuel 1:19 KJV).

For some, even for some who are young, death will come stealthily like a thief. If I am to be one of those, how then should I be living right now?

> Father, my physical death comes at the time of Your choosing, but living daily for Christ is the choice You have graciously given to me. And that is the choice I have made. For me to live is Christ and to die is gain.

MAY 8

The battle of Sharpsburg, Maryland, or Antietam, as it is called in the North was the first battle in which there were photographs. In October, 1862, the photographs were put on display by Matthew Brady at his New York gallery. Brady's colleague, Alexander Gardner, was the photographer, the first ever to display dead Americans on a field of battle. All of the dead were Confederate, but the poignant nature of the pictures had a great impact on people. Oliver Wendell Holmes wrote, "Let him who wishes to know what war is look at this series of illustrations." Another viewer said, "We recognize the battlefield as a reality, but a remote one, like a funeral next door. Mr. Brady has brought home the terrible earnestness of war. If he has not brought bodies and laid them in our dooryards, he has done something very like it."

"Thy men shall fall by the sword and thy mighty in war" (Isaiah 3:25 KJV).

If we could make a connection in our imaginations between sin and the ghastly carnage and death of a battle field, we could come closer to seeing sin as God sees it.

> Father, war and its killing must never be taken lightly. Even though it is forced upon us, and we must make war at times to survive, it is still the greatest example of man's inhumanity toward man. Grant that our nation may not go to war unless You so direct.

MAY 9

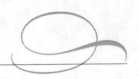

World War II hero, General George S. Patton III, had strong family ties to the Confederate States of America. One great uncle, Lieutenant Colonel John M. Patton, served in the 21st Virginia Regiment and saw action at the battle of Kernstown, Virginia. Suffering from poor health, he resigned his commission but survived the war, living until 1898. Another great uncle, Colonel Waller T. Patton, served in Pickett's division, Kemper's brigade, and was killed by artillery fire as he approached the stone wall on that fateful third day of the battle of Gettysburg. His grandfather, Colonel George S. Patton, was mortally wounded at the battle of 3rd Winchester, Virginia in 1864. Both great uncles and the grandfather were graduates of the Virginia Military Institute. General George S. Patton III attended there before graduating from West Point.

"I will pour My Spirit upon thy seed, and My blessing upon thine offspring" (Isaiah 44:3b KJV).

To have a distinguished name in Heaven is much more a blessing than to have a distinguished name here in the world. Christ will not erase from the Book of Life the names of those who overcome; rather He will confess those names before His Father and before His angels.

> Father, please pour out Your Spirit and blessing on those who come after me, those whom I influence, both those of my blood and those who are my children in the faith that their names may be confessed in Heaven.

MAY 10

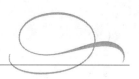

It is notable that church buildings were involved in many of the battles of the War. The battle of Shiloh, Tennessee, was named after Shiloh Church, a Methodist meeting house. (This battle was called the Battle of Pittsburg Landing in the South). Dunker Church figured greatly in the battle of Sharpsburg/Antietam, Maryland, as well as Sudley Church at II Manassas in 1862. There was also the battle of Salem Church, Virginia and the last phase of the battle of Chancelorsville, Virginia in May, 1863. Churches near the battle fields were immediately set up as field hospitals (as were school buildings and residences). Many a dying soldier took his last breath near the altar of a little country church.

"I was glad when they said to me, Let us go to the House of the Lord" (Psalm 122:1 KJV).

No doubt God, in His mercy, comforted the hearts of those about to die by letting their sight fall upon some of the symbols of eternal life.

> Father, what better place for a warrior to slip into
> eternity than from a church where Christ is central and His gospel is proclaimed? Help me to be
> an obedient and fruitful servant in Your church.

MAY 11

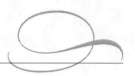

Having been fought to a standstill in the first phase of the battle of Sharpsburg, Maryland, the Union Army II Corps tried to break the center of the Confederate lines in what is called the second or mid-day phase of the battle. It involved a sunken road in which men from Georgia, Alabama, and North Carolina were well entrenched and repeatedly repulsed attacks from troops from Delaware, Maryland, and New York. The Union troops attacked in a broad line, and, row by row, they were cut down. At last they flanked the Southern position and were able to fire down into the road which would forever be known as Bloody Lane. Confederate dead were stacked three or four deep the entire length of the road as far as the eye could see. Many Southern soldiers were killed as they tried to retreat from Bloody Lane. The shooting continued for hours resulting in about five thousand casualties counting men from both sides.

"Therefore is my spirit overwhelmed within me. My heart within me is desolate" (Psalm 143:4 KJV).

The human race is a fallen race; in Christ alone is it restored.

> Father, when the human race fell into sin we lost
> reason and purpose. Only in Christ can we find it
> again. Help me to hold fast all that has been won
> by Jesus and graciously given to me.

MAY 12

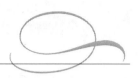

The afternoon or third phase of the battle of Sharpsburg, Maryland, was waged at the southern end of the battlefield at a stone bridge crossing Antietam Creek. Union General Ambrose Burnside and his 9th Corps had the assignment of crossing the creek at the bridge and flanking and crushing the Confederate right. Contesting the crossing of the bridge by the Union were five hundred Georgia and a few South Carolina riflemen. The fight at this point raged for four and a half hours until the 51st Pennsylvania and the 51st New York divisions rushed en masse across the bridge. They jumped over piled up Federal dead from prior attempts. This phase was called the Battle for

Burnside's Bridge. After pushing the few Confederate troops back, the Union Corps encountered A.P. Hill's division newly arrived from Harper's Ferry, Virginia who drove them right back across Burnside's Bridge. This along with the four and a half hour standoff by the riflemen saved the

Burnside's Bridge, Sharpsburg, Maryland, 1862.

Confederate Army. It marked the end of the battle which was called a draw after twenty-three thousand casualties.

"He that troubleth his own house shall inherit the wind" (Proverbs 11:29a KJV).

To live rightly requires physical courage sometimes, moral courage at all times.

> Father, it takes courage to live in a dark, dying world. Help me to be courageous like the men who fought at Sharpsburg.

MAY 13

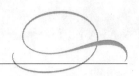

Seventeen year old William McDowell entered Virginia Military Institute just eight months before the battle of New Market, Virginia. He was one of ten cadets who died of wounds received during the fight. McDowell's classmate, John Wise, wrote of his friend's death: "A little removed from the spot where (VMI Cadet William) Cabell fell, and near the enemy, lay McDowell, it was a sight to wring one's heart. That little boy was laying there asleep, more fit, indeed, for the cradle than the grave. He had torn open his jacket and shirt, and, even in death, lay clutching them back, exposing a fair breast with its red wound."

"Remember how short my time is" (Psalm 89:47a KJV). "For what is your life? It is even a vapor, that appeareth for a little time, and then vanisheth away" (James 4:14b KJV).

The soul's a pearl preeminent of worth. The best way to respect its value is to be a disciple of Jesus Christ.

> Father, help me to remember that the content of my life is more important than its extent. Help me to live today for Christ.

MAY 14

Early in the war at the battle of Ball's Bluff, Virginia, Union General Charles Stone placed Colonel Edward Baker in command of Federal forces. Baker was a close friend of President Lincoln and was far more gifted in politics than battlefield strategy. As a result, on the afternoon of October 21, 1861, though the opposing powers were equal in number, the Confederates got the upper hand. Colonel Baker was killed with a shot in the head. The Confederates routed the Federal troops and forced

Potomac River, dividing the North from the South.

many down the eighty foot bluff and into the Potomac river. They shot many; others drowned and floated down the river to Washington D.C. and even as far as Mount Vernon, Virginia. After the battle the U.S. Congress created a Committee on the Conduct of the War. They cleared Colonel Baker of wrongdoing, but they charged General Stone with, "The most atrocious blunder in history." They ruined his military career and put him in prison at Fort Lafayette in New York Harbor. In later battles Federal commanders often failed to act for fear of Congressional reprimand.

"Lord, how they are increased that trouble me! Many are they that rise up against me" (Psalm 3:1 KJV).

It is best to do the right thing in the thick of the action without worrying about what armchair generals will think or do later.

> Father, help me to forgive those who treat me
> unfairly. Help me to leave the disposition of
> events in Your capable hands.

May 15

The horses ridden throughout the war by Generals Robert E. Lee and Stonewall Jackson were almost as renowned as their masters. Both outlived their masters. Jackson's horse, Little Sorrel, has been stuffed and mounted in the Virginia Military Institute Museum at Lexington, Virginia. Before the war Jackson taught at V. M. I. Traveller, Lee's horse, is interred on the front campus, outside of Lee's chapel at Washington and Lee University, also in Lexington. Lee was president of the college after the war until his death in 1870. Lee and his family are buried in a crypt at Lee's Chapel while Jackson and his family lie in the Lexington Cemetery.

"And the armies which were in heaven followed Him upon white horses, clothed in fine linen, white and clean" (Revelation 19:14 KJV).

Some day we will each have a white horse. Are you thinking of a name for yours?

> Father, in that last battle the One who is called Faithful and True, whose name is The Word of God will be victorious. Thank You that I am numbered in the ranks of His army by Your grace and His cross.

MAY 16

At the end of a school year the cadets hold a grand review on the parade grounds at the Virginia Military Institute in Lexington, Virginia. During the review someone calls the roll of the ten cadets killed at the battle of New Market, Virginia, on May 15, 1864. At the calling of each deceased cadet's name, a current cadet steps forward and answers, "Died on the Field of Honor, Sir!" Six of those cadets are buried at V. M. I., while have ten have

Graves and monuments of the ten V.M.I. cadets killed at New Market, Virginia, 1864.

memorials there. A statue called "Virginia Mourns" overlooks the graves and memorials.

"I am afflicted and ready to die from my youth up" (Psalm 88:15a KJV).

My object is not to make a name for myself, but rather to love and obey Jesus Christ. If He wills, He can make my name great. If not, still I am the winner because I have loved His name.

> Father, these ten young men were willing to die for their cause. Help me to live daily for the cause that saves men and sets them free—the Gospel of Christ.

MAY 17

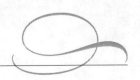

Early on May 3, 1863 General Stonewall Jackson's left arm was surgically removed after being wounded at the battle of Chancelorsville, Virginia. One week later he would die of pneumonia. When he left Jackson's hospital tent, his chaplain, Reverend B. Tucker Lacy, saw the General's amputated arm lying outside the door. He carried it to his brother's estate, Ellwood, and buried it in the family cemetery. In 1903 Reverend James Power Smith who had been on Jackson's staff during the War and who was the son-in-law of the estate's owner, erected a small granite marker over the buried arm.

"For our light affliction which is but for a moment, worketh for us a far more exceeding and eternal weight of glory" (II Corinthians 4:17 KJV).

To us our tribulations seem at times heavy beyond description. Yet God promises that they are both temporary and light compared to the eternal weight of glory that is in our future.

> Father, although we don't consider the loss of an arm and death light afflictions, still they cannot be compared to the joy and "exceeding and eternal weight of glory" that wait for those who have trusted You and Your promises. Thank You.

MAY 18

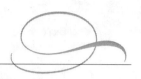

At the battle of Fredericksburg, Virginia, on December 13, 1862, Federal troops briefly broke through Confederate lines before being hurled back. However, before they were repulsed, they were misidentified by General Maxey Gregg of South Carolina. In the smoke and confusion he thought they were Confederate pickets returning to the battle line. He ordered his men to hold their fire until their identity could be determined. This was a fatal mistake; a Union bullet struck General Gregg and pierced his spine. Two days later he died after assuring the governor of his state, "I yield my life cheerfully, fighting for the independence of South Carolina."

"A good man out of the good treasure of the heart bringeth forth good things, and an evil man out of the evil treasure bringeth forth evil things" (Matthew 12:35 KJV).

It is my desire to yield my life cheerfully in the cause of Christ.

> Father, You said that a tree is known by its fruit.
> May everything that I think, say, and do identify
> me as a Christian, Christ's one.

MAY 19

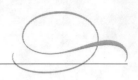

The last battle fought in the War Between the States raged near Brownsville, Texas on May 13, 1865. It was called the battle of Palmito Ranch; ironically it was a Confederate victory. A seventeen-year-old Confederate trooper fired the last shot in the war. Private John J. Williams of Company B, 34th Indiana, was the last soldier to fall. The last man had fallen, and the last shot had been fired. It was time for peace and reconciliation.

"And all things are of God, who hath reconciled us to himself by Jesus Christ, and hath given to us the ministry of reconciliation" (II Corinthians 5:18 KJV).

> Father, without knowing it I was once Your enemy. Then Christ saved me; by Him we are reconciled in love and trust. Help me to be a minister of reconciliation for people estranged from each other and for people estranged from God.

MAY 20

Sam Davis was a twenty-one-year-old Confederate spy captured and convicted by Federal authorities near Pulaski, Tennessee. His sentence was death by hanging unless he would divulge the name of his superior, who was the chief of scouts for General Braxton Bragg. This man was known as Captain E. Coleman, but his real identity was Captain Henry Shaw. Shaw had been arrested on a minor charge and was soon to be released. In the meantime he and Sam Davis were in the same jail. The Union authorities did not know that they had in custody the man they so desperately wanted. Sam Davis would tell them no differently; he went to his death on November 27, 1863. Shortly before his death he wrote his mother, "I have got to die tomorrow morning. Mother, I do not hate to die." The officer in charge of the execution made a last offer to Sam as he mounted the scaffold: surrender the name and be spared. Davis responded that he absolutely refused to purchase his own life by sacrificing that of a friend.

"Greater love hath no man than this, that a man lay down his life for his friend" (John 15:13 KJV).

True friendship and true loyalty are exceedingly rare. One should strive for such qualities as those strive who mine diamonds.

> Father, Sam Davis laid down his life for his friend Henry Shaw. Christ laid down His life for me. Help me to live for Him today in worship and obedience.

MAY 21

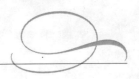

Private Wesley Culp was killed at the battle of Gettysburg, Pennsylvania. He died in action on his father's farm on the part of the battlefield later known as Culp's Hill. This was a strategic high ground that the Union army successfully held after repeated attempts by the Confederates to take it. Private Culp died in action serving in the 2nd Virginia Regiment. Army of Northern Virginia, Confederate States of America.

"Counsel is mine, and sound wisdom. I am understanding. I have strength" (Proverbs 8:14 KJV).

Wisdom consists in knowing how to live in the light of eternity whether life is lengthy or brief.

> Father, I don't know why Wesley Culp from Pennsylvania was serving in the Confederate Army. Even though he died, his decision to do so was not wrong unless he ignored You in making it. Keep me close to You and keen to know Your counsel in order that all my choices, large and small, may be right.

MAY 22

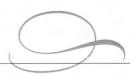

Major Roberdeau Wheat was a giant of a man, standing six feet four inches tall and weighing nearly three hundred pounds. At the battle of I Manassas, Virginia, July 21, 1861, things were going badly for the Confederates. Wheat and his "Louisiana Tigers" charged the mass of Union troops hoping to slow them enough to allow the Confederates to steady and strengthen their lines. Screaming and waving razorsharp Bowie knives, the Tigers slammed into the Federal lines, throwing them into confusion and disorder. The charge was successful, but Wheat was shot in the armpit. The bullet passed through the chest and left an exit wound on the other side. Having been told that his wound was mortal, he said, "I don't feel like dying yet." The surgeons told Wheat that they had never seen anyone recover from such a wound. He said, "Well then, I will put my case upon the record." He lived to fight again. Eleven months later he was killed while charging the Federal lines at the battle of Gaines Mill, Virginia.

"For Thou hast girded me with strength unto the battle. Thou hast subdued under me those that rose up against me" (Psalm 18:39 KJV).

After such a wound Major Wheat could have gone home with honor. He chose to get back in the fight.

> Father, strengthen me and gird me for battle that
> I might be a zealous and faithful warrior in the
> Army of the Lord. Give me the courage to hold
> to that which is good and to abhor evil.

MAY 23

General William Barksdale and his Mississippi Brigade had distinguished themselves at the battle of Fredericksburg, Virginia. Seven months later they would be part of a coordinated attack against the Federal left on the second day of the battle of Gettysburg, Pennsylvania. Their objective was a peach orchard held by the Union III Corps. Barksdale took his place before the 13th Mississippi and its battle flags. He drew his sword and gave the command, "Forward, men, forward!" From the throats of sixteen hundred Mississippians came the rebel yell. One Union colonel said, "It was the grandest charge ever made by mortal man." At nightfall the peach orchard was in Confederate hands with the Union salient broken in that area. But the Mississippi Brigade had lost their leader. As he led the charge, his long hair flowing, Barksdale was riddled with bullets. It was said that a Union officer ordered an entire company to fire at the Confederate commander.

"O God, the Lord, the strength of my salvation, Thou hast covered my head in the day of battle" (Psalm 140:7 KJV).

The spiritual battle is not with steel, gunpowder, and lead, but it is no less desperate. Its outcome is even more serious than that of Gettysburg.

> Father, strengthen me to charge the Devil's citadel and rescue a costly soul with the Gospel and Bible as my sword. Help me to build him up in the faith and with him to continue the war until the final victory.

MAY 24

On the third and final day of fighting at the battle of Gettysburg (soon after the Confederates failed to break the center of the Union lines), Union General Judson Kilpatrick ordered his subordinate, Brigadier General Elon J. Farnsworth to take his cavalry brigade and charge the Confederates on the right side of their line. Although the Confederates had been repulsed, they still had plenty of fight. Farnsworth argued strenuously over the order because cavalry charging massed formations of infantry had no chance of success. Even if there was a degree of success, it could not accomplish much. Certainly it would not be worth the great losses involved. Kilpatrick insisted and charged Farnsworth with cowardice. Farnsworth insisted that Kilpatrick should take back the false accusation. Kilpatrick did, and then Farnsworth chose to obey the order. The outcome was that the cavalry brigade was almost wiped out; Farnsworth himself received five bullet wounds and fell dead from his saddle. The men serving under Kilpatrick nicknamed him "General Kilcavalry."

"The way of a fool is right in his own eyes, but he that hearkeneth unto counsel is wise" (Proverbs 12:15 KJV).

I have considerable control over my choices. I have no control over their consequences.

> Father, my choices affect others, especially those I
> love. Help me to make wise choices that they may
> be blessed and not hurt.

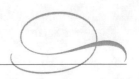

On July 4, 1865, nearly three months after Robert E. Lee surrendered to U.S. Grant and eleven days after the last Confederate force had surrendered to Federal authorities in what is now the State of Oklahoma, a group of approximately two hundred men, women, and children slipped across the Rio Grande from Texas into Mexico. Former Confederate general officers Kirby Smith, Jo Shelby, John Magruder, and Sterling Price along with former Confederate governors Pendleton Murrah of Texas and Henry Allen of Louisiana were in this group. They decided to go into exile rather than submit to the authority of the United States. How many eventually returned is not known, but some did.

"Obey them that have the rule over you and submit yourselves" (Hebrews 13:17a KJV).

God asks us to obey the authorities He has placed over us: parents, employers, church government, and civil government, etc. He is able to deal with those in authority and to protect us.

> Father, emotions and hurts run deep, but shouldn't these have followed the lead of Robert E. Lee and even the fiery Nathan Bedford Forrest? Help me to obey those in authority unless it violates Your law. Thank You that this has not yet been a problem.

MAY 26

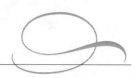

On April 10, 1865, one day after General Lee surrendered his army to General Grant, Lee issued his last general order to his men: "After four years of arduous service, marked by unsurpassing courage and fortitude, the Army of Northern Virginia has been compelled to yield to overwhelming numbers and resources. I need not tell the survivors of so many hard fought battles, who have remained steadfast to the last, that I have consented to the result from no distrust of them. But feeling that valor and devotion could accomplish nothing that would compensate for the loss that must have attended the continuance of the contest, I determined to avoid the useless sacrifice of those whose past services have endeared them to their countrymen."

"My flesh and my heart faileth but God is the strength of my heart, and my portion forever" (Psalm 73:26 KJV).

One burden of leadership is that one person's decision affects many people. Good leaders weigh issues and decide on principle rather than convenience. Good leaders are prepared to take the heat of those who disagree.

> Father, how difficult it is to put into words what
> is in our hearts. May what I do and say always be
> edifying to others and point them to Jesus.

MAY 27

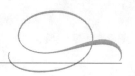

General Lee's last order concludes: "By the terms of the agreement officers and men can return to their homes and remain until exchanged.
You can take with you the satisfaction that proceeds from the con-
sciousness of duty faithfully performed; and I earnestly pray that a
merciful God will extend to you His blessing and protection. With an
increasing admiration of your constancy and devotion to your Country,
and a grateful remembrance of your kind and generous consideration of
myself, I bid you an affectionate farewell, R.E. Lee, General."

"Let us hear the conclusion of the whole matter: Fear God
and keep His commandments, for this is the whole duty of man"
(Ecclesiastes 12:13 KJV).

It must have seemed like a dream that the war at last was finished.
The men had been constant until the end. Such a magic moment looms
before every true saint. The privations of this long tribulation will suddenly vanish, and we will be in the presence of the Prince of Peace.

> Father, may I carry out the duties You have given
> me with the same fervor, constancy, and devotion
> with which the soldiers of General Lee's army
> performed so valiantly until the end.

MAY 28

On April 25, 1865, 2,580 people were packed on a river transport, the Sultana, at Vicksburg, Mississippi, for a cruise up the Mississippi River for ports to the north. A large number of horses and mules were also on board, a risky business for a boat built to accommodate 376 passengers. Nearly all of those on board were recently released Union prisoners of war. The captain of the Sultana was J. Cass Mason who was also a part owner. Charity had little to do with the overcrowding; the Federal enlisted men were charged five dollars, the officers ten—a huge profit for the owners. On April 27 shortly before 3:00 a.m. and seven or eight miles north of Memphis, the boilers on the Sultana exploded. The loss of life was horrendous with unofficial estimates being as high as seventeen hundred. Numbered among the dead was J. Cass Mason, master of the vessel.

"So are the ways of everyone that is greedy of gain which taketh away the life of the owners thereof" (Proverbs 1:19 KJV).

Greed clouds the judgment; poor choices then have the opposite effect of what the greedy person desired.

> Father, I must not judge the motives of another. Only You can do that, for all things are open before Your gaze. Help me to be wise and open to Your guidance in all the choices I make.

MAY 29

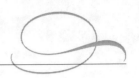

The greatest honor that could be bestowed on an enlisted man in the ranks was to bear the flag as a colorbearer. Officers carried the flag only when an enlisted man was unable. During the noise, smoke, and confusion of battle, verbal commands and bugle sounds were not often heard, so all eyes were on the flags. To charge, retreat, or remain in place depended on the position of the flag. A colorbearer was chosen because of his courage, devotion to duty, and exceptional soldiering skills. But this was dangerous duty as the opposing army knew the importance of the flag. The colorbearer was a target. If one fell, another would take his place. The flag of a regiment was its most precious possession; it bordered on being a religious symbol. The battle flag displayed the locations of battles in which the regiment had fought. It was a huge honor to capture the opponent's battle flag. On the first day of the battle of Gettysburg, Pennsylvania, the 26th North Carolina Regiment lost fourteen colorbearers, killed or wounded.

"Behold, he was honorable among the thirty but attained not to the first three and David set him over his guard" (I Chronicles 11:25 KJV).

Benaiah was truly a colorbearer for King David. He put loyalty before honor, and honor came to him.

> Father, Benaiah was satisfied in just serving David because he loved him. I am thankful and satisfied just serving Christ. Any honor that comes must belong to Him.

MAY 30

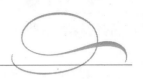

After the war there were no Federal cemeteries for the Confederate dead. Nearly all the Southern dead were buried in crude graves on the battlefield, some in mass graves such as at Shiloh, Tennessee. Several organizations such as the Fredericksburg, Virginia, Ladies Memorial Association, Spotsylvania Memorial Association, and the United Daughters of the Confederacy were responsible for buying land for the cemeteries and locating and bringing back the remains for burial. Efforts were still in motion up to ten years after the war ended by which time just a few bones or a skull might be found. This was a tremendous task for these ladies considering how destitute the South was after the war. Most of the dead in the Confederate cemeteries are unknown. Fredericksburg, Virginia Confederate Cemetery holds the remains of two thousand three hundred Southern soldiers from fourteen states. Two thousand one hundred eighty-four are unknown. Hagerstown, Maryland after the battle of Sharpsburg holds 2,468 with 2,122 unknown. Little Groveton Cemetery holds two hundred sixty-six after the battle of II Manassas; two hundred sixty-four are unknown.

"And the graves were opened and many bodies of the saints arose" (Matthew 27:52 KJV).

Not a single molecule or man in the universe escapes the notice and care of God.

> Father, when Your saints are raised from the dead, their bodies will be whole and perfect. I am thankful that all these dead are known to You although they are unknown to us.

MAY 31

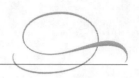

During the siege of Petersburg, Virginia by Federal forces, the 48th Pennsylvania Regiment, made up of men who had been coal miners before enlisting, began digging a tunnel. When finished the shaft would be five hundred eleven feet long, stretching from the Union lines to underneath the Confederate lines. Then four tons of black powder would be packed in magazines underneath a Confederate fort called Elliott's Salient. After the explosion, fifteen thousand federal troops would pour through the hole in the Southern line, very probably ending the war. The digging began on June 25, 1864. On July 30 at 3:15 a.m. the commander of the 48th Regiment, Colonel Henry Pleasants lit the fuse and scrambled out of the tunnel. The explosion was deafening and the damage indescribable. Body parts, pieces of artillery, and debris were everywhere. A crater, one hundred seventy feet long, ninety feet wide, and thirty feet deep appeared in what had been a Confederate fortress. Union forces took advantage of the confusion and chaos and seized one hundred fifty yards of works on each side of the crater. But there they stopped.

"This man began to build and was not able to finish" (Luke 14:30 KJV).

Ask God for the grace of perseverance.

> Father, instead of enveloping the Confederate lines and achieving victory, the Union troops stopped. What You have given me to accomplish, help me never to quit until it is finished.

JUNE 1

After immediate success at the crater, things began to unravel quickly for the Federal troops. Dazed, confused, and leaderless (for their commander had not accompanied them), the Union troops huddled in and around the crater for hours. As more troops poured in, the crater became filled with a great mass of men. This delay gave the Confederates time to launch a counterattack. First, eight hundred Virginians recaptured the trenches north of the crater. At 9:00 a.m. Confederate Brigadier General William Mahone's division rushed the depression, and after a terrible fight the Union forces retreated back to their original lines. The crater became a trap, filled with Union dead. One Confederate soldier said it was like shooting fish in a barrel. Out of fifteen thousand who made the attack, four thousand were casualties. A Union officer said, "This was a stupendous failure. It is agreed that the thing was a perfect success, except that it did not succeed."

"Whatever thy hand findeth to do, do it with thy might" (Ecclesiastes 9:10a KJV).

The most likely time for a counterattack is just after big success but before preparations are complete to secure the victory. It is this way also in the Christian walk; after a notable success, "Let him who thinks he stands take heed, lest he should fall."

> Father, nothing can be called a success until it is followed through and finished. Help me to learn to press on toward a secured victory.

JUNE 2

With so many notable people in the war, very, very few have ever heard of Henry Raisen, Company B, Seventh Tennessee Regiment, Heth's division, Army of Northern Virginia or Ferdinand Ushner, 12th Illinois Cavalry, Buford's Division, Union Army of the Potomac. Henry Raisen would be the first Confederate soldier to be killed at the battle of Gettysburg while Ferdinand Ushner would be the first Federal soldier to die in this battle. Before the three days were over the casualty count would be fifty-one thousand of which twenty-eight thousand were Confederate and twenty-three thousand were Union.

"We love Him because He first loved us" (I John 4:19 KJV).

God has all the nameless and unknown, the humble and obscure in His mind and on His heart.

> Father, there is no one who is unimportant to You; Your Son died for all. All are loved by You, and that is what gives us value. Help me to see others through the eyes of Christ and treat them with love.

JUNE 3

Even though he finished last in his class at West Point, George A. Custer of Michigan advanced rapidly in rank during the war. He was the youngest brigadier general in the Union army at twenty-one; he continued to impress his superiors until he had gained the rank of brevet major general at the war's end. Known for his dash and daring, for the colorful uniforms he designed for himself, and for his brash cavalry charges with his shoulder-length golden locks flowing in the wind, he seemed invincible as he escaped time after time in situations where certain defeats were turned into victories. His critics called him foolhardy and ambitious while his benefactors called him heroic and lucky. What had served him well during the war brought him down on June 25, 1876. Trying to impress the government in Washington, D. C. where he had fallen from favor, he disregarded the counsel of his scouts. Instead of waiting for more help, he attacked the combined camp of Sioux, Northern Cheyenne, and Arapaho numbering in the thousands at the Little Big Horn River in Montana. Five companies of cavalry were wiped out to a man, including Custer himself.

"Go from the presence of a foolish man when thou perceivest not in him the lips of knowledge" (Proverbs 14:7 KJV).

A wise heart examines its own motives and does not proceed until its motives are pure.

> Father, the men of Custer's command had to obey his orders. As a result two hundred twelve were killed on the bluffs overlooking the Little Big Horn. Please grant that my choices may not cause suffering or sorrow to anyone, especially to those I have authority over.

JUNE 4

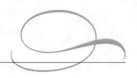

Maryland was a border state in the war, remaining in the Union but having strong Confederate sympathies. At the battle of Culp's Hill at Gettysburg, Pennsylvania, volunteers had enlisted on both sides and were facing each other in deadly combat. The First Maryland Regiment of the U. S. A. was directly opposite the First Maryland Regiment of the C. S. A. The regiments pitted against each other had been recruited from virtually the same section of the state. The same scene was played out at other battlefields by the other border states of Kentucky and Missouri. It is not too difficult to imagine that friend fought against friend, brother against brother.

"For it was not an enemy that reproached me; then I could have borne it; neither was it he that hated me that did magnify himself against me; then I would have hid myself from him. But it was thou, a man mine equal, my guide and mine acquaintance" (Psalm 55:12,13 KJV).

The enmity of those close to us is the most painful of all.

> Father, I can't imagine how difficult it was to look across the line of battle at the enemy with bayonet fixed and see a friend or brother or father. Thank You that I have never been in such a situation. Help me to be the best friend and brother that I can be.

JUNE 5

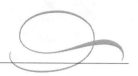

During the war, seventeen-year-old Jesse James and his older brother Frank, along with their cousins, the Younger Brothers, rode with the Confederate irregulars led by William Quantrill and Bloody Bill Anderson. Their main opponents were Federal troops in their home state of Missouri with Union irregulars from Kansas. The border war between Kansas and Missouri was raging long before the first cannon fire at Fort Sumter, South Carolina. The guerilla tactics they learned in the war served the James and Younger gang well afterwards. They became the most infamous outlaw gang in the history of our country. They flourished for sixteen years, even after the capture and imprisonment of the Younger brothers in 1876. Finally it ended with Jesse's murder by a friend in 1882. Frank James lived to old age and died in 1915. He had been tried and cleared of all charges.

"For they have sown the wind, and they shall reap the whirlwind" (Hosea 8:7a KJV).

We reap what we sow, with compound interest.

> Father, those were terrible and turbulent years. Help me to learn from the Bible and from history that I may not repeat poor choices.

JUNE 6

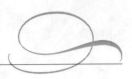

Upon hearing of the death of Lieutenant Preston Hampton in battle, General Robert E. Lee penned this letter to Lieutenant Hampton's father, General Wade Hampton, who at the time was General Lee's cavalry commander. "My dear General, I grieve with you at the death of your gallant son. So young, so brave, so true. I know how much you must suffer. Yet, think of the great gain to him; how changed his condition, how bright his future. We must labor in the charge before us, but for him I trust is rest and peace for I believe our merciful God takes us when it is best for us to go. He is now safe from all harm and from all evil and nobly died in the defense of the rights of his country. May God support you under your great affliction and give you strength to bear the trials He may impose upon you. Truly your friend, R. E. Lee." General Lee's daughter, Annie, had died two years previously at age twenty-three.

"Who comforteth us in all our tribulation that we may be able to comfort them which are in any trouble by the comfort wherewith we ourselves are comforted of God" (II Corinthians 1:4 KJV).

General Lee was able to commiserate with General Hampton only because of the pain of his own loss.

> Father, help me to be a comfort to others when
> they are hurting.

JUNE 7

One would be sore pressed to find anyone who suffered loss more than General Wade Hampton of South Carolina. Prior to the war, he was one of the richest planters on the continent, having vast holdings in Mississippi as well as South Carolina. Elected to the Senate, he gave a memorable speech against the reimportation of slaves to America. Horace Greely called it "a masterpiece of logic," directed by the noblest sentiments of the Christian and the patriot. He believed the institution of slavery was soon to be an unpleasant memory, and he was a staunch Unionist against secession. But at the outset of the war he raised the "Hampton's Legion" of infantry, cavalry, and artillery and offered it to the Confederacy. At the death of J. E. B. Stuart he became Robert E. Lee's cavalry commander. During the war he was wounded five times. He held his son, Preston, in his arms as he died at the battle of Hatcher's Run, Virginia. Federal troops burned down his mansion, and the war left him in financial ruins. Though he was great as a military leader, his greatest contribution was guiding his state through the horrors and bondage of the Reconstruction after the war. Opposing him were the carpetbaggers and scalawags of that era, a corrupt government in Washington, and Federal occupation troops. He was elected governor, and then served as a U. S. senator. After his death people said: "South Carolina had turned to General Wade Hampton who was to his people what Washington was to the colonies and for much the same reason."

"For whom I have suffered the loss of all things and do count them as dung that I may win Christ" (Philippians 3:8b KJV).

God has told us that the sufferings of this present time are light as feathers compared to the weight of glory that awaits us who are in Christ.

> Father, Wade Hampton suffered great loss but gained much more in Christ. Thank you that what I have in Christ cannot be burned, stolen, or lost. Help me to be faithful in the times of suffering as well as the times of joy and plenty.

JUNE 8

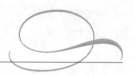

General Robert E. Lee did not issue much praise toward soldiers doing their duty as he felt it was the least they could do before God. But he did call General Joe Wheeler "outstanding." General Wheeler, from Georgia, did some of the greatest military exploits of the war during the most difficult times for the Confederacy. The Union grew stronger while the South grew weaker in forces and resources. Against overwhelming numbers and material, General Wheeler and his cavalry provided the only resistance to Union General Sherman's "March to the Sea." Wheeler and his small force scored victory after victory, but it was not enough to turn the tide. The end of the war did not end Wheeler's service. Beginning at age thirty he served two terms in the U. S. Congress; when the SpanishAmerican War exploded, President McKinley appointed him major general in command of all volunteers. He was at the battle of San Juan Hill, fought at Las Guasimas, and led a cavalry division in Cuba even though he was sixty years old and suffering from malaria. Later he commanded a brigade of cavalry in the Phillippines and gained the rank of brigadier general. He spent the last years of his life working to improve the conditions all over the South and in his adopted state of Alabama.

"As yet I am as strong this day as I was in the day Moses sent me. As my strength was then, even so is my strength now, for war, both to go out and to come in" (Joshua 14:11 KJV).

What greater honor can there be than to be useful to God and to people?

> Father, You preserved Caleb's strength at eighty-five years of age. Help me to fight the good fight and bear good fruit, to be forever young in Your service.

JUNE 9

On October 2, 1864, Albert Willis and a comrade were captured by the 2nd U. S. Cavalry. Because the two were a part of an elite Confederate Cavalry force called Mosby's Rangers, they were sentenced to hang. This order was issued by General Phillip Sheridan with the concurrence of General U. S. Grant. The sentence was so severe because of the havoc the Rangers were doing behind Union lines, harassing troops, capturing supply trains, disrupting communication, and destroying wagons and Federal stores. In one six-month period the Rangers, under the command of John S. Mosby, inflicted one thousand two hundred Federal casualties and collected sixteen hundred horses and mules, two hundred thirty cattle, and eighty-five wagons. What infuriated the Union command was their inability to capture and destroy Mosby and his men. Thus, any ranger captured was to be hung. Albert Willis, a seminary student, was offered a chaplain's exemption. Willis declined, but gave his exemption to his comrade who was married. The twenty-year-old Willis gave himself as a substitute so his fellow prisoner could go free. On October 14, 1864, as the rope was placed around his neck, Willis professed his Christian faith and his readiness to die. He prayed for his executioners and was hanged.

"He that loveth his life shall lose it and he that hateth his life in this world shall keep it unto life eternal" (John 12:25 KJV).

Albert Willis demonstrated to the utmost the principle that it is more blessed to give than to receive.

> Father, young Albert Willis gave up something very precious to save the life of another. He gained something far more precious that he will have forever. Thank You for making it so.

JUNE 10

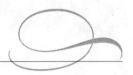

Major John S. Mosby was small in stature, weighing just 125 pounds, but what he lacked in size he made up in daring and military brilliance. He was the commander of an elite Confederate ranger force that disrupted the Union war effort for two years. They attacked supply lines, trains, and Federal troop emplacements, even capturing a Union general. Mosby operated out of two counties in Northern Virginia which gave him access to Union supply routes and rail lines. His tactic was to make lightning raids; he and his men carried two .44 caliber pistols each. He was known as the Gray Ghost to friend and foe; the two counties from which he operated were called "Mosby's Confederacy." Two of the best Union cavalry companies had the sole assignment to hunt down and kill Mosby, but they never could. A hundred of the best horsemen in the Union Army were armed with new repeating rifles and ordered to search for and destroy Mosby's Rangers. On November 18, 1864, Mosby and the Rangers ambushed the Union contingent and wiped them out, except for two men. Mosby survived the war, though wounded seven times. The Rangers totaled fewer than two thousand for the entire war, though they never numbered as much as a thousand at a time. The war lasted arguably a year longer due to Mosby's Rangers.

"I am small and despised yet do I not forget Thy precepts" (Psalm 119:144 KJV).

It is good to be as bold as a lion for God's Kingdom.

> Father, my size is not important; only my heart
> and commitment matter. May I never be lacking
> in that.

JUNE 11

In 1875 a large gathering of black citizens met at the Shelby County Fairgrounds east of Memphis, Tennessee to hear a speech by a man who had been the first Grand Wizard of the Ku Klux Klan. He had given his life to Christ and trusted Him as Lord and Savior. He also broke away from the Klan. This is a portion of the words spoken that day by Nathan Bedford Forrest: "I come to meet you as friends, and to welcome you to the white people. I want you to come nearer to us. When I can serve you I will do so. We have but one flag, one country; let us stand together. We may be different in color but not in sentiment. I have been in the heat of battle when colored men have asked me to protect them. I have placed myself between them and the bullets of my men, and told them they should be kept unharmed. Go to work, be industrious, live honestly, and act truly, and when you are oppressed I'll come to your relief."

"Therefore, if any man be in Christ, he is a new creature. Old things are passed away; behold all things are become new" (II Corinthians 5:17 KJV).

Every creature needs the new birth; in Christ alone we may have it.

> Father, these words were spoken by one of the South's greatest war heros. He was fierce in battle, giving no quarter and asking none. After trusting Christ, he became a man of peace and reconciliation. Help me to live as a new creature in Christ and to follow the example of Forrest.

JUNE 12

As the Army of Northern Virginia found itself surrounded by over-whelming Federal forces, Union General Phillip Sheridan coun-seled General Grant to turn loose the full power of Union forces and completely annihilate the "Rebel" army. Lee's army had no route of escape and was outnumbered ten to one in arms. Lee had said, "Then there is nothing left for me to do but go to General Grant and I would rather die a thousand deaths." Now the choice to destroy the Southern army to the man or offer it an opportunity to surrender was up to General Grant. To his credit he accepted the surrender, and the terms he offered were generous.

"It is of the Lord's mercies that we are not consumed, because His compassions fail not. They are new every morning. Great is Thy faithfulness" (Lamentations 3:22,23 KJV).

As we grow in the faith, we also grow in the revelation of our depravity. This gives us a bigger view of the amazing mercy of God.

> Father, mercy was extended here, but nothing can compare to the mercy You have shown fallen man. Help me to be merciful to those who need to be shown mercy, because Your mercy has been shown to me.

JUNE 13

In this war the United States formulated a "total war" policy against the Confederacy. For the first time, war would be made on the civilian population as well as the military. The justification behind this was that through total war, the war would be shortened. Several Union generals excelled at allowing and even ordering all manner of devastation, destruction, arson, looting, and in some cases, murder and rape of noncombatants. The most notable were William T. Sherman in his "March to the Sea" through Georgia, South Carolina, and North Carolina, Thomas Ewing in Missouri, John Pope in Northern Virginia, Phillip Sheridan and David Hunter in the Shenandoah Valley, Virginia, and Benjamin Butler in New Orleans. None of this could have been possible, however, without the concurrence of the Commanding General of the Army, U.S. Grant and President Abraham Lincoln.

"I beheld the transgressors and was grieved because they kept not Thy word" (Psalm 119:158 KJV).

The confusion and difficulty of war do not justify evil, nor does a good end justify evil means.

> Father, Your word teaches that we must be merciful and charitable toward noncombatants. Help me to distinguish clearly between combatants and noncombatants and to be the best warrior I can be.

JUNE 14

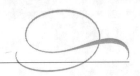

After the War, the policy of "Total War" would be carried out still. The new victims would be the plains Indians west of the Mississippi. When General Sheridan was explaining his actions of "Total War" against Indian villages, he said, "Did we cease to throw shells into Vicksburg or Atlanta because women and children were there?" To a surrendering Comanche chief he said, "The only good Indian I ever saw was dead." Sheridan ordered the attack on a sleeping Cheyenne village in what was called the Battle of the Washita (in what is now Oklahoma). The attack was carried out by the 7th U.S. Cavalry under the command of Lieutenant Colonel George A. Custer. A hundred and three Cheyenne were killed of whom only eleven were warriors. Fifty-three women and children were also taken captive and marched through severe wintry conditions to Fort Supply, Oklahoma. With the band playing and the fort turned out, the cavalrymen marched in with their captives and waved the scalps of the Cheyenne Chief Black Kettle and the other dead "savages."

"And this is the condemnation, that light is come into the world, and men loved darkness rather than light because their deeds were evil" (John 3:19 KJV).

It is one thing to kill in war a uniformed enemy or a terrorist; it is quite another to target deliberately his woman or his little child even though he has no qualms about targeting your civilians.

> Father, I know that apart from You I am capable of all manner of atrocities and sin. May I always walk in the Spirit on the path You have blazed for me. Help me to be a true warrior for Your glory and never to allow the concept of "collateral damage" become an excuse for deliberate shedding of innocent blood.

JUNE 15

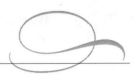

As the war raged in 1864, General Robert E. Lee penned a letter to Mrs. Lee from the field. A portion of it says, "I received today a kind letter from Reverend Mr. Cole of Culpepper Court House. He is a most excellent man in all the relations of life. He says there is not a church standing in all that country, within the lines formerly occupied by the enemy. All are razed to the ground, and the materials used often for the vilest purposes. Two of the churches at the Court House barely escaped destruction. The pews were all taken out to make seats for the theater. The fact was reported to the (Union) commanding officer by their own men of the Christian Commission, but he took no steps to rebuke or arrest it. We must suffer patiently to the end, when all things will be made right."

"And God shall wipe away all tears from their eyes, and there shall be no more death, neither sorrow, nor crying, neither shall there be any more pain for the former things are passed away" (Revelation 21:4 KJV).

Because God is real, both justice and mercy will prevail finally. But justice will be merciless to those who have shown no mercy.

> Father, is there anything I need to make right? If
> so, may I waste no time to do it.

JUNE 16

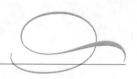

The Constitution of the Confederate States of America is copied almost word for word from the United States Constitution. Shortly before his death, James Henley Thornwell of South Carolina, one of America's greatest theologians, petitioned the Confederate Congress on behalf of the General Assembly of the Presbyterian Church to amend the Constitution to reflect a clear and distinct Christian worldview. Thornwell wrote, "We are constrained, in candour, to say that, in our humble judgment, the Constitution, admirable as it is in other respects, still labors under one capital defect. It is not distinctively Christian. It is not bigotry, but love to our country, and an earnest, ardent desire to promote its permanent wellbeing, which prompts us to call the attention of your honorable body to this subject, and, in the way of respectful petition, to pray that the Constitution may be amended so as to express the precise relations which the government of these states ought to sustain to the religion of Jesus Christ."

"Wherefore, God also hath highly exalted Him and gave Him a name which is above every name; that at the name of Jesus every knee should bow, of things in heaven, and things in earth, and things under the earth, and that every tongue should confess that Jesus Christ is Lord, to the glory of God the Father" (Philippians 2:9-11 KJV).

To have a life in which Christ is not merely present but preeminent is greatly to be desired.

> Father, James Thornwell was unsuccessful in his earnest desire that the Confederate Constitution be amended. Please let me be successful in amending my life, that Christ may be preeminent in it.

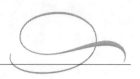

James Thornwell continued his plea: "We must contemplate people and rulers as alike subject to the authority of God. If then the State is an ordinance of God, it should acknowledge the fact. Let us guard in this new Confederacy against the fatal delusion that our government is a mere expression of human will. It is not enough for a State which enjoys the light of Divine Revelation to acknowledge in general terms the supremacy of God; it must also acknowledge the supremacy of His Son, whom He hath appointed heir to all things, by whom also He made the worlds. To Jesus Christ all power in heaven and earth is committed. To Him every knee shall bow, and every tongue confess. He is Ruler of the nations, the King of kings, the Lord of lords."

"Let the redeemed of the Lord say so, whom He hath redeemed from the hand of the enemy" (Psalm 107:2 KJV).

The world system is in rebellion against the true King. It is for us to establish His kingdom in our hearts, homes, and spheres of influence until the King comes back and casts out the usurper.

> Father, James Thornwell wanted the Confederate States of America to be recognized as a nation yielded to and centered in Christ. This I pray for my dear country today, and for myself.

James Thornwell continued his exhortation to amend the Constitution: "But it may be asked—has the state any right to accept the Scriptures as the Word of God? If by 'accepting the Scriptures' it is meant that the State may itself believe them to be true and regulate its own conduct and legislation in conformity with their teachings, the answer must be in the affirmative. Nevertheless we, the people of these Confederate States distinctly acknowledge our responsibility to God, and the supremacy of His Son, Jesus Christ, as King of Kings and Lord of Lords, and hereby ordain that no law shall be passed by the Congress of these Confederate States inconsistent with the will of God, as revealed in the Scriptures."

"Trust in the Lord with all thine heart and lean not unto thine own understanding. In all thy ways acknowledge Him, and He shall direct thy paths" (Proverbs 3:5,6 KJV).

Our responsibility, as was Thornwell's, is to play our part in this great republic, to be salt and light, whether or not we succeed in changing things for good.

> Father, bless our government officials with Your wisdom. May no laws be passed or policies adopted that are not consistent with Scripture.

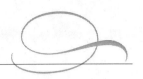

James Thornwell concluded his appeal: "The separation of Church and State is a very different thing from the separation of religion and the state. Here is where our fathers (America's founders) erred. In their anxiety to guard against the evils of a religious establishment, and to preserve the provinces of Church and State separate and distinct, they virtually expelled Jehovah from the government of the country, and left the State an irresponsible corporation, or responsible only to the immediate corporators. God is the Ruler among the nations, and the people who refuse Him their allegiance shall be broken with a rod of iron or dashed in pieces like a potter's vessel. Our republic will perish like the pagan republics of Greece and Rome, unless we baptize it into the name of Christ. We long to see, what the world has never yet beheld, a truly Christian Republic, and we humbly hope that God has reserved it for the people of these Confederate States to realize the grand and glorious idea."

"Blessed is the nation whose God is the Lord, and the people whom He hath chosen for His own inheritance" (Psalm 33:12 KJV).

Some would use the idea of separation of Church and State to expel the Christian faith from public life altogether, an idea utterly foreign to the founding fathers.

> Father, how very much it would have grieved James Thornwell and our founding fathers, to see the terrible shame that has gripped our nation through the misinterpretation by the courts of the concept of separation of Church and State. Please place godly judges in positions of authority to interpret the Constitution rightly and to restore and establish, as Thornwell envisioned, a nation in which You have your rightful place as the heart and soul of America.

JUNE 20

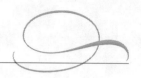

R. L. Dabney, who was Stonewall Jackson's chaplain and served on his staff until Jackson's death, wrote this: "Thus God teaches how good, how strong a thing His fear is. He makes all men see and acknowledge that in this man (Jackson) Christianity was the source of these virtues which they so rapturously applauded; that it was the fear of God which made him so fearless of all else, that it was the love of God which animated his energies; that the lofty chivalry of his nature was but the reflex of the Spirit of Christ. Even the profane admit, in their hearts, this explanation of Jackson's power and are prompt to declare that it was his religion that made him what he was. His life is God's lesson, teaching that "it is righteousness that exalteth a nation."

"Righteousness exalteth a nation, but sin is a reproach to any people" (Proverbs 14:34 KJV).

Each of us is profoundly different, but, if animated by the Holy Spirit of Christ, our lives, too, may become God's lesson to a needy world.

> Father, may I be so filled with the Holy Spirit that others, Christian and non-Christian, may see clearly in me what was so evident in the life of Stonewall Jackson.

JUNE 21

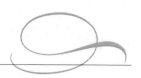

At the beginning of the war President Lincoln took upon himself what many believed to be dictatorial powers, such as suspending the writ of habeas corpus which led to arrest and imprisonment of any who voiced disagreement with the government or the president. The city of Baltimore, Maryland, was taken over by the Federal military at the point of the bayonet. Civil rights were defined at the pleasure of a centralized Federal government in Washington, D.C. Chief Justice of the Supreme Court, Roger B. Taney, gave an opinion in the "Merryman Case" that John Merryman from Maryland had not broken the law, but that Lincoln had broken it by arresting and imprisoning Merryman. Judge Taney wrote for the U. S. Supreme Court: "If the President of the United States may suspend the writ (of habeas corpus) then the Constitution of the United States has conferred upon him more regal and absolute power over the liberty of the citizen than the people of England have thought it safe to entrust to the crown—a power which the Queen of England cannot exercise to this day, and which could not have been lawfully exercised by the sovereign even in the reign of Charles the First." As a result of this, President Lincoln issued a warrant of arrest for the eighty-five year old Chief Justice which the Federal Marshall did not serve.

"For He cometh to judge the earth. With righteousness shall He judge the world, and the people with equity" (Psalm 98:9b KJV).

One day we shall stand before an impartial Judge who will examine our lives and who, alone, knows our motives.

> Father, in this incident President Lincoln proceeded as if he believed the end justified the means. Help me to deal justly toward all those influenced by my life for the sake of Your reputation and Your glory.

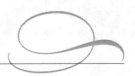

During the War, Union General William Sherman had this to say of Confederate Cavalry General Nathan Bedford Forrest: "That devil Forrest! I would like to have Forrest hunted down and killed." On another occasion Sherman issued orders to "follow Forrest to the death if it costs ten thousand lives and breaks the treasury. There will never be peace in Tennessee until Forrest is dead." Forrest and his cavalry won a host of battles with the Federals including Brice's Cross Roads, Holly Springs, Okolona, and Cedar Bluff. Among Forrest's horse soldiers were several dozen black troopers whom Forrest had said, "Better Confederates did not live." Having a very limited education because of having to support his family as a youth, and no military training, Forrest made a fortune before the war trading in cotton, real estate, and slaves. Forty-four of his own slaves went to war with him, and forty-two remained with him the entire war. After the war ended and peace had come, General Sherman said that Forrest "was the most remarkable man our Civil War produced on either side."

"And after him was Shamgar, the son of Anath which slew of the Philistines six hundred men with an ox goad, and he also delivered Israel" (Judges 3:31 KJV).

Few of us will be counted great or mighty in generations to come. Still, we can use our limited resources, our broken swords, to strike our small blows for the Kingdom of God. And who knows, perhaps God will use our efforts more profoundly than we could imagine.

> Father, General Forrest Bedford, like Shamgar, used what he had where he was and did what he could. Help me to do the same today for duty, honor, country, and the cause of Christ.

JUNE 23

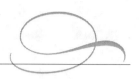

In a two week period in the fall of 1864, Confederate General Nathan Bedford Forrest and his cavalry, in an area south of Nashville, Tennessee, captured 2,360 Federal soldiers and killed or wounded an estimated one thousand more. The cost to the Confederates was three hundred forty wounded, of whom forty-seven died. Forrest had destroyed eleven blockhouses along with the extensive trestles and bridges they were meant to guard. He and his men took seven U. S. Cannon, eight hundred horses, more than two thousand rifles, and fifty wagons loaded with spoils, all of which he brought with him. Best of all, he had wrecked the Tennessee and Alabama railroad so thoroughly that even the skilled Union work crews would need six full weeks to put it back into operation. When asked about his successes against the West Point-trained Federal commanders, he said, "Whenever I met one of them fellers that fit (fought) by note, I generally whipped him before he got his tune pitched." His famous axiom about military success was, "Get there first with the most." After many attempts to capture or kill Forrest and his four thousand five hundred troops, Sheridan exclaimed, "It's a physical impossibility to protect the roads now that Hood, Forrest, Wheeler, and the whole batch of devils are turned loose without home or habitation."

"In the days of Shamgar the son of Anath, in the days of Jael, the highways were unoccupied and the travellers walked through byways" (Judges 5:6 KJV).

What an honor to be a man both hated and respected by the enemy!

> Father, as Shamgar so terrorized the Philistines that they abandoned the highways, and as Forrest so disrupted and confused his enemies, so strengthen me to war against Your enemies, both offensively and defensively.

JUNE 24

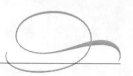

Shortly after his conversion to Christ in 1875, Nathan Bedford Forrest, formerly a general in the Confederacy, attended worship services with his wife. The sermon centered on Jesus' parable of the builders (One built his house on rock, one on sand). After the service, Forrest approached the pastor who had delivered the message and who had known him for twenty-five years. Reverend George Stainback said that Forrest took his arm, suddenly leaned back against the wall, his eyes filling with tears, and said, "Sir, your sermon has removed the last prop from under me. I am the fool that built on sand; I am a poor miserable sinner." Stainback counseled the shaken Forrest to study Psalm 51 for help and comfort. The next evening the minister visited Forrest and, after a prayer together, Forrest rose from his knees and said he was, "satisfied. All is right. I put my trust in my Redeemer."

"Therefore, whoever heareth these sayings of mine and doeth them, I will liken him unto a wise man, which built his house on a rock" (Matthew 7:24 KJV).

Through the years we build our lives with thoughts, words, choices, and deeds. At the end, each person has built an edifice. Some of those edifices are built on sand; they will fall. Some are built on rock; they will stand.

> Father, thank you that all who love Christ and live
> for Him have built their house on the Rock of salva-
> tion; they shall not be moved.

JUNE 25

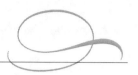

Shortly after he had trusted Christ as Savior and Lord, General Nathan Bedford Forrest was visiting with his former aide, Charles Anderson, who had ridden into battle with Forrest and had seen his savagery in combat. He had seen firsthand why his enemies were frozen in fear at the mention of his name. But this was a different Forrest. The burning light of a warrior still simmered in his eyes, but it was gentler. When asked about the difference in his countenance, Forrest was silent for a moment. Then he took hold of the lapel of Anderson's coat so that they faced each other squarely and said, "Major, I'm not the man you were with so long and knew so well. I hope I am a better man. I've joined the Church and am trying to live a Christian life."

"Therefore, if any man be in Christ, he is a new creature. Old things are passed away. Behold all things are become new" (II Corinthians 5:17 KJV).

There is a hideous worm that enters a cocoon and emerges as a beautiful butterfly. This is a picture of the new birth in Christ.

> Father, thank You that, in Christ, the old has
> passed away and the new has come. Help me to
> live as the new man today.

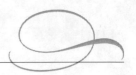

In 1877, twelve years after the war ended and two years after he gave his life to Christ, Confederate General Nathan Bedford Forrest lay dying. On his deathbed at age fifty-six he confided in his friend, Reverend Stainback, that he regretted words spoken in anger and deeds done thoughtlessly and in haste. Nevertheless he said, "I want you to understand now that I feel that God has forgiven me for all. I have an indescribable peace. All is peace within. I want you to know that between me and the face of my Heavenly Father, not a cloud intervenes. I have put my trust in my Lord and Savior."

"As for me, I will behold Thy face in righteousness: I shall be satisfied when I awake, with Thy likeness" (Psalm 17:5 KJV).

Every single human soul will see Christ face to face, either as Savior or Judge. We who die in Christ will wake in Heaven fully satisfied to know that all is well between us.

> Father, what a joy it will be to look upon the face
> of my Master. May He return soon and may He
> find me faithful.

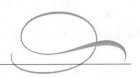

After he surrendered in 1865 Confederate General Nathan Bedford Forrest wanted to be sure his men knew that the fighting was over and that it was time for peace. He said to them: "Civil war as you have just passed through naturally engenders feelings of animosity, hatred, and revenge. It is our duty to divest ourselves of all such feelings and so far as it is in our power to do so, to cultivate feelings toward those with whom we have so long contested, and heretofore so widely but honestly differed. Whatever your responsibilities may be to government, to society, or to individuals, meet them like men." Forrest spent the rest of his life financially supporting disabled Confederate veterans and the widows and orphans of dead soldiers with money that he earned after the war. Not a penny was received for these from the U. S. Government though the Government gave millions to Union veterans.

"The steps of a good man are ordered by the Lord, and He delighteth in his way" (Psalm 37:23 KJV).

A Christian leader does not lord it over people; he is a servant leader.

> Father, General Forrest spent the last years of his
> life doing good. Please order my steps that I may
> finish well and that You may delight in my way.

JUNE 28

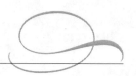

Dr. J. William Jones, chaplain in the Army of Northern Virginia had this to say of a Sunday morning in the camp of General Stonewall Jackson: "General Lee used frequently to attend preaching at Jackson's headquarters; and it was a scene which a master hand might have delighted to paint—those two great warriors, surrounded by hundreds of their officers and men, bowed in humble worship before the God and Savior in whom they trusted." It has been estimated that during the four years of war, one hundred thousand Confederate soldiers had professed their faith in Christ as Savior and Lord. This does not count those who were Christians prior to entering the army. There are few examples in military history before or since that such a large number of men in an army have given their lives to Christ and embraced orthodox Christianity.

"Then Simon Peter answered Him, Lord, to whom shall we go? Thou hast the words of eternal life. And we believe and are sure that Thou art that Christ, the Son of the living God" (John 6:68,69 KJV).

The proximity of sudden, violent death gives a certain clarity of thinking to warriors. The utter certainty of death should do the same for the rest of us.

> Father, thank You for the overwhelming proof
> You have given regarding who You are and what
> You came to do. Help me to respond to You in
> faith as did many of the soldiers of the South.

JUNE 29

Fearing what he believed to be worldliness throughout the Southern army, Stonewall Jackson said, "The only thing which gives me any apprehension about my country's cause is the sin of the army and the people." As a result he wrote a letter to the General Assembly of the Southern Presbyterian Church requesting more chaplains to be assigned to the ranks. Jackson wrote, "Each branch of the Christian Church should send into the army some of its most prominent ministers who are distinguished for their piety, talents, and zeal; and such ministers should labor to produce concert of action among chaplains and Christians in the army. These ministers should give special attention to preaching to regiments which are without chaplains, and induce them to take steps to get chaplains, to let the regiments name the denominations from which they desire chaplains selected, and then to see that suitable chaplains are selected. A bad selection of a chaplain may prove a curse instead of a blessing. If the few prominent ministers thus connected with each army would cordially cooperate, I believe that glorious fruits would be the result. Denominational distinctions should be kept out of view and not touched upon, and, as a general rule, I do not think that a chaplain who would preach denominational sermons should be in the army. His congregation is his regiment, and it is composed of various denominations. I would like to see no question asked in the army of what denomination a chaplain belongs to; but let the question be, Does he preach the Gospel?"

"Preach the Word! Be instant in season, out of season; reprove, rebuke, exhort with all longsuffering and doctrine" (II Timothy 4:2 KJV).

Every chaplain, pastor, and Christian leader must pray for grace to speak the truths that are nearest to the heart of God.

> Father, as the question is asked, "Does he preach the Gospel?" may the answer be "yes" for the chaplains in the military and for the pastors in our churches.

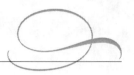

Union General U. S. Grant believed the war to be all but over after he had victories over the Confederate army at Fort Henry on the Tennessee River, February 6, 1862 and then at Fort Donelson on February 16, 1862. He wired his superiors in Washington, D.C., "The war is on its last legs and the enemy too demoralized to constitute a danger. The temper of the rebel troops is such that there is but little doubt but that Corinth (Mississippi) will fall much more easily than Donelson did when we do move. All accounts agree in saying that the great mass of the rank and file are heartily tired." Then the bloody battle of Shiloh, Tennessee was fought on April 6. Grant, though victorious, came close to losing his entire army. There was a combined total of 23,741 casualties, most being Grant's. This exceeded the total of all the nation's three previous wars. After Shiloh, Grant said, "I gave up all idea of saving the Union except by complete conquest." By this he meant the idea of "Total War."

"Go to now, ye that say, today or tomorrow we will go into such a city ... For that ye ought to say, If the Lord will, we shall do this or that" (James 4: 13a, 14a, 15 KJV).

Not one of us knows what will happen tomorrow; it is unwise, then, to make rash predictions.

> Father, help me not to make presumptions on the future by racing ahead, but to wait on You in submission to Your will.

JULY 1

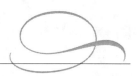

The only hope for the Confederacy to win its independence was for the war to be short. It was not. Those of the South hoped that the people of the North would grow war-weary because of the great loss of life and limb the North suffered in every battle. But the Union had so much more of everything, and the longer the war continued, the less chance the Confederacy had of winning. Of population the North had eighteen and a half million, the South nine million; of factories it was one hundred thousand five hundred versus twenty thousand six hundred; of railroads, twenty thousand miles versus nine thoudand miles; of workers, one million one hundred thousand versus one hundred eleven thousand; of value of products, $1,500,000,000 versus $155,000,000. The North had a navy; the South did not. The North produced iron, coal, and copper; the South tobacco and cotton.

"Thus saith the Lord: Let not the wise man glory in his wisdom, neither let the mighty man glory in his might. Let not the rich man glory in his riches. But let him that glorieth glory in this; that he understandeth and knoweth Me, that I am the Lord who would exercise lovingkindness, judgment, and righteousness in the earth. For in these things I delight, saith the Lord" (Jeremiah 9:23,24 KJV).

The temptation of every highly gifted individual and nation is an overweening pride, as if somehow our achievements were related to our own greatness of soul. But if we do achieve something, it is only with the brains, strength, and intelligence given us from above.

> Father, the Union won because You willed it so. Give me wisdom as I spend time with You to rejoice more over our relationship than over the very best thing I ever accomplish while I am here in the world.

JULY 2

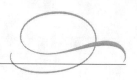

On December 20, 1860, the State Government of South Carolina voted to secede from the United States. On January 9, 1861, Mississippi followed suit. Then came Florida on January 10, Alabama on January 11, Georgia on January 19, Louisiana on January 26, and Texas on February 1, 1861. After the Union's Fort Sumter was fired upon on April 12, 1861, President Abraham Lincoln called upon the states to furnish seventy-five thousand volunteers to put down the "Rebellion" and force the "Rogue States" back into the Union. After Lincoln's call to arms, Virginia voted for secession on April 17, 1861, followed by Arkansas on May 6, Tennessee on May 7, and North Carolina on May 20, 1861. These eleven states formed the Confederate States of America with its first capital located at Montgomery, Alabama; later they moved it to Richmond, Virginia. This was one hundred miles from the United States capital at Washington, D.C.

"Thy throne, O God, is forever and ever. The scepter of Thy Kingdom is a right scepter" (Psalm 45:6 KJV).

Some day the United States of America will be no more. But God's Kingdom is eternal.

> Father, nations come and go, rise and fall, but
> Your Kingdom is firmly established forever. Help
> me to be a good citizen in it.

JULY 3

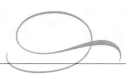

"On to Richmond" became the battle cry of the Union army and the people of the North after the successful landing of General George McClellan on the east coast of Virginia with his force of one hundred twenty thousand troops. As McClellan moved steadily toward the Confederate capital against a Southern force half its size, optimism rose in the North. They would avenge the defeat at I Manassas and bring the war to an end! Their spirits were high as they arrived at a place eight miles from the city limits of Richmond. After all, the Confederate general in command, Joe Johnston, had been wounded and replaced by another who, they thought, was well past his prime—Robert E. Lee.

"Lord, Thou hast heard the desire of the humble. Thou wilt prepare their heart. Thou wilt cause Thine ear to hear" (Psalm 10:17 KJV).

To make a presumption on the future and to make a presumption about someone's abilities are equally erroneous.

> Father, it appeared that many had the proud antic-
> ipation of an easy and early victory, only to find
> that it was neither easy nor early. Help me never
> to take anyone or anything for granted; help me
> never to make presumptions on the future.

JULY 4

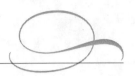

At the Battle of the Wilderness in 1864 the Texas Brigade formed in line to counterattack the Union forces. Brigadier General Evander Law's Alabama Brigade moved alongside the Texas Brigade. General Lee asked, "What troops are these?" Upon hearing the answer, he said, "God bless the Alabamians!" Then to everyone's horror, General Lee spurred Traveller forward to lead the attack at the head of the Texas Brigade. Soldiers shouted, "Lee to the rear! Lee to the rear! General Lee, go back!" But Lee refused until the soldiers were pleading, "We won't go unless you go back," and a sergeant took his horse's reins and led him back. The Texans and Alabamians were ready to die in the attack, and many would, but no one was willing to lose General Lee. They knew that the war would be lost if Lee were lost. He was the primary inspiration for all the soldiers.

"And the three brake through the host of the Philistines and drew water out of the well of Bethlehem that was by the gate and took it and brought it to David" (I Chronicles 11:18a KJV).

What kind of love can lead men to do daring, reckless deeds for someone? Why would they risk their lives in such a tumult?

> Father, these three warriors loved David so much that they fought a host of Philistines just to bring him a cup of water. Lee's soldiers loved him in the same way. This is the kind of love that comes from You. Please let this love be seen in me as I love others and especially as I love You.

July 5

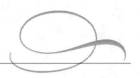

After the Confederate effort to end the war failed in the defeat of the Southern Army at the battle of Gettysburg, Pennsylvania in 1863, all of the general officers involved in the battle except two fought to absolve themselves of any blame. The two were General Richard Ewell, who confessed to committing many errors, and General Robert E. Lee, who assumed total responsibility for the defeat. General Pickett's report to General Lee was highly critical of other units and their leaders. General Lee returned the report, suggesting that Pickett destroy it along with all its copies. He said to Pickett, "You and your men have covered yourselves with glory. But we have the enemy to fight and must carefully, at this critical moment, guard against dissensions which the reflections in your report would create. I hope all will yet be well."

"To wit, that God was in Christ, reconciling the world to himself, not imputing their trespasses to them, and hath committed unto us the word of reconciliation" (II Corinthians 5:18 KJV).

God has said in the Scripture that he hates sowers of discord among brethren, but "blessed are the peacemakers."

> Father, how easy it is to blame others while seeing
> no fault in myself. Help me to be a reconciler and
> peacemaker and not a sower of discord.

July 6

In 1864 at the battle of the Wilderness in Virginia, the Confederate line was on the point of breaking due to a Union advantage in men and resources. At a critical time the Southern reinforcements began forming, on the run, behind General Lee as he sat astride Traveller. He cried out, "Who are you, my boys?" "Texas boys!" was the loud response. These were Lee's "immortals," Hood's Texans who were now under the command of Brigadier General John Gregg. Gregg's was the lead brigade of General Field's division. Lee shouted, "Hurrah for Texas!" as he took off his hat and waved it; then, standing in his stirrups, again he yelled, "Hurrah for Texas!" These were the men he needed to drive the Union back. The army was saved, and the battle won.

"I will say of the Lord, 'He is my refuge and fortress, my God; in Him will I trust'" (Psalm 91:2 KJV).

Things that happen in war demonstrate God's sovereign control of history. Although He gives us freedom to make decisions and take action, what we do cannot thwart His sovereign and mysterious purpose.

> Father, the Texas Brigade arrived just in time;
> thank You that You also are never late; You have
> always intervened just in time to protect me, and
> so You do with all your saints.

JULY 7

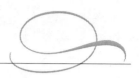

As the Texas Brigade filed into line at such a crucial time during the battle of the Wilderness, they were cheered on by General Lee. Observers had never seen the usually dignified and reserved general so animated. Long after the war his subordinates recalled the event saying, "His blood was up." When General Lee shouted, "The Texans always move them," the brigade commander, General John Gregg gave the order, "Attention, Texas Brigade! The eyes of General Lee are upon you. Forward, March!" The Texas Brigade suffered severe casualties while successfully driving back the Union surge. General Gregg survived this battle, but was later killed in action at age 36 during the battle of Petersburg, Virginia on the Darbytown Road.

"Be strong and of a good courage, fear not, nor be afraid of them, for the Lord thy God, He it is that doth go with thee. He will not fail thee nor forsake thee" (Deuteronomy 31:6 KJV).

We seldom think of the huge importance encouragement plays in helping us do the right thing and make decisions untainted by fear.

> Father, please impart to me the kind of courage those Texas soldiers had going into battle, some to their death. Thank You for encouraging me in the daily battles as General Lee encouraged the Texas Brigade.

JULY 8

Southern politician Benjamin H. Hill of Georgia had this to say of Robert E. Lee after his death: "He was a foe without hate, a friend without treachery, a soldier without cruelty, a victor without oppression, and a victim without murmuring. He was a public officer without vices, a private citizen without wrong, a neighbor without reproach, a Christian without hypocrisy, and a man without guile. He was a Caesar without his ambition; Frederick without his tyranny; Napoleon without his selfishness; and Washington without his reward."

"Mine eyes shall be upon the faithful of the land, that they may dwell with Me. He that walketh in a perfect way, he shall serve Me" (Psalm 101:6 KJV).

Faithfulness means to be steadfast in allegiance and firm in observance of duty.

> Father, it appears that General Lee was faithful,
> that he walked in a perfect way and served You.
> He dwelt with You. May that be the course of my
> life too, that I may dwell with You.

JULY 9

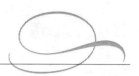

After the war and shortly before his death, Confederate President Jefferson Davis had this to say: "Nothing fills me with deeper sadness than to see a Southern man apologizing for the defense we made of our inheritance. Our cause was so just, so sacred, that had I known all that has come to pass, had I known what was to be inflicted upon me, all that my country was to suffer, all that our posterity was to endure, I would do it all over again."

"Let integrity and uprightness preserve me, for I wait on Thee" (Psalm 25:21 KJV).

If we could know that a particular decision followed by action would result in profound suffering, shouldn't we do it anyway, so long as it was right?

> Father, President Jefferson Davis believed with all his heart in the rightness of Southern independence. The cause was just and sacred to him, and he would leave the truth and error of that in Your hands. Help me to be as passionate for the cause of Christ.

JULY 10

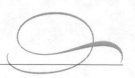

Just a few days prior to the battle of Gettysburg, Pennsylvania, in 1863, the command of the Union Army of the Potomac had changed for the sixth time in approximately a year and a half. The new commander was General George Meade of Pennsylvania. The subordinates and staff of Robert E. Lee laughed about this new change and this new commander of Federal forces. They considered Meade a mediocre appointee who would fare no better than those who came before him. General Lee set their thinking straight by saying, "General Meade will commit no blunder on my front, and if I make one he will make haste to take advantage of it." His words, to some extent, proved true.

"Humble yourselves in the sight of the Lord, and He shall lift you up" (James 4:10 KJV).

An example of a presumptuous sin is to boast about a supposed outcome of a future event.

> Father, General Lee resisted pride and boasting
> before the battle was fought. He humbled himself
> before You; may I do the same.

JULY 11

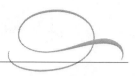

When General Lee surveyed the town of Fredericksburg, Virginia after his great victory over the Federal army at Marye's Heights (south of the town) in December of 1862, he was shocked and angered at the wanton destruction and desolation by the Union troops when they had occupied the town. The Union had launched a tremendous artillery shelling of Fredericksburg before their attack when there were but a small number of Confederates in the town. But that could not compare to the looting, destruction, and vandalism by Union troops before they abandoned the town in retreat. A Federal officer admitted that their behavior was like a mob out of control. As he looked at the carnage General Lee said, "These people delight to destroy the weak and those who can make no defense. It just suits them." One of Stonewall Jackson's staff asked what should be done to such people. Jackson replied, "Why, shoot them."

"See that none render evil for evil unto any man, but ever follow that which is good, both among yourselves and to all men" (I Thessalonians 5:15 KJV).

The warriors who are most fondly remembered are those who acted, to the extent humanly possible, on the principles of respect for the life and dignity of human beings.

> Father, I can understand the anger because of the suffering of the innocent non-combatants in this war. I am thankful that Generals Lee and Jackson did not behave in like manner. Help me to strengthen the weak and never render evil for evil.

JULY 12

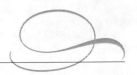

The battle of McDowell, Virginia, May 8, 1862 was the second battle fought by Stonewall Jackson against Union forces in what is known as Jackson's Valley Campaign. The Confederates held the high ground, especially two key positions. One was called Bull Pasture Mountain and the other, Sitlinger's Hill. If Jackson could get his artillery up these heights, the Federal forces would be in grave danger in the valley. About 4:30 p.m. twenty-three hundred Union soldiers started up the steep incline to force the twenty-eight hundred Confederate soldiers waiting for them off the mountain. The battle raged for four hours, hand to hand, with clubs, Bowie knives, and bayonets until the Federals withdrew. Captain James H. Wood, Company D, 37th Virginia described the action: "The whole scene is vivid in my mind as I saw it. Our Brigade was well down the mountain when the battle began and the roar of the musketry and shouts of the contending forces came up the mountainside to us as we hurried on. There was a kind of horrible grandeur about it all that allured and inspired some, and struck others with trepidation. We moved on. Louder and still fiercer the battle grows. Reinforcements are now entering on the Federal side with battle shouts and huzzahs, which are answered in grim defiance by the Confederates."

"A time to love and a time to hate; a time of war, and a time of peace" (Ecclesiastes 3:8 KJV).

There is a great spiritual conflict that has raged throughout man's history; the many wars of history are but small manifestations of it. And there really is a "horrible grandeur" in the Christian soldier's service on whatever front, because it is as grand to stand for righteousness and justice as it is horrible to behold the defiling works of Satan.

> Father, due to man's sin nature war has always been with us. After Christ has forever defeated his enemies, peace will reign and His glory will blaze forever. Thank You for this hope.

JULY 13

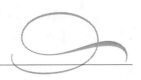

Captain Wood continues to describe the battle of McDowell, Virginia: "Our Brigade has now reached the base of the ridge, where we find Jackson who quickly points our position. Here, too, we find the field hospital, the ground strewn with the wounded, the dead, the dying; and still others came down the ridge from the front, wounded and red with blood, assisted or carried on litters. Surgeons and assistant surgeons are doing all they can to save suffering and life, but the scene is too sickening to pause and consider. On we go up the ridge, take our position in the line, and open fire upon the enemy. The battle now rages ten times fiercer than before. Men fall on every side, some never to rise, while others are wounded and helped to the rear. The smoke of battle settles upon us so dense and dark that we cannot see happenings around us. Begrimed, drinking and tasting the smoke of battle seemed to increase courage and determination, and thus with defiant war cries, the battle goes on for some hours."

"He shall redeem their soul from deceit and violence, and precious shall their blood be in His sight" (Psalm 72:14 KJV).

Perhaps the greatest mystery is that Almighty God has not yet brought an end to the wrath of man. Though we do not understand, yet we trust Him, for He is good.

> Father, You love every warrior, and the shed blood of warriors is precious to You. Christ's blood, shed for us, is most precious. Thank You for His sacrifice.

JULY 14

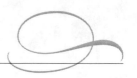

At the battle of Spotsylvania, Virginia, on May 12, 1864, a scene was repeated that had occurred one week earlier at the battle of the Wilderness. The Union had overwhelming numbers concentrated in key places; these threatened to cut the Southern army in half. General John Gordon was about to give the order for his three brigades to attack the four Union divisions when he saw General Lee in the center of the line, ready to lead the counterattack as he had tried to do at the Wilderness. General Gordon rode his horse at a gallop over to Lee and said, "General Lee, this is no place for you. Go back, General, we will drive them back." As the soldiers gathered around them, Gordon continued: "These men are Virginians and Georgians. They have never failed you. They never will. Will you, boys?" Their answer was loud and clear: "No! No! General Lee to the rear; Lee to the rear! We will drive them back for you, General." And as at the Wilderness, Traveller was led back to a safe area with General Lee astride him. The attack took the Union forces by surprise, stopped the Federal advance, and made time for the Confederate line to stabilize.

"Then the men of David sware unto him, saying, Thou shalt go no more with us to battle, that thou quench not the light of Israel" (II Samuel 21:17b KJV).

Loyalty is a much eroded virtue in this present time. Yet it is an eternal virtue.

> Father, at this point in the war the men were fighting for General Lee. To lose him was to lose the war. Help me to follow You as these men followed "Marse Robert."

JULY 15

During Stonewall Jackson's brilliant military campaign in the Shenandoah Valley in Virginia in 1862, his adjutant general and closest friend, Lieutenant Colonel Alexander (Sandie) Pendleton described the steep and forbidding countryside as follows: "This is the meanest country I ever saw, but it is still old Virginia, and we must have it." Colonel Pendleton was the person who dressed General Jackson's body and prepared it for burial just short of a year after his victories in the Valley. Later Pendleton became chief of staff for General Richard Ewell and General Jubal Early. This "mean country" witnessed the death of Sandie Pendleton during the battle of Fisher's Hill, September 22, 1864 while fighting Union General Phillip Sheridan's cavalry.

"But God will redeem my soul from the power of the grave, for He shall receive me. Selah" (Psalm 49:15 KJV).

Death for each of us is a certainty. Can we die better than those who die contending for truth?

> Father, there are not many things worth dying for.
> Sandie Pendleton believed that "old Virginia" was
> one of them. Surely the cause of Christ is worth
> living for and dying for. Give me grace to do so.

JULY 16

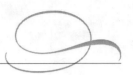

After the battle of Spotsylvania, Virginia in 1864, Union Commander U. S. Grant said in his dispatches to Washington that he "was satisfied that the enemy are very shaky." This opinion was not shared by all in the Union camp. Federal Colonel Theodore Lyman wrote: "Lee is not retreating. He is a brave and skillful soldier and will fight while he has a division or a day's ration left." Lyman had this to say of the poorly fed and ill clad soldiers who served in Lee's army: "These rebels are not half starved. A more sinewy, tawny, formidable-looking set of men could not be. In education they are certainly inferior to our native born people, but they are usually very quick-witted, and they know enough to handle weapons with terrible effect. Their great characteristic is their stoical manliness. They never beg or whimper or complain, but look you straight in the face with as little animosity as if they had never heard a gun fired."

"Of Zebulun such as went forth to battle, expert in war with all instruments of war, fifty thousand which could keep rank. They were not of double heart" (I Chronicles 13:33 KJV).

Commitment means to suffer privation for the cause without complaint.

> Father, help me to be strong in battle and never
> wavering or double-minded.

JULY 17

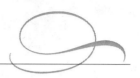

After Stonewall Jackson's series of victories in his famous Valley campaign in 1862, he shared with one of his staff his axioms for victory. One was "to always mystify, mislead and surprise the enemy, if possible. And when you strike and overcome him, never let up in the pursuit so long as your men have strength to follow; for an army routed, if hotly pursued, becomes panic stricken, and can then be destroyed by half their number."

"And when the Philistines saw their champion was dead they fled. And the men of Israel and Judah arose and shouted and pursued the Philistines until they came to the valley and to the gates of Ekron" (I Samuel 51b, 52a KJV).

We are often defeated by fear rather than by a superior enemy.

> Father, thank You that the battle is not only waged
> defensively, but also offensively. Thank You that
> the outcome has already been decided—victory at
> the cross and at the empty tomb.

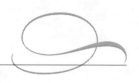

Another discovery that Stonewall Jackson had made regarding combat was "never fight against heavy odds if by any possible maneuvering

Confederate cannon, Chancellorsville, Virginia, 1863.

you can hurl your own force on only a part, and that the weakest part, of your enemy and crush it. Such tactics will win every time, and a small army may thus destroy a large one in detail, and repeated victory will make it invincible." He carried this out at the battle of Chancellorsville, Virginia in 1863.

"But thanks be to God, which giveth us the victory through our Lord Jesus Christ" (I Corinthians 15:57 KJV).

Our victory in Christ may not be immediately visible. Christ's death on the cross appeared to be the most colossal defeat ever, and yet it was the most colossal victory ever.

Father, thank You that the warrior who has put his trust in Christ serves in the "invincible" army of the Lord of Hosts. Total victory is certain in the end.

JULY 19

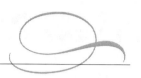

At the battle of Seven Pines, Virginia in 1862, Confederate Commanding General Joseph Johnston was very seriously wounded with a bullet wound in the right shoulder and a shell fragment striking him in the chest. He would survive his wounds and distinguish himself later in the war by great leadership and military brilliance. But at the time the command of his army fell into the hands of a man who, up to this point, had been a military disappointment. He had been unable to deal with headstrong subordinates in the field, causing reversals in what is now West Virginia. The army that he would now be commanding was filled with high strung and headstrong troop commanders. He had not been in combat since the Mexican-American War at Chapultepec fifteen years before. The entire South was hoping and praying that Robert E. Lee was up to the task.

"And we know that all things work together for good to them that love God, to them who are called according to His purpose" (Romans 8:28 KJV).

How often suffering comes bearing precious gifts, and how vigorously we flee from it!

> Father, General Johnston later said his wounding was the best thing that could have happened for the good of his country. Help me to accept with thanksgiving all that You bring into my life, because You will work it for good.

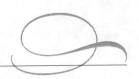

After General Lee surrendered the Army of Northern Virginia to General Grant and the Federal forces on April 9, 1865, he rode back to his men who stood in column. Soon the men broke ranks and crowded around General Lee asking, "General, are we surrendered? Are we surrendered?" Lee answered, "Men, we have fought the war together, and I have done the best I could for you. You will all be paroled and go to your homes until exchanged." Then with his eyes filling with tears he said, "Goodbye." From many emotion-choked throats came cries of, "General, we'll fight 'em yet." Though most responded with stunned silence, one warrior dropped to his knees and cried out, "Blow, Gabriel, blow! My God, let him blow, I'm ready to die!" One told his brigade commander, "We'll go home, make three more crops, and try 'em again." Though General Lee's ragged and starved army was just a shell of its former self, it was ready to fight to the death if Lee so ordered.

"Most men will proclaim every one his own goodness, but a faithful man who can find?" (Proverbs 20:6 KJV).

These men demonstrated their faithfulness with deeds.

> Father, General Lee's men loved him more than
> their own lives. Help me to love Christ so.

July 21

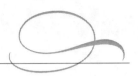

After General Lee wrote a farewell to his army, Confederate Captain Henry Perry copied, "General Orders, No. 9" on a piece of paper and asked Lee to sign it. Lee graciously consented. This was Perry's account of the event: "There were tears in his eyes when he signed it for me, and when I turned and walked away there were tears in my own eyes. He was in all respects the greatest man who ever lived, and as a humble officer of the South, I thank heaven I had the honor of following him."

"The steps of a good man are ordered by the Lord, and He delighteth in his way" (Psalm 37:23 KJV).

The beautiful attributes of character in every truly good man come from the indwelling Spirit of Christ.

> Father, General Lee would be the first to deny
> that he was "the greatest man who ever lived." He
> would humbly attribute that title to Christ. Help
> me to walk in humility and submission to the real
> "greatest One who ever lived"—Jesus.

July 22

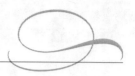

On the morning of March 21, 1865, shortly before the end of the war, sixteen-year-old Willie Hardee, after months of pleading, got permission from his father, General William J. Hardee to take part in the battle at Bentonville, North Carolina. Young Hardee was assigned to the 8th Texas Cavalry Regiment which charged the Federal lines on this, the last day of the battle. Greatly outnumbered, the Confederates pulled back toward Smithfield. Their casualties numbered 1,694 wounded and 912 killed. Among the dead lay young Willie Hardee.

"O my son Absalom, my son, my son Absalom! Would God I had died for thee, O Absalom, my son, my son!" (II Samuel 18:33b KJV).

Whether in time of war or time of peace, death may be an unwelcome visitor. In either time Christ is our comfort.

> Father, I'm sure General Hardee felt for his son as David did for his. Thank You for being the God of comfort when we are grieved and broken.

July 23

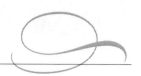

After the terrible ordeal of "Reconstruction" was in full swing, General Phillip Sheridan was given charge of one of the military districts in the South. His district included Texas and Louisiana. Sheridan, not noted for kindness, said this: "If I had a choice between living in hell or Texas, I would live in hell and rent out Texas." A Texan replied, "Every man to his own country." Due to Sheridan's harshness and depredations upon the people in his district, President Johnson found it necessary to remove him from that assignment and move him north. In 1875 the New Orleans newspaper had this to say of Sheridan: "If there is one man responsible for the misfortunes of Louisiana, that man is General Phil Sheridan."

"For a small moment I have forsaken thee, but with great mercies will I gather thee" (Isaiah 54:7 KJV).

Sometimes God's people appear to be forsaken by Him when our perspective takes in only time and circumstance. But in the mystery of the deep things of God, he works it all for eternal good.

> LORD, You have always been merciful to me, and I have never felt forsaken. I cannot imagine the agony of Your only begotten Son when You turned away from Him as He hung on the cross for me. Thank You for the cross.

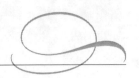

Confederate Brigadier General Turner Ashby was well known for his dash and bravery. He seemed driven to kill as many Federals as he could. People said it was because he wanted to avenge his brother who was murdered while trying to surrender to Union troops. Whatever the truth may be, Ashby left this life in a blaze of glory. He was killed while leading a cavalry charge, sword in hand, at the battle of Harrisburg, Virginia. His last words were: "Charge, men! For God's sake charge!" His commanding officer, Stonewall Jackson, had this to say of him, "As a partisan officer, I never knew his superior."

"O Lord God, to whom vengeance belongeth; O God, to whom vengeance belongeth, show Thyself" (Psalm 94:1 KJV).

We do not have the knowledge necessary to bring judgment on someone. We don't know all the motives and circumstances, as God does, and we have our own sins to deal with. It is best to pray for our enemies and to wait patiently until God brings about perfect justice.

> Father, there appears to be much in this life that isn't fair or just. I must leave the righting of it to You and simply do my duty as You equip me to do it.

JULY 25

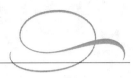

Major R. L. Dabney was Stonewall Jackson's chief of staff. He was also a pastor who delivered sermons to various Confederate camps when it was possible. One Sunday morning Major Dabney inquired of General Jackson if any military operations would be held on this day. General Jackson replied, "Major, you know I always try to keep the Sabbath if the enemy will let me."

"Remember the Sabbath day, to keep it holy" (Exodus 20:8 KJV).

The enemy of our souls does indeed try to keep us from observing the Lord's day.

> Father, thank You that You did not create men for
> the Sabbath, but the Sabbath for men. Help me
> to keep the Lord's day holy and set apart, a special
> day of rest focusing on the good things of God.

July 26

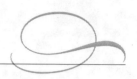

Confederate General Stonewall Jackson demanded much of those who served under him, but not nearly as much as he demanded of himself. During his valley campaign of 1862, there had been a mixup during the movement of his army near Strasburg, Virginia. Men, wagons, horses, and equipment had become entangled on a narrow road. Incensed, Jackson rode up to an infantry commander and ordered him to get his troops in line and move them away from the confusion. He said, "Colonel, why do you not get your brigade together, keep it together, and move on?" "It's impossible, General. I can't do it," replied the colonel. "Don't say it's impossible! Turn your command over to the next officer. If he can't do it, I'll find someone who can, if I have to take him from the ranks."

"Open rebuke is better than secret love" (Proverbs 27:5 KJV).

It is difficult to confront a wrong; it is more difficult to accept rebuke, especially if it is needed.

> Father, even though rebuke is often painful, when it is needed and lovingly applied, it leads to character building and Christlikeness. Help me to accept correction and rebuke in a humble and contrite spirit.

JULY 27

After a resounding Confederate victory at the battle of II Manassas, Virginia, in 1862, troops commanded by General Stonewall Jackson pursued the retreating Union army, looking for opportunity to destroy it totally. A stiffened resistance by the Federal force and a violent rainstorm slowed the Confederate advance. One Southern commander requested permission to retreat because the cartridges his men were firing had become too wet to ignite. Jackson answered, "My compliments to your Colonel. Tell him the enemy's ammunition is just as wet as his."

"The slothful man saith, 'There is a lion without; I shall be slain in the streets" (Proverbs 22:13 KJV).

We can demoralize ourselves by thinking of what might happen instead of what our duty is.

> Father, help me to be more concerned with obey-
> ing You and carrying out Your instructions than
> trying to rationalize why I can't.

JULY 28

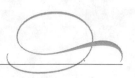

Just days before the Battle of Gettysburg, Pennsylvania, Lieutenant Colonel J. A. L. Fremantle, a military observer representing the British government and assigned to the Army of Northern Virginia, said this: "General Lee is, almost without exception, the handsomest man of his age I ever saw. He is 56 years old, tall, broad shouldered, very well made, well set up—a thorough soldier in appearance; and his manners are most courteous and full of dignity. He is a perfect gentleman in every respect. I imagine no man has so few enemies, or is so universally esteemed. He has none of the small vices, such as smoking, drinking, chewing, or swearing, and his bitterest enemy never accused him of any of the greater ones. He generally wears a well worn gray jacket, a high black felt hat, and blue trousers tucked into his Wellington boots."

"Now he was ruddy and withal of a beautiful countenance, and goodly to look to" (I Samuel 16:12a KJV).

A man may look only on the outward appearance, but God sees the heart.

> Father, General Lee and King David had the appearance of warriors and the strength of character to back it up. Help me to keep a dignified appearance and to be a real warrior of Christ in the heart.

JULY 29

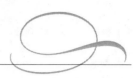

Lieutenant Colonel Fremantle continues his description of General Lee: "I never saw him carry arms, and the only mark of his military rank are the three stars on his collar. He rides a handsome horse, which is extremely well-groomed. He himself is very neat in his dress and person, and in the most arduous marches he always looks smart and clean. I believe he has never slept in a house since he has commanded the Virginian army, and he invariably declines all offers of hospitality, for fear the person offering it may afterwards get into trouble for having sheltered the Rebel General. His only faults, so far as I can learn, arise from his excessive amiability."

"For I knew that Thou art a gracious God, and merciful, slow to anger, and of great kindness, and repentest Thee of evil" (Jonah 4:2b KJV).

Some of God's character traits may also dwell in human hearts, though imperfectly; among these are graciousness, mercy, and kindness.

> Father, General Lee submitted to Your lordship in his life, thus "putting on Christ." Help me to do likewise, and grant that I may be accused of "excessive amiability."

JULY 30

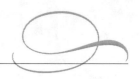

How easy it is to be joyous and have a right attitude when we are victorious. But what about the times of disaster and defeat, as when the Confederate Army of General Robert E. Lee was repulsed at the battle of Gettysburg, Pennsylvania in July, 1863? General Lee then knew better than anyone that the war would be lost. How did he respond to this disastrous battle? Lieutenant Colonel J. A. L. Fremantle, the British observer, said this: "He was engaged in rallying and in encouraging the broken troops and was riding about a little in front of the wood, quite alone. His face, which is always placid and cheerful, did not show signs of the slightest disappointment, care, or annoyance, and he was addressing to every soldier he met a few words of encouragement. He spoke to all the wounded men that passed him, and the slightly wounded he exhorted to 'bind up hurts and take up a musket' in this emergency. Very few failed to answer his appeal, and I saw many badly wounded men take off their hats and cheer him."

"The Lord gave, and the Lord hath taken away. Blessed be the name of the Lord" (Job 1:21b KJV).

The great test of faith is to weather disastrous times without doubting God's goodness.

> Father, General Lee believed that You are sovereign and in control of all things. He accepted that for good or ill. Help me to accept all that You bring into my life with a grateful and humble spirit.

July 31

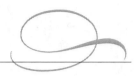

General Lee's battered and bloodied soldiers returned after failing to break the Union line at Gettysburg. Lieutenant Colonel Fremantle described this as follows: "He said to me, 'This has been a sad day for us, Colonel, a sad day; but we can't expect always to gain victories.' He was also kind enough to advise me to get into some more sheltered position, as the shells were bursting around us with considerable frequency." Fremantle then saw General Wilcox approach and report, tearfully, that his brigade had been all but destroyed. In a voice filled with kindness and understanding, General Lee responded, 'Never mind, General, all this has been my fault. It is I that have lost this fight, and you must help me out of it in the best way you can."

"In all this, Job sinned not, nor charged God foolishly" (Job 1:22 KJV).

We need not try to exonerate ourselves. If guilty of failure we should not try. If not guilty, then the accusations will ultimately fail. If God is for us, who can be against us?

> Father, General Lee assumed complete responsibility for this defeat, not accusing You or anyone else foolishly. Not all the blame was his, but he took it all. May I never shift blame to anyone else when the blame lies with me.

AUGUST 1

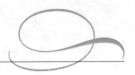

It has been said of Confederate General Stonewall Jackson that his men respected him because of his military genius and the victories he brought them. He seemed personally stern and shy and hard to get close to. General James Longstreet said of Robert E. Lee that "his men respected him as a soldier but loved him as a man." Though Generals Jackson and Lee were very different, they had much in common. Along with military brilliance, they had a great affection and trust for each other and an undying love for Christ.

"That ye may be blameless and harmless, the sons of God, without rebuke, in the midst of a crooked and perverse generation, among whom you shine as lights in the world" (Philippians 2:15 KJV).

Our personality differences were designed by Christ; He can transform any personality to shine as a light in the world.

> Father, the Confederate States were no more crooked and perverse than the United States. Yet Generals Lee and Jackson had such a close walk with You that they were truly blameless in the midst of a perverse generation. Even their enemies could not cast blame on them. May it be so with me.

AUGUST 2

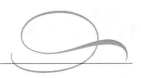

At the battle of Bethel Church, Virginia, June 10, 1861, Federal forces attacked a Confederate encampment. Major Theodore Winthrop of Massachusetts, a descendant of its first governor, a Yale graduate and a favorite of the Northeastern elite, stood on a fence waving his sword. At a distance of about two hundred yards, Confederate soldier Sam Ashe took aim and fired, killing Major Winthrop instantly. Major Winthrop was the first Union officer killed in the War. Sam Ashe was one of the many blacks fighting in the Confederate Army for the only country he ever knew.

"A prudent man forseeth the evil and hideth himself, but the simple pass on and are punished" (Proverbs 27:12 KJV).

For every human being the world is a minefield, and we walk through it only at great hazard. The only effective mine detector is God's Word. With God's guidance we can pass through safely.

> Father, it cost Major Winthrop his life to expose himself needlessly. Help me to foresee "the evil" and to be prudent.

AUGUST 3

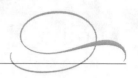

President Theodore Roosevelt of New York had this to say of General Lee, "Robert E. Lee was without any exception the greatest of all the great captains that the English-speaking peoples have brought forth." Robert E. Lee penned these words: "You have only always to do what is right. It will become easier by practice, and you will enjoy in the midst of your trials the pleasure of an approving conscience. That will be worth everything else." Also, "There is a true glory and a true honor: the glory of duty done, the honor of the integrity of principle."

"And herein do I exercise myself, to have always a conscience void of offense toward God and toward men" (Acts 24:16 KJV).

The slave who has integrity is happier than the king who has a defiled conscience.

> Father, help me to make right choices, directed by the Holy Spirit, that I might have a clean conscience.

AUGUST 4

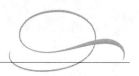

At the battle of Bethel Church, Virginia, 1861, seventeen Federal soldiers were killed. Major Winthrop was among them. In the same battle Private Henry Wyatt of North Carolina was killed, the first Confederate soldier to die in the war. Before the end of the carnage four years later, Private Wyatt would be numbered with two hundred sixty thousand Confederate soldiers and sailors to die, along with three hundred sixty thousand Union military men. Nearly an entire generation of young Americans perished in the fighting.

"I will pour it out upon the children abroad, and upon the assembly of young men together, for even the husband with the wife shall be taken, the aged with him that is full of days" (Jeremiah 6:11b KJV).

Peace and freedom are purchased only by the sacrifice of warriors.

> Father, those who fought in this war were young and old. The body of a boy of twelve might lie next to that of a grandfather of seventy. What a terrible tragedy. Help me today to be an instrument of peace even though I am girded for battle.

AUGUST 5

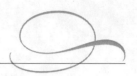

The last four states to secede from the Union and join the Confederacy were Virginia, Arkansas, Tennessee, and North Carolina. These states had hoped that a compromise might be attained; they consented to secede only when President Lincoln ordered each state to provide troops to invade the Confederacy, put down the "rebellion," and force the rebel states back into the Union. Many of the men who wore the gray were Unionists, but felt, as Robert E. Lee, they had been given no other choice.

"Trust in the Lord with all thine heart, and lean not unto thine own understanding. In all thy ways acknowledge Him, and He shall direct thy paths" (Proverbs 3:5,6 KJV).

It is for us to make our decisions prayerfully and then to trust God with the outcome.

> Father, I'm sure that the governing bodies of each state took very seriously the choices that lay before them. No doubt individuals did too as they donned the blue or the gray. Guide me in my decisions today as I acknowledge You in all that I do.

AUGUST 6

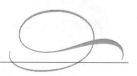

After the War a great victory parade (the Grand Review) lasted two days in Washington, D.C. The Army of the Potomac marched on the first day; General Sherman's Army of Georgia and Army of Tennessee marched on the second day. Missing from the Grand Review were soldiers from the United States Colored Troops. One hundred eighty thousand black soldiers had served the Union and had fought bravely in many bloody battles; the only blacks in the Review were laborers, dressed in their civilian clothes, hired by Sherman to dig ditches and cut down trees. General Sherman had threatened to pull his troops out of the parade if any black soldiers marched near his troops. Therefore, all black troops were assigned duty far from the Grand Review.

"Of a truth I perceive that God is no respecter of persons. But in every nation he that feareth Him and worketh righteousness is accepted in Him" (Acts 11:34b, 35 KJV).

Men look on the outward appearance, but God knows our hearts. He is moved by a contrite heart, by one who trembles at His word.

> Father, thank You that you are not partial to any color, sex, or rank. Your kingdom is open to anyone who puts his trust in Christ.

AUGUST 7

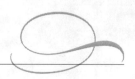

In February of 1862 Union forces captured Roanoke Island, North Carolina. As they moved inland they were attacked, probably by Confederate militia. After beating off the attackers, Colonel Rush C. Hawkins of the 9th New York Regiment ordered the sacking and burning of the town of Winton, North Carolina to exact revenge. Winton was the first town to suffer this fate, but certainly not the last. One New York soldier penned this in a letter home: "Court houses, churches, beautifully furnished dwellings with velvet carpets, pianos, etc., all sharing the same fate, and you may be sure that we gave it a pretty good ransacking while the flames were doing their work."

"Terrors are turned upon me. They pursue my soul as the wind, and my welfare passeth away like a cloud" (Job 30:15 KJV).

All our stuff and even our very lives are temporary; to know Jesus Christ is to have the hope of an eternal dwelling.

> Father, thank You that in a world filled with hurt and terror, Christ the overcomer brings peace, hope, and reason.

August 8

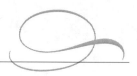

In April of 1862 Federal forces, led by General George McClellan and numbering one hundred eight thousand were at the outskirts of the Confederate capital of Richmond, Virginia. Facing them were twenty-three thousand of the Army of Northern Virginia with another thirty-one thousand five hundred marching to join them. Under orders from General Robert E. Lee to make a strong and bold front to the enemy, General John Magruder devised a scheme. Directly in the Union Army's point of advance there was a heavily wooded area with a single clearing. Magruder had a single battalion to march through that clearing all day, circling around out of sight of the Federals and marching through over and over. Union outposts counted the troops passing through the clearing. In a near panic, the ever cautious McClellan telegraphed President Lincoln that "at least two hundred thousand rebels" were facing him, and he had to have more men. The bluff worked. The Union advance stalled until the Confederate reinforcements arrived on the scene.

"Let them be turned backward and put to confusion that devise my hurt" (Psalm 70:2b KJV).

The victory that overcomes the world is our faith.

> Father, may the enemies of the Gospel be thrown into confusion and defeated. May the righteous, equipped by the Holy Spirit, make a strong and bold front to the enemy.

AUGUST 9

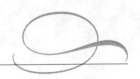

Upon hearing of the death of a dear friend's son at the battle of Petersburg, Virginia, Emma Mordecai wrote these words in her diary: "Went to see Mrs Levy whose son Isaac was killed near Petersburg on Sunday 21st. Was greatly interested in my visit to the family. Isaac was an example to all young men of any faith—to those of his own most especially. A true Israelite without guile—a soldier of the Lord and a soldier of the South. A noble Patriot. His parents and sisters mourn for him as those mourn who, while full of love, are full of faith and hope and submission. If all our people were like that family, we would already arise and shine for our light would have come."

"Jesus saw Nathanael coming to him and saith of him, "Behold, an Israelite, indeed, in whom is no guile" (John 1:47 KJV).

What a high honor—that God so complimented a mortal man!

> Father, thank You for Israel and for the plan and purpose You have always had for her. May the time arrive quickly when Israel will at last recognize Jesus as Messiah. And help me to live without guile.

AUGUST 10

When Dwight D. Eisenhower was president of the United States, he received a very critical letter from one who took him to task for his admiration for Robert E. Lee. This is how the president answered: "Dear Dr. Scott: Respecting your August 1 inquiry calling my attention to my often expressed admiration for General Robert E. Lee, I would say, first, that we need to understand that at the time of the War Between the States the issue of secession had remained unresolved for more than seventy years. Men of probity, character, public standing, and unquestioned loyalty, both North and South, had disagreed over this issue as a matter of principle from the day our Constitution was adopted. General Robert E. Lee was, in my estimation, one of the supremely gifted men produced by our nation."

"A soft answer turneth away wrath, but grievous words stir up anger" (Proverbs 15:1 KJV).

One of the marks of greatness is the ability to respond wisely to criticism.

> Father, President Eisenhower took time from his numerous duties to respond to a searing letter in a graceful and informative way. May I respond to criticism, whether deserved or not deserved, in a like manner.

AUGUST 11

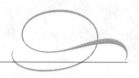

President Eisenhower continued in his letter: "He (Lee) believed unswervingly in the Constitutional validity of his cause which until 1865 was still an arguable question in America; he was thoughtful yet demanding of his officers and men, forbearing with captured enemies but ingenious, unrelenting, and personally courageous in battle, and never disheartened by a reverse or obstacle. Through all his many trials, he remained selfless almost to a fault and unfailing in his belief in God."

"These things I have spoken to you, that in Me ye might have peace. In the world ye shall have tribulation, but be of good cheer; I have overcome the world" (John 16:33 KJV).

It is one thing to be stoic in the face of defeat; it is another to persevere after defeat through faith in the One who overcame the world.

> Father, help me to accept reversals and adversity
> knowing that all things are directed by You and
> will, in time, work together for good.

AUGUST 12

President Eisenhower concluded his letter as follows: "Taken together, he (Lee) was noble as a leader and as a man, and unsullied as I read the pages of our history. From deep conviction I simply say this: a nation of men of Lee's caliber would be unconquerable in spirit and soul. Indeed, to the degree that presentday American youth will strive to emulate his rare qualities, including his devotion to this land as revealed in his painstaking efforts to help heal the nation's wounds once the bitter struggle was over, we, in our own time of danger in a divided world, will be strengthened and our love for freedom sustained. Such are the reasons that I proudly display the picture of the great American on my office wall. Sincerely, Dwight D. Eisenhower."

"Be of good courage and He shall strengthen your heart, all ye that hope in the Lord" (Psalm 31: 24 KJV).

There is not a shortage of American heroes for American youth to look up to; there is merely a want of diligence to find out about them and a failure of parents and teachers to identify them.

> Father, General Lee took courage and was strengthened because his hope was in Christ. May I draw from that all-sufficient well of courage and strength that never runs dry as I trust You in everything today.

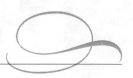

In the spring of 1864 the Federal war plans were for U.S. Grant to defeat Robert E. Lee in Virginia and for William Sherman to beat Joe Johnston in Georgia. Several other campaigns to defeat the Confederate armies were put into motion. One was in the deep Southwest. General Nathaniel Banks was to lead twelve thousand Union troops from Alexandria, Louisiana up the Red River to capture the city of Shreveport. Opposing Banks were nine thousand Southern troops commanded by Generals Richard Taylor and Kirby Smith. Taylor had served under Stonewall Jackson in his brilliant Valley Campaign. Nathaniel Banks had led one of the Union armies defeated in that campaign. On April 4 Banks wired President Lincoln: "We hope to be in Shreveport by the 10th of April. I do not fear the concentration of the enemy at that point. My fear is that they may not be willing to meet us." Lincoln had heard such talk from his generals before. When he received the report he said, "I am sorry to see this tone of confidence. The next news we shall hear from there will be a defeat."

"When pride cometh, then cometh shame, but with the lowly is wisdom" (Proverbs 11:2 KJV).

The danger of pride is that often the proud man does not even realize his presumption.

> Father, how easy it is to claim victory before the
> battle is waged. If I should have success, it is only
> through the grace of God. To Him be the glory.

AUGUST 14

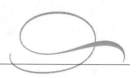

After being soundly defeated at Sabine Crossroads, Louisiana, on April 8, 1864, and the next day at Pleasant Hill, Louisiana, General Nathaniel Banks' army had been routed; it was in full retreat. Out of the twelve thousand Union soldiers, over thirty-six hundred had been killed, wounded, or captured. They lost twenty cannon and two hundred wagons. As the Federal soldiers retreated through the town of Grand Ecore, they derided their commander with this song: "In eighteen hundred and sixty-one we all skedaddled to Washington. In eighteen hundred and sixty-four we all skedaddled to Grand Ecore. Napoleon P. Banks."

"A prudent man concealeth knowledge, but the heart of fools proclaimeth foolishness" (Proverbs 12:23 KJV).

One way that we learn humility is through humiliating failures. It is then that we are most likely to be teachable.

> Father, how painful it must have been for General Banks to hear this song from his own men after a stinging failure. Help me to learn humility so as not to hurt others or myself.

AUGUST 15

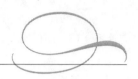

Boasting and overconfidence by Union commanders prior to battles proved costly to the Union cause. Examples were: John Pope before the battle of II Manassas, Virginia, George McClellan before the battle of Sharpsburg, Maryland, Joe Hooker before Chancelorsville, Virginia, and Nathaniel Banks before Shreveport, Louisiana. Their reasons, no doubt, were varied. Could it have been a cover for fear or just sinful pride? Whatever the cause, it had dire consequences, cost thousands of lives, and prolonged the conflict.

"A man's pride shall bring him low, but honor shall uphold the humble in spirit" (Proverbs 29:23 KJV).

Am I a selfmade man? No. God made my spirit, soul, and body. Even if I have done something with these gifts, that, too, is only by His grace.

> Father, pride unchecked is so destructive. I know I'm so capable of being a prideful man to the harm of many, including myself. May I yield to the Holy Spirit so that humility may reign instead of pride.

AUGUST 16

After serving in the western theater of operations in Tennessee and Alabama for eight months, the First Corps of the Army of Northern Virginia had been returned to the command of Robert E, Lee. He reviewed them astride his horse, Traveller. He removed his hat as these veterans from South Carolina, Georgia, Alabama, Mississippi, Arkansas, and Texas unfurled their war-torn battle flags. The men in the ranks responded with a visceral, heartfelt rebel yell. Lee's eyes then filled with tears. One of his staff said, "Does it not make the General proud to see how these men love him?" Another answered, "Not proud. It awes him."

"And now abideth faith, hope, charity, these three. But the greatest of these is charity" (I Corinthians 13:13 KJV).

Our Commander-in-Chief, Jesus Christ, will one day review us. On that day we will honor Him with a visceral, heart-felt shout. Why wait till then?

> Father, Lee's warriors trusted him and hoped he would lead them to victory. More than that, they loved him to the end. Help me to love Christ with the kind of devotion these bloodied warriors had toward General Lee. Wouldn't it be grand if Jesus were awed by my love for Him?

AUGUST 17

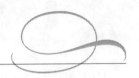

Some of the largest problems in the Union Army of the Potomac were envy, jealousy, infighting, and backbiting. No one was more adept at this than General Joe Hooker. After the disastrous defeat at Fredericksburg, Virginia, in December, 1862, General Ambrose Burnside was removed from command and replaced by Hooker on the order of President Lincoln. Lincoln sent Hooker a letter after he took command, saying: "General: I have placed you at the head of the Army of the Potomac. Of course I have done this upon what appear to me to be sufficient reasons, and yet I think it best for you to know that there are some things in regard to which I am not quite satisfied with you. I believe you to be a brave and skillful soldier, which of course I like. I also believe you do not mix politics with your profession, in which you are right. You have confidence in yourself which is a valuable if not an indispensable quality."

"It is better to trust in the Lord than to put confidence in men" (Psalm 118:8 KJV).

The builder of the Titanic reportedly said, "God Himself couldn't sink this ship." He was wrong.

> Father, confidence can be a valuable asset if it is placed in a trustworthy object. Help me to have confidence in my abilities to the extent that it is appropriate. Help me to have complete confidence in You.

AUGUST 18

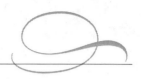

President Lincoln's letter to General Hooker continues: "You are ambitious which, within reasonable bounds, does good rather than harm; but I think that during General Burnside's command of the army you have taken counsel of your ambition and thwarted him as much as you could, in which you did a great wrong to the country and to a most meritorious and honorable brother officer. I have heard, in such a way as to believe it, of your recently saying that both the army and the government needed a dictator. Of course it was not for this, but in spite of it, that I have given you command. Only those generals who gain successes can set up dictators."

"(The Lord hates) a false witness that speaketh lies, and he that soweth discord among brethren" (Proverbs 6:19 KJV).

It is for us live by every word that comes from the mouth of God, and all the more to note the things He loves and the things He hates.

> Father, help me to abhor what You abhor and to
> cleave to what is good, helps others, and glorifies
> You.

AUGUST 19

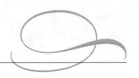

President Lincoln's letter to General Hooker concludes, "What I ask of you is military success, and I will risk the dictatorship. The government will support you to the utmost of its ability, which is neither more nor less than it has done and will do for all commanders. I fear that spirit which you have aided to infuse into the army, of criticising their commander and withholding confidence from him, will now turn upon you. I shall assist you as far as I can to put it down. Neither you nor Napoleon, if he were alive again, could get any good out of an army while such a spirit prevails in it. And now, beware of rashness, but with energy and sleepless vigilance go forward and give us victories. Yours very truly, A. Lincoln." Two months later after another disastrous defeat at the battle of Chancelorsville, Virginia, with a casualty count of seventeen thousand, Hooker was removed from command and replaced by General George Meade.

Those who plant wheat will reap it; likewise, those who plant trouble will reap it. Perhaps the crop will be bigger than they would want.

"Be not deceived, God is not mocked. Whatever a man soweth, that also shall he reap" (Galatian 6:7 KJV).

> Father, I understand I am responsible for the choices I make. The good ones bring blessing, the bad ones, pain and hurt.

AUGUST 20

As 1864 ended and the fortunes of the South continued to wane, President Jefferson Davis concluded his message to the Confederate Congress with these words: "The patriotism of the people has proved equal to every sacrifice demanded by their country's need. We have been united as a people never were united under like circumstances before. God has blessed us with success disproportionate to our means, and under His divine favor our labors must at least be crowned with the reward due to men who have given all they possessed to the righteous defense of their inalienable rights, their homes, and their altars."

"Blessed is the man that trusteth in the Lord, and whose hope the Lord is" (Jeremiah 17:7 KJV).

God, in His sovereignty and wisdom, brings about things that we cannot understand. Though we do not understand, we still trust Him, because we know that His plan is best.

> Father, You are my hope. Even though You bring
> about events that are not as I want, I trust You. At
> the very end I know I will not be disappointed.

AUGUST 21

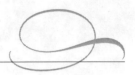

In May of 1864 at the battle of the Wilderness, Virginia, General James Longstreet, commander of the 1st Corps of Lee's army was returning to his lines after a second reconnaissance of Union positions. His troops had successfully exploited a weakness in the left flank of the Federal lines, and, in the words of the Union commander, General Hancock, after the war, "You rolled me up like a wet blanket." As Longstreet returned, his own troops fired muskets at him, having mistaken him and his staff for Northern Cavalry. This was reminiscent of a tragic mistake a year earlier when Stonewall Jackson was shot and later died by friendly fire. Three of Longstreet's staff were killed; he himself was severely wounded, but survived.

"They fell down and there was none to help" (Psalm 107:12b KJV).

Life in this world is transitory and marred by tribulation. Until the King returns.

> Father, tragedy struck just as the battle was won.
> I long for a time when the fighting's done, the
> victory's won, and the Prince of Peace, God's Son,
> reigns forever.

AUGUST 22

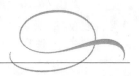

Twenty-eight year old Brigadier General Micah Jenkins of South Carolina was a rising star in the command structure of the Army of Northern Virginia. He served on the staff of General James Longstreet's 1st Corps. As he rode back to his lines after observing the results of a successful attack on the enemy's flank he said, "I am happy; I have felt despair for the cause for some months, but now I am relieved, and feel assured that we will put the enemy back across the Rapidon River before night. We will smash them now." Then he was struck by friendly fire; a bullet lodged in his brain. Two hours later he died, along with two of his comrades.

"Then are they glad because they be quiet; so he bringeth them unto their desired haven" (Psalm 107:30 KJV).

We think we are in the land of the living on our way to the place of the dead. The converse is true; we are in the land of the dying, on our way to the place of life.

> Father, when You bring us home from the battle
> we'll be forever in the place You have prepared for
> us where peace, joy, and love abide forever. We'll
> thank You forever.

AUGUST 23

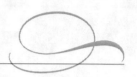

At the battle of I Manassas, Virginia, on July 21, 1861, superior Union forces initially drove the Confederates back. Brigadier General Francis Bartow commanded the 7th, 8th, and 9th Georgia Regiments and the 1st Kentucky. He tried to stem the flood of Federal troops. This battle ended in a decisive Southern victory, but General Bartow was not there to celebrate. He was mortally wounded while rallying his troops. He was the first Confederate officer to give his life on the battlefield.

"Gather My saints together unto Me; those that have made a covenant with Me by sacrifice" (Psalm 50:5 KJV).

Who are the people most revered in the records of history? Is it not those who have lived sacrificially for the good of others?

> Father, how noble is the man who is willing to sacrifice his life for something precious, something greater than himself. Help me to commit all I do for Your Kingdom and glory.

AUGUST 24

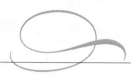

In February of 1864 President Lincoln issued a military draft call for five hundred thousand men followed a month later by calling up two hundred thousand. Half a million men was more than the Confederacy had throughout all their camps. Having bled for three years in the loss of manpower, all the South could do was to lower the draft age to seventeen and raise it to fifty. What they feared most had come upon them—a war of attrition.

"And said unto Jeremiah the prophet, 'Let, we beseech thee, our supplication be heard before thee, and pray for us unto the Lord Thy God, even for all the remnant, for we are but a few left of many as thine eyes do behold us'" (Jeremiah 42:2 KJV).

God winnows, the chaff flies away, and the grain remains. Press on to know the Lord.

> Father, there appears to be attrition of those who once stood in close fellowship with You. The battles of life rage heavy and hot. Please bring spiritual awakening among the lost and revival among Your people. Keep me close to You always.

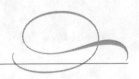

Shortly after the war ended (and its wounds ran deep) there was a Sabbath worship service in Richmond, Virginia. A black man walked down from the balcony, the section reserved for blacks, and knelt in the front of the sanctuary to pray and receive communion. There was a stunned silence in the church. Then, very quietly, a dignified white gentleman got up from his pew and knelt beside the black man. Then one by one, then twos, then groups of people from both races came forward to pray and receive communion. Robert E. Lee had again set an example of Christlikeness.

"There is neither Jew nor Greek. There is neither bond nor free, there is neither male nor female, for ye are all one in Christ Jesus" (Galatians 3:28 KJV).

The ground is level at the foot of the cross.

> Father, forgive us for putting up barriers that separate us from You and each other. Help us to remove them.

AUGUST 26

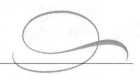

In 1865 after the war ended and the U. S. Congress convened, Representative George Julian of Indiana spoke before the House: "As for Jeff Davis, I would indict him, I would convict him and hang him in the name of God. As for Robert E. Lee, unmolested in Virginia, hang him too. And stop there? Not at all. I would hang liberally while I had my hand in."

"Ye have heard that it hath been said: Thou shalt love thy neighbor and hate thine enemy. But I say unto you, Love your enemies..." (Matthew 5:43,44 KJV).

In nations that have never heard the gospel one often finds blood feuds that go on from generation to generation in bloody acts of revenge. Only the grace of Jesus Christ can break those cycles of violence.

> Father, it was said of Robert E. Lee that he was a gallant foe in the fight, and a brother when the fight was over. Thank You that reason and charity prevailed instead of unbridled hate. Help me to deal quickly with anger so that it does not take root and grow into hate.

AUGUST 27

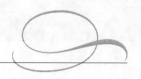

At his first battle Colonel William Nelson Pendleton of Virginia commanded an artillery battery of four cannon. He was a West Point graduate and an Episcopal minister. He named the cannon Matthew, Mark, Luke, and John. Before giving the order to fire, he said, "May the Lord have mercy on their poor souls."

"And David came to the trench, as the host was going forth to the fight, and shouted for the battle" (I Samuel 17:20b KJV).

A disciplined life is essential in order to be a good soldier. We must train in the use of weapons.

> Father, as Colonel Pendleton had four cannon in the battle, You have given us four effective weapons for the spiritual conflict: the Bible, prayer, fellowship, and witnessing. Help us to make skillful use of those weapons in order to glorify You and gain the victory.

AUGUST 28

In 1864 General James Longstreet's Confederate Corps of thirty thousand moved by overloaded trains from Virginia to the western theater of war. A lady who saw them passing through her village in South Carolina recorded this in her diary: "God bless the gallant fellows; not one man intoxicated, not one rude word did I hear. It was a strange sight. What seemed miles of platform cars, and soldiers rolled in their blankets lying in rows with their heads all covered, fast asleep. In their gray blankets packed in regular order, they looked like swathed mummies. A feeling of awful depression laid hold of me. All these fine fellows going to kill or be killed, but why? A word took to beating about my head like an old song, 'The unreturning brave.' when a knot of boyish, laughing young creatures passed, a queer thrill of sympathy shook me. Ah, I know how your homefolks feel. Poor children!"

"Therefore He said He would destroy them had not Moses His chosen, stood before Him in the breach" (Psalm 107:23a KJV).

We should continually thank God for our soldiers; not just on Memorial Day and the Fourth of July.

> Father, thank You for the military of our dear nation who have stood in the breach on our behalf to preserve our freedom. They are our best and bravest; many have sacrificed all they had to give. Thank You for Christ who stood in the breach for all mankind.

AUGUST 29

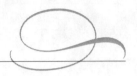

In 1861 the 14th Tennessee Regiment marched out of Clarksville, Tennessee with bands playing and banners waving for nine hundred sixty men going to war. After two years of bitter fighting on every major battlefield, the regiment charged across an open field at Gettysburg, Pennsylvania on the first day of battle with three hundred sixty five men. When the sun set the regiment had sixty combatants left. At the end of the third day (after a failed attempt to break the center of the Federal line in the Pickett/Pedigrew charge) all that remained of this proud regiment was three. This was not the only band of warriors to suffer in such a way, but that was no comfort to the people of Clarksville, all of whose young men, save three, had fallen. One in the city said, "A gloom rests over the city; the hopes and affections of the people were wrapped in that regiment."

"And whether one member suffer, all the members suffer with it" (I Corinthians 12:26b KJV).

We all experience suffering. It is better to suffer in fellowship than alone.

> Father, thank You that all in Christ are members
> of one body. What affects one affects all. Help me
> to be sensitive to those who suffer or grieve and
> to take action to decrease their pain.

AUGUST 30

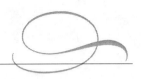

At the battle of Okolona, Mississippi in February, 1864, the Confederate Cavalry under General Nathan Bedford Forrest charged the Union lines. At the front of the charge was Colonel Jeffrey Forrest who was fatally shot from his horse with a bullet through his throat. His commander and older brother knelt beside him. Jeffrey was the youngest of the six Forrest brothers and had been raised by Nathan, sixteen years his senior, as a son. After a few minutes General Forrest remounted and ordered the bugler to blow the charge again. Forrest and his men crashed into the Federal lines. For an hour they fought savagely, hand to hand, until the Union troops broke and retreated. In this violent combat General Forrest had two horses killed under him; he himself killed three enemy soldiers with pistol and saber.

"He maketh wars to cease unto the end of the earth. He breaketh the bow, and cutteth the spear in sunder. He burneth the chariot in the fire" (Psalm 46:9 KJV).

Because of soldiers who shed blood to protect America we have been kept from the iron boots of tyranny.

> Father, the terrible fact of war is the death of those we hold dear. After Your last great victory over evil war will not even be remembered. Until then please help us always to remember with thanksgiving those who have sacrificed all in the cause of truth and right.

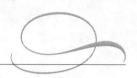

On February 11, 1864, an elite, handpicked Union cavalry force of seven thousand men with repeating rifles set out from Collinsville, Tennessee under the command of General W. Sooy Smith to find and destroy General Nathan Bedford Forrest and his command. Forrest had been disrupting and destroying Federal communication and supply lines. The two forces met in a series of battles. The first was in West Point, Mississippi where Forrest's force of thirty-five hundred attacked the much larger Union cavalry. The rebels consisted mostly of green troops newly recruited from western Tennessee. As the battle opened, one young Confederate turned and ran back and right into his commanding officer. Forrest cut a switch from a brush pile and gave the young man a solid whipping. Then he brought him to his feet, pointed him back to the battle, and said, "Now, blast you, go back to the front and fight! You might as well be killed there as here, for if you ever run away again you will not get off so easy." The young man returned to his comrades as the Confederates drove the Federals from the field. Emboldened by this victory, the Southerners won three more battles and chased the Union cavalry back to Memphis, Tennessee. The green troops became veterans, and "the Wizard of the Saddle" continued to wreak havoc in the Union rear.

"Be not afraid of sudden fear, neither of the desolation of the wicked when it cometh" (Proverbs 3:25 KJV).

If only we had a greater awareness of the immense resources available to us in Christ! He is for us.

> Father, there is much in life that can bring fear.
> Thank You that You are with me, much bigger
> than anything I fear. Your perfect love casts out
> fear.

SEPTEMBER 1

In Alabama in 1863 Confederate General Nathan Bedford Forrest and his cavalry were chasing a larger Federal force, trying to capture or destroy it. The Union cavalry had crossed Black Creek near Gadsden, Alabama, and had burned the bridge behind them. A sixteen-year-old farm girl, Emma Sanson, guided the Southern troopers downstream to a shallow ford where they could cross. Eventually the Confederates caught the Union force and captured it. In gratitude General Forrest (better known for his courage and military brilliance than his spelling) wrote her a note: "Hedquaters in Sadle, May 2, 1863. My highest regardes to Miss Ema Sanson for hir gallent conduct while my posse was skirmishing with the Federals across Black Creek near Gadsdan, Allabama. N. B. Forrest, Brig Genl, Comding N. Ala."

"A little one shall become a thousand and a small one a strong nation: I the Lord will hasten it in his time" (Isaiah 60:22 KJV).

All true heroism gives a demonstration of God's attributes of love and courage.

> Father, heroes come in different sizes and sexes. Emma Sanson guided the Confederate Cavalry under fire. She was a Southern heroine. But the greatest hero of all time for all people is the itinerant Carpenter from Nazareth. Thank You for Him.

SEPTEMBER 2

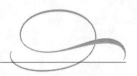

At the beginning of the War in 1861 the overall Commanding General of the United States Army was Winfield Scott, hero of the Mexican-American War. In 1846 he had been victorious at Vera Cruz, Cerro Gordo, Chapultepec, and finally Mexico City. When the War Between the States broke out he instituted the "Anaconda Plan" which was the blockade of all Southern seaports by the U. S. Navy. In time the South would be "squeezed" from receiving any supplies outside its borders. Thus, unless the war ended quickly, the South would literally starve and lack the materials to wage war. The plan proved successful, but General Scott's position was coveted, and taken, by a very talented and ambitious "success story" in the person of George B. McClellan.

"Incline my heart unto Thy testimonies, and not to covetousness" (Psalm 119:36 KJV).

Our lives are happier and safer because of many who have lived sacrificially for the public good.

> Father, General Scott was a Virginian but committed to keeping the Union together. His lifelong service and sacrifice for his country was all but forgotten as he was pushed aside. Please keep me far from covetousness; instead, may my heart be filled with gratitude for people like Winfield Scott and, most of all, for You.

SEPTEMBER 3

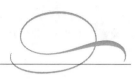

With his spirit and health broken, a victim of political intrigue, Winfield Scott resigned from the service. His successor, George McClellan, saw him off at the train depot in Washington. McClellan wrote this account to his wife: "The sight of this morning was a lesson to me which I hope not soon to forget. I saw there the end of a long, active, and industrious life, the end of the career of the first soldier of this nation; and it was a feeble old man scarce able to walk; hardly anyone there to see him off but his successor. Should I ever become vainglorious and ambitious, remind me of that spectacle." Probably no one had more to do with the tragic scene at the train depot than George McClellan. When asked by President Lincoln if the addition of General Scott's position to his current duties might be too burdensome, McClellan answered, "I can do it all."

"A man's pride shall bring him low, but honor shall uphold the humble in spirit" (Proverbs 29:23 KJV).

Instead of by intrigue, it is better to obtain promotion by diligence and faithfulness.

> Father, please make me keenly aware of the hideous effects of pride and ambition. Within a year and a half General McClellan was removed from his command, his military career at an end. Even an attempt at politics failed. May the Holy Spirit keep the pride in my life bound until it is forever gone.

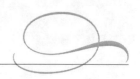

Thomas J. Jackson was opposed to secession, but when Virginia voted to secede, Jackson offered his services to Virginia. This was after President Lincoln had called for seventy-five thousand volunteers to force the seceding states back into the Union. At the same time Colonel Jackson (before he was nicknamed Stonewall) believed that the whole issue had to do with honor and freedom. These were his words: "What is life without honor? Degradation is worse than death. We must think of the living and of those who are to come after us, and see that by God's blessing we transmit to them the freedom we have ourselves inherited."

"A good man leaveth an inheritance to his children's children" (Proverbs 13:23a KJV).

Inheritance means infinitely more than mere material goods.

> Father, help me to pass on to those who come after me an inheritance of character, truth and righteousness that points them to Jesus.

September 5

Many things have been said and written about Stonewall Jackson, not the least being his eccentricities. He thought his body was out of balance and often rode Little Sorrel with one arm thrust in the air as if imploring divine help. His diet consisted of plain bread, milk, raspberries, and a constant supply of lemons. He refused any seasoning on his food, complaining that pepper caused pain in his left leg. Also his appearance did not match his reputation. Until Jeb Stuart gave him a new uniform prior to the battle of Fredericksburg, Virginia, he wore a worn out coat that he had worn in the Mexican War, an old V. M. I. Cadet cap with a broken visor that drooped down to his pale blue eyes, the eyes that seemed to blaze fiery red when battle raged. He was branded a religious fanatic who often walked through the camp interrupting poker games and games of chance by passing out Gospel tracts. He desired that his army might become "an army of the living God as well as of its country." There seemed to be two things that he strongly held to in waging war: "The vigorous use of the bayonet and the blessings of Providence." The one thing all could agree upon, friend and foe alike, was Jackson's military genius and his ability to win battles.

"For Thou hast girded me with strength unto the battle. Thou hast subdued under me those that rose up against me" (Psalm 18:34 KJV).

Since God is not a "respecter of persons" victory is there, not just for people like Stonewall Jackson, but also for you and me to claim.

> Father, strengthen me as I wage war against the evil that surrounds me in this fallen world. Thank You that the victory has been won already in Christ. We know this because we've read the last chapter in Your word.

SEPTEMBER 6

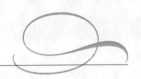

In the winter of 1862 Robert E. Lee wrote to his brother: "I am glad you derive satisfaction from the operations of the army. I acknowledge nothing can surpass the valor and endurance of our troops, yet while so much remains to be done, I feel as if nothing has been accomplished." And in a letter to Mrs. Lee he wrote: "I tremble for my country when I hear of confidence expressed in me. I know too well my weakness, and that our only hope is in God."

"Blessed are the meek, for they shall inherit the earth" (Matthew 5:5 KJV).

The word "meek" means something very different in the Scripture than in how people use it from day to day. A meek man may be as strong as the Rock of Gibraltar before men, yet he is totally submissive before God.

> Father, General Lee was meek but not weak. This same meekness comes from Jesus who endured the cross and in whose strength I can do all things.

SEPTEMBER 7

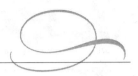

In one of his letters General Lee wrote: "But we must endure to the end, and if our people are true to themselves and our soldiers continue to discard all thoughts of self and to press nobly forward in defense alone of their country and of their rights, I have no fear of the results. We may be annihilated, but we cannot be conquered. No sooner is one (Union) army scattered than another rises up. This snatches from us the fruits of victory and covers the battlefield with our dead. Yet, what have we to live for if not victorious?"

"But thanks be to God, which giveth us the victory through our Lord Jesus Christ" (I Corinthians 15:57 KJV).

As General Lee said (in view of the eternal perspective), we may be annihilated, but we cannot be conquered. In Christ we are more than conquerors.

> Father, in this world we will have tribulations and defeats, but the ultimate victory has been won for us by Christ. We will share in the fruits of it with Him in glory forever. Thank You.

SEPTEMBER 8

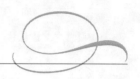

During some successes by Confederate forces early in the war, Senator Herschel V. Johnson of Georgia, who had been a candidate for the position of Vice President of the United States in the 1860 election, and now a member of the Confederate Congress wrote to a friend: "You ask me if I have confidence in the success of the Southern Confederacy? I pray for success but I do not expect success. The enemy in due time will penetrate the heart of the Confederacy and the hearts of our people will quake and their spirits will yield to the force of overpowering numbers. The enemy is superior to us in everything but courage and therefore it is quite certain, if the war is to go on until exhaustion overtake the one side or the other, that we shall be the first to be exhausted." His words proved to be prophetic.

"And He said unto me: It is done! I am the Alpha and Omega, the beginning and the end. I will give unto him that is athirst of the fountain of the water of life freely" Revelation (21:6 KJV).

To be human is to be subject to exhaustion at some point. Woe to the one who comes to the end of his own resources and does not know to trust Jesus Christ.

> Father, when I am exhausted, You energize and empower me. When I lift my cup to drink of Your fountain of life, truth, and righteousness, You fill it to overflowing. Thank You.

SEPTEMBER 9

Confederate General Jubal Early compared the achievements of France's Napoleon and England's Duke of Wellington to those of Confederate General Robert E. Lee. "Napoleon was of extraordinary genius, but he had to have complete success. Defeats such as the retreat from Moscow and his defeat at Waterloo were ruinous to him. This caused him to make errors in judgement that 'cost lives, liberties, and happiness to others.' He could not have withstood any of the campaigns that General Lee waged against such forces that came against him. Wellington, on the other hand was successful because all the odds were on his side. All of Europe had allied with him against Napoleon. He had such resources as the Union had against the Confederacy. At the Battle of Waterloo, he fought a Napoleon who was but a shell of what he once had been and who was driven to a desperate, losing gamble. General Lee never had the benefits Wellington enjoyed. If he had, the outcome of the War for Southern Independence might surely have ended differently. It can be defensibly argued that General Lee exceeded both Napoleon and Wellington in military genius."

"He keepeth the paths of judgment and preserveth the way of his saints" (Proverbs 2:8 KJV).

Even the gift of genius is just that—a gift. The credit must be given to the Giver of genius.

> Father, General Lee never took credit for his victories, always took responsibility for defeat, and accepted both with grace and humility. Help me to do likewise.

SEPTEMBER 10

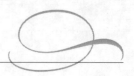

One of the hardships Union soldiers faced as they advanced farther south was the onslaught of various insects. Malarial mosquitos were an especially grievous enemy to the Federals. But the one that caused the most discomfort and annoyance was the chigger. A private from Illinois wrote home: "Chiggers are big and red as blood. They will crawl through any cloth and bite worse than fleas, and poison the flesh very badly. Many of the boys will anoint their bodies with bacon rines which chiggers can't go. Salt water bathing would cure them but salt is too scarce to use on human flesh."

"Surely He shall deliver thee from the snare of the fowler and from the noisome pestilence" (Psalm 91:3 KJV).

Chiggers and mosquitos have chafed and attacked us since the fall of man when the "fowler" deceived him and led him outside God's will. That was the true beginning of pestilence.

> Father, thank You for delivering me ultimately from the noisome pestilence through Jesus Christ.

SEPTEMBER 11

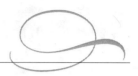

Beginning with the battle of the Wilderness on May 5, 1864, and ending with the battle of Cold Harbor on June 12, 1864, the Union Army of the Potomac sustained 54,929 casualties. Especially hard hit was the officers' corps with literally hundreds killed. The regimental commanders were especially devastated. At the battle of Cold Harbor, 2nd Corps lost seven colonels in a matter of minutes. Union Brigadier General John Gibbon had this to say about such loss: "The effect of such slaughter on a military organization can be readily imagined. The very best officers fell. When they were gone, the number who served as leaders was fearfully reduced." One Federal colonel was struck so many times by bullets, he was identified only by the buttons on his sleeve. In four of the five major battles during this time, twenty-one regimental commanders were either killed outright or mortally wounded: twelve colonels, eight lieutenant colonels, and one major.

"They lifted up their voice and wept, and they rent every one his mantle, and sprinkled dust upon their heads toward heaven" (Job 2:12b KJV).

The Biblical picture of true leadership is not of lording it over others; it is of sacrifice and service.

> Father, often leadership comes at great risk and at horrific cost. If you call me to a position of leadership, help me to be a servant of those I lead and never to direct them to any place that I am not willing to go.

SEPTEMBER 12

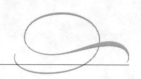

Field Marshall Viscount Wolseley, commander of British forces who were victorious in the Sudan had this to say of Robert E. Lee: "I have met but two men who realize my ideas of what a true hero should be: my friend Charles Gordon was one, General Lee was the other. When all the angry feelings roused by the secession are buried with those which existed when the Declaration of Independence was written, when Americans can review the history of their last great rebellion with calm impartiality, I believe all will admit that General Lee towered far above all men on either side in that struggle. I believe he will be regarded not only as the most prominent figure of the Confederacy, but as the great American of the 19th Century, whose statue is worthy to stand on an equal pedestal with that of Washington, and whose memory to be enshrined in the hearts of all his countrymen."

"With the merciful Thou shalt show Thyself merciful. With an upright man Thou wilt show Thyself upright" (Psalm 18:25a KJV).

God pays especial attention to the man who is totally committed to Him.

> Father, I must be filled with the Spirit that I might live uprightly before You and before others. Please let my life demonstrate the difference it makes to be fully committed to You.

SEPTEMBER 13

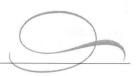

Lieutenant Thomas Jonathan Jackson who later became "Stonewall" was born January 21, 1824 in Clarksburg, Virginia. His parents died while he was still a child, so his uncle raised him at Jackson's Mill in what is now West Virginia. At the age of eighteen he was appointed to West Point. The academics were difficult for young Jackson, but he disciplined himself and persevered. He graduated in 1846 receiving the brevet rank of second lieutenant. His religious character began to develop early in his military career; he started to study the Bible and joined the Church in 1851. His devotion to Christ and his desire to obey the Scripture gradually became a major part of his character.

"Study to show thyself approved unto God, a workman that needeth not to be ashamed, rightly dividing the word of truth" (II Timothy 2:15 KJV).

For some people the prospect of reading the Bible all the way through seems impossible. It is done in the same way one eats an elephant—a bite at a time.

> Father, help me to be diligent in spending time with you, studying the Bible and praying that I might be a workman in Your harvest who does not need to be ashamed.

SEPTEMBER 14

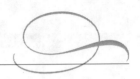

In the thirty years between 1820 and 1850, settlers in the United States pushed the frontier farther westward. The land available for settlement was tremendous. Regional concerns began to arise as each part of the country became more and more concerned with regional interests. The North demanded protective trade tariffs, a strong central government, and a strong federal banking system. The agricultural South demanded free trade and stood strongly for states rights and a less intrusive central government. The people of the West wanted an easy money system and a strong central government to provide protection and free land. These differences increased while attempts at reconciliation became futile.

"Blessed are the peacemakers for they shall be called children of God" (Matthew 5:9 KJV).

True peacemakers are very concerned about justice.

> Father, though I am a warrior, let me be a peacemaker by fighting for justice and gaining it and staying on guard to maintain it.

SEPTEMBER 15

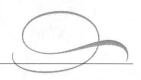

Some things in a soldier's life never lose their importance, such as mail or a word from home. Often when the battle rages the thing that motivates us and keeps us going is the letter from a loved one at home reminding us of happier times in the past and making us think of the joy of reunion in the future. This is part of a letter written by Private Thomas Winton Fisher of the 51st Virginia Infantry to his parents: "My dear parents, I am now on picket and I thought I would write to you one more time and see if I could ever hear from home. I have written two letters since I came back and yet I have not had a scratch of a pen since I left Glade Springs Depot. I wrote once at Staunton and once on the road between that place and Winchester. In those two letters I gave you a sort of history of our march and as I commenced I will finish."

"A merry heart maketh a cheerful countenance, but by sorrow of the heart the spirit is broken" (Proverbs 15:13 KJV).

How good it is to hear from home when far away. We have means to contact home, and we have other means to contact our true home, heaven.

> Father, help me to maintain a merry heart that I might be an encourager of others in whatever ways we may communicate. Help me to uplift the weak and encourage the strong as we serve Christ together.

SEPTEMBER 16

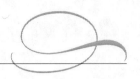

In Fredericksburg, Virginia, a young lady was asked if she was from Virginia. Her reply was that she was not just from Virginia, but that she was a Virginian. "There is a difference." Knowing who we are is a large part of our heritage.

"The Lord is the portion of mine inheritance and of my cup; Thou maintainest my lot. The lines are fallen unto me in pleasant places. Yea, I have a goodly heritage" (Psalm 16:5,6 KJV).

I am not just from the Church. I am a Christian.

> Father, You are my portion, my inheritance. In You I have my identity; I am fully complete. Let me never be satisfied with anything less than being a warrior grateful for the wonderful heritage of the Lord.

SEPTEMBER 17

In 1862, because of his slowness of movement against the capital of the Confederacy and the subsequent defeat of the Union Army by much smaller Southern forces in the Seven Days Battles, George McClellan had been removed as the General-in-Chief of all Federal armies and replaced by a rival, Major General Henry W. Halleck. President Lincoln was displeased with McClellan because his army had been at the outskirts of Richmond just a short time before, and victory had seemed imminent. Now the Confederate Army had pushed the Federals down the peninsula. Lincoln ordered their return to Washington. McClellan wrote his wife: "In all these things the President and those around him have acted so as to make the matter as offensive as possible. He has not shown the slightest gentlemanly or friendly feeling, and I can not regard him as in any respect my friend. I am confident that he would relieve me tomorrow if he dared to do so. His cowardice alone prevents it. I can never regard him with other feelings than those of contempt."

"Do all things without murmurings and disputings" (Philippians 2:14 KJV).

If we know that the all-powerful and all-knowing God is for us, it becomes unnecessary to be defensive or to try to manipulate outcomes in our own favor.

> Father, how much better it is to receive the things that come into our lives, knowing they are directed by the One who loves us and desires to do us good.

In December, 1862 just before the battle of Fredericksburg, Virginia, the two armies faced each other across the Rappahannock River. A huge snowfall came down. Many of the Confederate soldiers from the deep South had never seen snow before. While waiting for the Yankees to make their move they had many snowball battles of great proportion. General Robert E. Lee's young daughter had died a month

The Rappahannock River, Virginia. Two great armies faced each other across it.

before. In the same snowfall and stillness before this battle Lee wrote: "In the quiet hours of the night, when there is nothing to lighten the full weight of my grief, I feel as if I should be overwhelmed. I have always counted, if God should spare me a few days after this war is ended, that I should have her with me, but year after year my hopes go out, and I must be resigned."

"These things I have spoken unto you, that in Me you might have peace. In the world ye shall have tribulation, but be of good cheer, for I have overcome the world" (John 16:33 KJV).

Our hopes for happiness in this life often do go out; our hope for happiness in the life to come can never be snuffed out, for we are in Christ and He has overcome the world.

> Father, it is true that in this world there is much to grieve and mourn. But the cross and the empty tomb point us to Jubilee and joyous days ahead. Although the day is dark and overcast, the sun is still there above the clouds.

SEPTEMBER 19

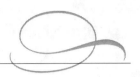

In the spring of 1862 as Confederate troops were marching through Richmond, Virginia on their way to oppose Union forces moving up the peninsula, the air was filled with patriotic music. It was a festive time with crowds lining the streets and leaning out of windows, waving handkerchiefs and cheering the troops as they marched past. From one of these windows a lady and a pale young man were cheering. The soldiers saw them from the street. One called out, "Come along, sonny. The lady will spare you. Here's a little musket for you." "All right boys," was the reply. "Have you got a leg for me too. I lost mine at Manassas." He then placed the stump of his missing leg on the window sill. The soldiers halted, apologized, and presented arms; then they cheered loud enough to drown out all else.

"I beseech you therefore, brethren, by the mercies of God, that ye present your bodies, a living sacrifice, holy, acceptable unto God which is your reasonable service" (Romans 12:1 KJV).

Most of us will not be led to sacrifice life or a limb. But all who would be warriors must sacrifice at least our time which is the stuff life is made of.

> Father, help me to be willing to sacrifice all for the cause of Christ and the furtherance of His Gospel. Being a warrior involves sacrifice. May any sacrifice I make be for the right and the good.

SEPTEMBER 20

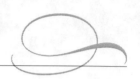

During the war some spiteful and injurious words were spoken about President Lincoln such as, he "was a long-armed creature," "the original gorilla," and that one would not have to travel to Africa to find the missing link since he resided in Washington, D.C. These words were not said by people of the South as one might have suspected, but by the General-in-Chief of all the Union armies, George McClellan, and Lincoln's Secretary of War, Edwin Stanton. On another occasion President Lincoln, Secretary of State Seward, and Lincoln's secretary, John Hay, called upon General McClellan at his residence in Washington, D.C. Told that McClellan was not present but would return soon, they decided to wait. After an hour McClellan returned and was told by his servant of his visitors. Without acknowledging them he went upstairs. After another thirty minutes they sent the servant upstairs to tell General McClellan that they were still there. When the servant returned, he told them that the general had retired for the night. On the way home Secretary Seward angrily condemned McClellan's rudeness and insolence. All Lincoln said was, "I would hold McClellan's horse if he would give us success."

"But whosoever shall say, 'Thou fool,' shall be in danger of hell fire" (Matthew 5:22b KJV).

The Scripture forbids us to make a railing accusation even against Satan. How much more should we be careful when we talk about our fellow men, made in God's image?

> Father, there are times when my eyes are the eyes of an enemy and other times when I see the value of a person because of the price paid for him on the cross. Help me to see others through the eyes of Christ today.

SEPTEMBER 21

In 1862 at his second inauguration, Jefferson Davis was made a permanent, rather than temporary, President of the Confederate States of America. The weather was wet and unseasonably cold. This adverse weather seemed to demonstrate the adverse fortunes of war at the time. Gone were the early successes of I Manassas and Ball's Bluff; fortune now frowned, and the South experienced military defeats, especially in the west. In his inaugural address Davis said, "A million men, it is estimated, are now standing in hostile array and waging war along a frontier of thousands of miles. Battles have been fought; sieges have been conducted, and although the contest is not ended and the tide for the moment is against us, the final result in our favor is not doubtful. We have had our trials and difficulties. That we are to escape them in the future is not to be hoped. It was to be expected when we entered upon this war that it would expose our people to sacrifice and cost them much, both of money and blood."

"For which of you, intending to build a tower, sitteth not down first, and counteth the cost, whether he have sufficient to finish it" (Luke 14:28 KJV).

We must count the cost of following Christ, but we must do so with the right information—what it will cost versus what it will gain. We must prepare beforehand to pay the price.

> Father, in their attempt to build and preserve a nation, the people of the South thought the price paid was worth it. The people of the North thought it was worth the price to try to preserve the Union. The cost of being a disciple of Christ cannot be compared to the benefits. It has been said that a man is no fool to give up what he cannot keep to gain what he cannot lose. Help me to have this perspective.

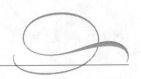

President Davis continues: "But the picture has its lights as well as its shadows. This great strife has awakened in the people the highest emotions and qualities of the human soul. It was perhaps, in the ordination of Providence that we were to be taught the value of our liberties by the price we pay for them. The recollection of this great contest, with all its common traditions of glory, of sacrifice and blood, will be the bond of harmony and enduring affection amongst the people, producing unity in policy, fraternity in sentiment, and just effort in war." Davis closed his address with this prayer: "My hope is reverently fixed on Him whose favor is ever vouchsafed to the cause which is just. With humble gratitude and adoration, acknowledging the Providence which has so visibly protected the Confederacy during its brief but eventful career, to Thee, O God, I trustingly commit myself and prayerfully invoke Thy blessing on my country and its cause."

"Except the Lord build the house, they labor in vain that build it. Except the Lord keep the city, the watchman watcheth but in vain" (Psalm 127:1 KJV).

If we call Christ Lord, it means that He has the right to tell us what to do, and we have the responsibility to do it. It is not for us to set our own course and expect God to ratify it.

> Father, keep me from making my own plans and expecting You to bless them. Apart from You I can do nothing, but through Christ I can do all things.

SEPTEMBER 23

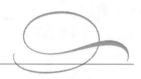

Several months after the battle of Sharpsburg, Maryland in 1862, President Lincoln was very dissatisfied with the progress of the Union Army under the command of George McClellan to pursue and do battle with the Confederates. McClellan had requested more horses because the ones he had were fatigued and broken down. Lincoln answered: "Will you pardon me for asking what the horses of your army have done since the battle of Antietam (Sharpsburg) that fatigues anything." McClellan responded in a letter to his wife: "It was one of those little things that I can't get used to when they are not merited." Later he wrote to one of his corps commanders: "I may not have command of the army much longer. Lincoln is down on me." He was correct on both counts.

"Turn away mine eyes from beholding vanity, and quicken me in Thy way" (Psalm 119:37 KJV).

Many men have had a meteoric rise and fall because they did not have the resources to keep pride in check.

> Father, how quickly pride and vanity can bring a
> man down. Please abide in me that I might see You
> as You are and myself as I am.

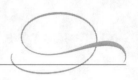

In 1862 after being pushed back from the outskirts of Richmond by a much smaller force, his army in retreat, Union Commanding General George McClellan wired his superiors in Washington, D.C.: "I know the full history of the day. I have lost this battle because my force was too small. I again repeat that I am not responsible for this, and I say it with the earnestness of a general who feels in his heart the loss of every brave man who has been needlessly sacrificed today. If, at this instant, I could dispose of ten thousand fresh men, I could gain a victory tomorrow. I know that a few thousand more men would have changed the battle from a defeat to a victory. As it is, the Government must not and can not hold me responsible for the result. I feel too earnestly tonight. I have seen too many dead and wounded comrades to feel otherwise than that the Government has not sustained this army. If you do not do so now the game is lost. If I save this army now, I tell you plainly that I owe no thanks to you or to any other person in Washington. You have done your best to sacrifice this army."

"And the man said, the woman whom Thou gavest to be with me, she gave me of the tree, and I did eat.… And the woman said, the serpent beguiled me, and I did eat" (Genesis 3:12, 13b KJV).

As men of integrity we must take responsibility for our deeds.

> Father, how easy it is to blame others, even You,
> when things don't go as we plan. I understand
> You hold me responsible for the choices I make.
> Help me to make wise decisions that glorify You.

In the battle of Cold Harbor, Virginia, June 3, 1864, Union forces attacked fortified Confederate positions with a casualty count of five thousand in less than twenty minutes and another two thousand before the day was done. The dead and wounded lay between opposing lines. Union General Grant was hesitant to call a truce because the first side to ask that was admitting loss of the battle. President Lincoln was in the middle of a tough re-election campaign; the news of another lost battle would be a blow to his re-election. Finally on June 7 Grant asked for a truce for the purpose of collecting his wounded and burying the dead. In the Virginia heat decomposition had set in—a sickening sight. Also, after the passing of the days, many suffering wounded succumbed to their wounds. Although he was never one to second guess himself, Grant said of the charge at Cold Harbor: "I should never have ordered that last attack."

"The sorrows of death compassed me and the pains of hell got hold on me. I found trouble and sorrow" (Psalm 116:3 KJV).

Heavy are the crowns that kings wear and heavy on the shoulders of leaders are their responsibilities.

> Father, it is so difficult being in leadership and having to order men into combat. I pray for wisdom for all our military leaders, high-ranking and low.

SEPTEMBER 26

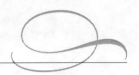

General Joseph Johnston penned this last order to his troops after receiving orders removing him from command of the Confederate army in the west and being replaced by General John Bell Hood, July 17, 1864: "I cannot leave this noble army without expressing my admiration of the high military qualities it has displayed. A long and anxious campaign has made conspicuous every soldierly virtue, endurance of toil, obedience to orders, brilliant courage. The enemy has never attacked but to be repulsed and severely punished. You, soldiers, have never argued but from your courage, and never counted your foes. No longer your leader, I will still watch your career, and will rejoice in your victories. To one and all I offer assurances of my friendship, and bid an affectionate farewell." General Johnston regained leadership of his army but surrendered it in North Carolina to Union General William Sherman a short time after Lee surrendered to Grant in April 1865.

"Behold, how good and how pleasant it is for brethren to dwell together in unity" (Psalm 133:1 KJV).

We Christians have three terrible and merciless foes: the world, the flesh, and the Devil. Should we not love each other all the more as we participate in this war?

> Father, General Johnston and his men had a deep affection for each other. They would fight and die for him, and he would lead them wisely. Help me to be a peace maker and a preserver of unity among my brothers."

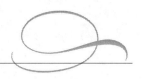

It has been said that Confederate General John Bell Hood, in trying to teach his army a lesson in courage sacrificed that army as they launched repeated attacks against strongly fortified Union positions at the battle of Franklin, Tennessee in 1864. The remnant of that force was virtually destroyed a short time later at the battle of Nashville, Tennessee. As the survivors marched away from the slaughter of so many of their comrades, the soldiers sang this to the tune of "The Yellow Rose of Texas": "My feet are torn and bloody and my heart is full of woe. I'm going back to Georgia to see my Uncle Joe. You may talk about your Beauregard and sing of Bobby Lee, but the gallant Hood of Texas, he played h___ in Tennessee."

"The way of a fool is right in his own eyes, but he that hearkeneth unto counsel is wise" (Proverbs 12:15 KJV).

We are often blind to our own stupidity until we pay for it.

> Father, General Hood rejected the counsel of his subordinates regarding this attack. It resulted in a great and tragic loss of life and the destruction of his army. This one wrong decision negated Hood's long record of bravery, courage, and sacrificial service. Since my decisions affect others, help me to listen to counsel and to choose wisely.

September 28

During the war it was said that the time was divided between the utter boredom of camp life and the terror of combat. During the march and around campfires music played a large part in lifting morale or comforting the troops. Confederate cavalry General J. E. B. Stuart had in his command a man named Sweeney who had no equal as a banjoist. And there were lively tunes played by regimental bands as the men marched or attended concerts. Favorite songs by the Union troops were "Battle Hymn of the Republic" and "When Johnnie Comes Marching Home." Those that were popular for the Confederates were "Dixie," "The Yellow Rose of Texas," and "The Bonnie Blue Flag." Around the campfires in the evenings the men of both sides thought of home with songs like "Home, Sweet Home," "Lorena," and "All's Quiet Along the Potomac Tonight." Music affected the men both with melancholy and nostalgia.

"I got me men singers and women singers and the delights of the sons of men, as musical instruments, and that of all sorts" (Ecclesiastes 2:8b KJV).

Beautiful music glides past our defenses and touches the emotions and the hidden things of the heart that can not be expressed in words.

> Father, what a grand concert it will be when all of Your saints and all of the heavenly host lift their voices in praise and glorify the Lamb who was slain, who lives and reigns. May we worship You with music that is worthy of such a great end.

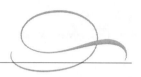

One story that Robert E. Lee loved to tell was about his conversation with a young Confederate soldier who was a courier between the different commands. Knowing how dangerous this duty was, Lee asked the man if he had ever been wounded as so many of the soldiers had. The soldier answered that much of his time was spent among the various generals, and he felt very safe there. Unfortunately this was not really the case because many of the general officers on both sides were killed or wounded. But an attempt at humor was always welcome in the unhappy circumstances of war.

"All the days of the afflicted are evil, but he that is of a merry heart hath a continual feast" (Proverbs 13:13 KJV).

Humor is the rare gift that helps soothe a troubled mind.

> Father, many do not know that General Lee had
> a great sense of humor which was never degrad-
> ing to others. Help me to have fun, but never at
> someone else's expense.

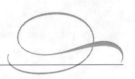

It is a puzzle as to why Union General James H. Wedlie was given command of a division at the battle of Petersburg, Virginia. His performance throughout the war had been less than stellar. During the battle of Whitehall he had directed artillery fire that had wounded many of his own men. At the North Anna River he performed poorly. Now at Petersburg his troops had been selected to charge the Confederate lines after the mine had exploded under the Southern works. He never left the safety of a bombproof bunker, drinking ample amounts of rum, and issuing orders without knowing what was really happening in the battle. In the absence of strong leadership, what could have been a great Union victory, shortening the war, turned into a terrible Union nightmare. Of the fifteen thousand who made the attack, four thousand were killed, wounded, or captured before the eleven thousand limped back to their lines. General Wedlie played a great part in this colossal failure. Amazingly he was never charged with misconduct; he was sent home on medical leave to await further orders that never came.

"Where there is no vision the people perish, but he that keepeth the law, happy is he" (Proverbs 29:18 KJV).

How can a man obtain vision? He can seek it in the great store of the treasury of Christ. He can access it by meditating on God's Word.

> Father, many young men died needlessly because
> of the want of character and vision in the leaders.
> I pray that character and vision will be strong in
> all those in authority over us.

OCTOBER 1

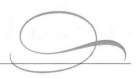

After many invitations were turned down to accompany President and Mrs. Lincoln to attend Ford's Theatre on April 14, 1865, Union Major Henry R. Rathbone and his fianceé, Clara Harris accepted. The play was "Our American Cousin," a comedy that the President eagerly anticipated watching. The theater had been an outlet of relief for the President in the four long years of the war. Now that the end was so near, Lincoln yearned for a more peaceful time. That was not to be. John Wilkes Booth stole into the President's box and shot him in the back of the head. Rathbone struggled with Booth trying to subdue him and received a deep knife slash to his forearm. Booth jumped from the box to the stage; he broke his leg in the escape. Major Rathbone resigned his commission in 1870, married Miss Harris, and moved to Germany. But the story ended tragically. Rathbone lost his mind, murdered his wife, and spent the rest of his life in an asylum for the criminally insane.

"For God hath not given us a spirit of fear, but of power, and of love, and of a sound mind" (II Timothy 1:7 KJV).

We have two sorts of guilty feelings: those we deserve and those we don't deserve.

> Father, it appears that Major Rathbone may have struggled with the demons of guilt, wondering if he might have been able to do more to save the President's life. I understand how vital it is to abide in You that I might have a sound mind and be delivered both from true moral guilt and from guilty feelings that I don't really deserve.

OCTOBER 2

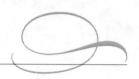

On May 24, 1861, the day after Virginia seceded from the Union, Federal Colonel Elmer Ellsworth was ordered to cross the Potomac River and seize Alexandria, Virginia which was right across the river from Washington. DC. Ellsworth, a close friend of President Lincoln, had established an elite drill team with rifle and bayonet as well as a regiment of New York City firemen called the New York Fire Zouaves modeled after the French Zouaves of the Crimean War. The young and handsome Ellsworth soon became the darling of the North. Upon reaching the Virginia shore he noticed a large Confederate flag flying from the top of the Marshall House, an inn in Alexandria. He positioned troops throughout the town while he and three others rushed to the inn, up the stairs, and they cut down the flag. As they came down, James W. Jackson, the innkeeper was waiting on the third level with a shotgun. Corporal Francis E. Brownell tried to deflect the weapon, but not before it discharged into Ellsworth's chest killing him instantly. Brownell then shot Jackson and bayoneted him, killing him. The North gave Ellsworth a memorial service in the White House where his body lay in state; also he had a memorial service in his home state of New York before burial. He became the poster boy for getting "Revenge against the Rebels." Meanwhile Jackson became a hero in the South for defending what was his.

"Good understanding giveth favor, but the way of transgressors is hard" (Proverbs 13:15 KJV).

There is such as thing as a just war. World War II was clearly a defense of free peoples against despicable barbarism. Defending one's own country from invaders is just.

> Father, this was the opening scene of a long and
> bloody and tragic war. Help me to think and give
> me understanding before I take any aggressive or
> violent action. Help me to be sure that the cause
> is just and my motives right.

OCTOBER 3

After one sinking off the coast of Mobile, Alabama and at least three at Charleston, South Carolina with the loss of thirty-three lives including the inventor, H. L. Hunley, the Confederate military ceased any more tests and experiments on the submergible vessel, a submarine. Finally Confederate army lieutenant George E. Dixon convinced his superiors to restart the tests. After some degree of success the Hunley went into Charleston bay with Dixon commanding and a crew of eight to do battle with the Federal ships blockading the port. The Hunley's torpedo was detonated under the hull of the USS Housatonic. It went to the bottom as the first victim of a submarine. Unfortunately the Hunley never surfaced, and years later it was discovered lying next to the wreckage of the Housatonic at the bottom of Charleston Bay.

"Thy cry hath filled the land for the mighty man hath stumbled against the mighty, and they are fallen both together" (Jeremiah 46:12b KJV).

Although a long life might give us more time to serve Christ, it might also give us more opportunities to fail Him.

> Father, the men of the Hunley went out into what they knew would be a suicide mission. A warrior is willing to give what it takes, even his life, in a cause that is true and right. Help me to live and fight and, if need be, die for Christ and His Kingdom.

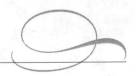

In 1864 while Varina Davis, wife of Confederate President Jefferson Davis, was riding in her carriage in Richmond, Virginia, she came across a large black man beating a small black child. Mrs. Davis grabbed the little boy and placed him beside her in the carriage. He was taken to live in the Confederate White House as a member of the Davis family, although it is not known whether he was ever adopted. At age four he was unable to give much information about himself other than he was an orphan. He was much loved by all, especially the Davis children who gave him the name of Jim Limber Davis. President and Mrs. Davis gave him as much love and care as they did their own children; he soon became a special member of the family. After several Southern armies surrendered, President Davis and his family left Richmond and journeyed south, the Federal cavalry in pursuit. They were overtaken in lower Georgia, and President Davis was taken prisoner. Union troops dragged little Jim from Mrs. Davis' arms screaming and crying. This little boy, raised and educated by President and Mrs. Davis in the Southern White House, was never seen again.

"He that despiseth his neighbor sinneth, but he that hath mercy on the poor, happy is he" (Proverbs 14:21 KJV).

One reason that showing mercy is appropriate is that every individual human being needs it, whether he realizes it or not. Even the best of us desperately needs mercy from God. And God gives it generously.

> Father, the mercy showered upon Jim Limber by the Davis family was considerable, but it cannot compare to the mercy God has given all mankind. Thank You for showing mercy to me.

OCTOBER 5

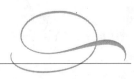

One of the most vilified men to the people of the South was Union General David Hunter, known as Black Dave because of his extreme cruelty and wanton destructiveness. He had brought destruction to the Shenandoah Valley on a par with Phillip Sheridan's carnage later in 1864. Lexington, Virginia suffered especially under Hunter. Hunter burned the home of Governor John Letcher to the ground. Smoking debris was all that was left of Washington College and the Virginia Military Institute. Stonewall Jackson's grave site suffered damage and desecration. Hunter continued this vile behavior until Southern forces under General Jubal Early defeated him and diminished his involvement in the war. Had he been captured, or if the South had won, he would have been tried for crimes against humanity. Hunter was born and raised in Virginia; this made him even more abhorrent to those of the South.

"What persecutions I endured, but out of them all the Lord delivered me" (II Timothy 3:11b KJV).

Have you ever heard of General David Hunter? Probably not unless you are a history scholar. Have you ever heard of General Robert E. Lee? This question is rhetorical. History favors the compassionate, not the cruel.

> Father, David Hunter cannot be condemned for choosing to serve the Union, but rather for his egregious cruelty. Thank You for restoring Lexington, Virginia, through the service of Your servant, Robert E. Lee, who became president of Washington College after the war. And thank You that our present tribulations in the service of Jesus cannot compare with the joy of knowing Him and belonging to Him.

OCTOBER 6

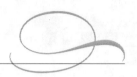

After the death of President Lincoln Federal cavalry hunted down and killed his assassin, John Wilkes Booth. They also made widespread arrests of anyone thought be have a part in the crime. Eight people were finally put to a trial the outcome of which was predetermined. They forced the accused to wear canvas hoods when not in the courtroom; they were constantly in chains. Hardly any of their legal rights were observed; as a result all were found guilty with four to be hanged and four to endure long prison terms. Sentenced to die was George Atzerodt whose part in the plot was to kill Vice president Andrew Johnson; instead he panicked and fled. Also sentenced to death was David Herrold, a close companion of Booth who surrendered at the time Booth was killed. Lewis Paine was sentenced to hang for slashing Secretary of State William Seward near the jugular; he failed to kill him. The final death sentence was for Mrs. Mary Surratt whose only apparent crime was to own the boarding house where the crimes were planned. The other defendants testified to her innocence, but to no avail. The sentences were carried out on July 7, 1865.

"Who leave the paths of uprightness, to walk in the ways of darkness" (Proverbs 2:13 KJV).

Am I the same person alone and secluded that I am when with other people? I should be.

> Father, plots devised in darkness come to no good and prove too costly. Please grant that all I plan, say, and do may be done intentionally in Your presence, in the awareness that nothing is hidden from You.

OCTOBER 7

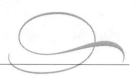

John Surratt, son of Mary Surratt, was in the conspiracy with John Wilkes Booth to kidnap President Lincoln but not to assassinate him when the kidnap failed. After Lincoln was killed he fled the country. Many thought this played a large part in his mother's death sentence. Two years later Surratt was recognized, arrested, and returned to the United States to stand trial before a civil court rather than the military court that had convicted his mother. The court dropped the charges against him because the statute of limitations pertinent to his case had expired. He lived until the age of seventy-two and died at home in Maryland. Four men were charged and convicted of complicity in the assassination of the President. Edman Spangler received six years in prison. Dr. Samuel Mudd, Michael O'Laughlin, and Samuel Arnold received life sentences at a prison in the Dry Tortugas. These were islands off the Florida coast where conditions were terrible, disease was rampant, and death was the most likely way out.

"We are become a reproach to our neighbors, a scorn and derision to them that are round about us" (Psalm 79:4 KJV).

Justice means giving people their due whether good or bad. Criminal justice means a punishment commensurate with the crime.

> Father, there is much injustice in our fallen world. Bless our judicial system in order that that fair judgments may abound. Thank You that one day Christ will make all things right.

OCTOBER 8

The conviction of Dr. Samuel Mudd was unusual in that the only connection between him and the assassin, John Wilkes Booth, was that he gave medical treatment to a man with a broken leg who knocked at his door. That man was Booth along with David Herrold. After Dr. Mudd, Michael O'Laughlin, Edman Spangler, and Samuel Arnold began serving their sentences, a yellow fever epidemic spread throughout the prison. In 1867 many died including Michael O'Laughlin and the prison doctor. Dr. Mudd offered his services and was credited with saving many lives of both prisoners and prison officials. Those officials and many other people appealed for Dr. Mudd's release. President Andrew Johnson responded by releasing Mudd, Spangler, and Arnold. Spangler was dying of tuberculosis; Dr. Mudd brought him back to his Maryland home to live until his death two years later.

"Forbearing one another, and forgiving one another, if any man have a quarrel against any: even as Christ also forgave you, so also do ye" (Colossians 3:13 KJV).

Sin is cosmic treason against the One who made the cosmos. In the end there will be perfect justice. That means the awful sentence of eternal hell for those who have spurned the pardon God has offered in Christ.

> Father, there is doubt about Dr. Mudd's guilt, but there is no doubt that I am guilty of sin, of cosmic treason against You. My only hope is the atoning blood of Christ that He shed on the cross for me. Thank You that it is a sure hope.

OCTOBER 9

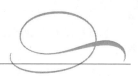

At the battle of the Wilderness in Virginia, which was considered a Confederate victory, Federal officers were exclaiming over Robert E. Lee's tactics and maneuvering of his troops. They wondered what he would do next. Union Commander U. S. Grant, normally a quiet and docile individual exploded. "Oh I am heartily tired of hearing about what Lee is going to do. Some of you always seem to think he is suddenly going to turn a double somersault and land in our rear and on both flanks at the same time. Go back to your command and try to think what we are going to do ourselves instead of what Lee is going to do." Union General George Meade said later, however, that General Grant was beginning to understand that Robert E. Lee and the Army of Northern Virginia were not the same as the Confederate army Grant had faced and defeated in Tennessee. Later, after the battle of the Cold Harbor, Virginia, some officers on Lee's staff were deriding Grant for the wanton slaughter of his own Federal troops in ordering attacks against strong Confederate fortifications. General Lee silenced Grant's critics by saying, "I think General Grant has managed his affairs remarkably well up to this present time."

"The wisdom of the prudent is to understand his way, but the folly of fools is deceit" (Proverbs 14:8 KJV).

It is good to anticipate what the enemy will do. It is better to take the initiative. It is best to do both.

> Father, both generals Lee and Grant respected each other; yet each had confidence in his own abilities. Please strengthen my weaknesses and sustain my strengths that Christ may continually be glorified.

OCTOBER 10

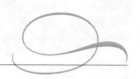

Brigadier General Abner Perrin of South Carolina had distinguished him-self valiantly in every battle of General Lee's Army of Northern Virginia. On May 12, 1864, the thirty-seven year old Perrin was ordered to take his command and defend against an attempted breakthrough of Confederate lines by the Union at the battle of Spotsylvania at Courthouse, Virginia. As he rushed forward before his men he exclaimed, "I shall come out of this fight a live major general or a dead brigadier." Soon afterwards he was shot from his saddle; his body had seven bullet wounds. Brigadier General Abner Perrin's body lies in the Confederate Cemetery at Fredericksburg, Virginia, along with five other Southern generals and three thousand three hundred comrades. Only 1,116 of those have been identified by name.

"Surely goodness and mercy shall follow me all the days of my life and I will dwell in the house of the Lord forever" (Psalm 23:6 KJV).

Sentry standing guard over unknown Confederate dead, Fredericksburg, Virginia Confederate Cemetery.

Death means separation of the soul from the body and of the loved one from his family. It has been a certainty through-out human history. Now in the fullness of time Christ has come and has abol-ished death. The one who dies in Christ goes immediately to His presence and to reunion with his Christian ancestors. Some day he will have reunion with his resurrected body, when God resurrects the dead. For the true believer, "To live is Christ, to die is gain."

Father, I have witnessed with awe the courage and heroism of so many warriors who gave their lives for something they believed to be greater than them-selves. Where can this devotion come from except from You? Help me to love Christ more than my own life.

OCTOBER 11

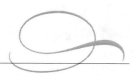

In February of 1864 a Union cavalry raid was ordered on the Confederate capitol of Richmond, Virginia. Thousands of Union prisoners were imprisoned at that time in the capitol which was sparsely defended. The purpose of the raid was to free the POW's and pass out thousands of amnesty proclamations signed by President Lincoln to influence any Southerners who might have second thoughts about the war. General Judson Kilpatrick led the raid with a force of thirty-five hundred troopers. He divided his force, sending Colonel Eric Dahlgren to attack the city from the south while Kilpatrick struck from the north. In trying to find a place to ford the James River, Dahlgren enlisted the aid of a young black youth named Martin Robinson to guide. When they reached the usual ford, they found that the recent rains made it impossible to cross. Enraged, Dahlgren had the young guide hanged. He found a place to cross only after long delays; all chances of a simultaneous attack on Richmond had faded away.

"The lot is cast into the lap, but the whole disposing thereof is of the Lord" (Proverbs 16:33 KJV).

The battle is not always won by the strong.

> Father, often in warfare plans written on paper are not carried out in the field. How often Your Providence brings the victory or the defeat.

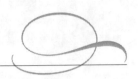

The Kilpatrick/Dahlgren raid on Richmond was a failure before it started. The weather opposed them with snow, sleet, strong wind, and ice. Some militia units whose wounded were being treated in local hospitals and a few military men who happened to be in the area were the defenders. This ragtag force not only repulsed both attacks, but they chased the Union forces away from the capitol. When the Dahlgren group finally united again with Kilpatrick, they had lost two hundred of their comrades, killed or wounded, including the commander. The total casualty count was three hundred forty as they turned away from Richmond. The Confederates found secret orders on Colonel Dahlgren's body (which had four bullet wounds, each of which would have been fatal). The orders were to free the POW's, distribute amnesty papers, and find and kill President Jefferson Davis and as many Rebel leaders as could be found. Washington, D.C. denied any part in the plot. The orders, later viewed as genuine, could not have been issued without the knowledge of someone very high in the Federal Government.

"For God will bring every work into judgment, with every secret thing, whether it be good or whether it be evil" (Ecclesiastes 12:14 KJV).

We err when we imagine that we are alone or that we have secrets. God has been present with us in our most shameful moments. Yet He loves us anyway.

> Father, nothing is hidden from Your eyes. Let me remember that any secret that I have hidden from men is not hidden from You. Help me to confess these things daily, and to repent of the wrong things.

OCTOBER 13

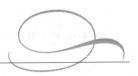

Some described Confederate Captain Charles Edward (Ned) Meriwether as brave, dashing, and handsome. He was killed in a cavalry battle with Federal forces at Sacremento, Kentucky on December 28, 1861. His commanding officer, General Nathan Bedford Forrest said of him, "Had he lived, Captain Ned Meriwether would have been one of the great cavalry officers of the Confederacy. He had all the qualities that make a man a commander among men." A study of Captain Meriwether's life and the lives of other Meriwethers who served in the Confederacy led to the writing of this devotional book; one of the authors is his descendant.

"I will pour My Spirit upon thy seed, and My blessing on Thy offspring" (Isaiah 44:3b KJV).

Men of integrity leave a good legacy for their descendants.

> Father, many have a rich heritage from their ancestors. What better heritage can there be than having godly parents, grandparents, and great-grandparents? God blesses the children of those who love Him. Help me to be a person of integrity and a true follower of Christ for the sake of my descendants.

OCTOBER 14

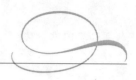

Illustrative of the nation's serious divisions in 1861 was the graduating class at the West Point Academy of 1857. Thirty-eight graduated that year. One of the cadets died in 1859. When the war opened twenty-two of the class chose to serve the Union. Of the twenty-two, four were killed in battle, one died of disease, three were wounded, and two were captured in the course of the war. Of the fifteen cadets who served the Confederacy, three died of disease and one was captured. This war split apart classes, families, and businesses; it literally pitted brother against brother.

"Endeavoring to keep the unity of the Spirit in the bond of peace" (Ephesians 4:3 KJV).

Most of the things that we divide over are not worth the evil consequences of division and enmity.

> Father, help me to exert all effort to walk in trust and obedience to my sovereign King that His church would be unified in the bond of peace.

OCTOBER 15

At the battle of Fredericksburg, Virginia on December 13, 1862, the Confederate defensive lines were so formidable that the commander of the Southern artillery, Colonel E. Porter Alexander exclaimed to General James Longstreet, "General, we cover that ground so well now that we will comb it as fine as a tooth comb. A chicken could not live on that field when we open on it." General Lee showed concern that repeated Federal attacks might break the Confederate lines where Longstreet's men were defending. General Longstreet assured him, "General if you put every man now on the other side of the Potomac River in that field to approach me over that same line, and give me plenty of ammunition, I will kill them all before they reach my line." As the battle neared its conclusion someone remarked, "It is no longer a battle but butchery." The twelve thousand five hundred thirty-five Union soldiers killed, wounded, or captured could attest to this.

"For the indignation of the Lord is upon all nations and His fury upon all their armies. He hath utterly destroyed them. He hath delivered them to the slaughter" (Isaiah 34:2 KJV).

The Bible instructs us to be subject to the governing authorities. It is right to respond to a draft notice, because God has so commanded. Yet even the government does not have the right to command us to do something that is clearly opposite to God's laws. This calls for discernment for each believer.

> Father, man in his fallen state is going to make war and kill. Yet there is such a thing as a just war. I am a warrior, and a warrior fights. Give me discernment to take part only in a just war. Please give our leaders wisdom to initiate war only for a just cause.

October 16

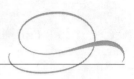

Part of the Confederate defensive force behind the stone wall at the crest of a rise known as Marye's Heights was the 24th Georgia Regiment. The stone wall bordered a sunken road; this provided the Southern soldier protection and enabled him to fire his musket at chest level. The 24th Georgia was made up entirely of Irish immigrants who had settled in the South. On December 13, 1862 at the battle of Fredericksburg, Virginia, the fifth brigade to charge the stone wall in its second wave was comprised of Irish immigrants from Philadelphia, New York, and Boston. With a green sprig in their hats the one thousand three hundred men of the Irish Brigade attacked their fellow Irishmen of the 24th Georgia. Men on both sides had fought together as comrades in the 1848 rebellion to free Ireland. Now they trained their muskets on each other. Although the Irish Brigade came closer to the stone wall than any other Federal force, the attack, along with ten others, failed. The Brigade suffered a forty-two 42 percent casualty rate, five hundred forty-five men. Many of the Confederates were seen to be weeping as they fired their terrible barrages into the massed ranks of their former comrades.

"Oh that my head were waters, and mine eyes a fountain of tears that I might weep day and night for the slain of the daughter of My people" (Jeremiah 9:1 KJV).

War is a part of the insanity of living in a depraved and fallen world that is in rebellion against God. The Christian soldier can but choose to be in subjection to his government, entrust his life to God, and acquit himself like a man.

> Father, some victories bring joy while others, even though they are victories, bring tears. All true victories are Yours. I am a warrior in Your service. Please give me victories that bring You glory, whether on the battlefield or in resisting the world, the flesh, and the Devil.

OCTOBER 17

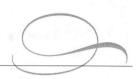

The noted Southern historian Douglas Southall Freeman said this about the flag of the Confederate 61st Virginia Regiment: "This flag was in the Seven Days Battles. This flag flapped at Chancelorsville. This flag was on the ridge at Gettysburg. This flag went through all the experiences and all the blood and slaughter of the Wilderness and of Spotsylvania Court House. This flag was at Ream's Station. This flag—my father saw it—came up the hill when the Crater was recovered at Petersburg at the end of July in 1864, and this flag with the tears of the men who bore it, was laid down on that red clay at Appomattox and surrendered.

"Thus my heart was grieved and I was pricked in my reins. Nevertheless I am continually with Thee. Thou hast holden me by my right hand" (Psalm 73: 21, 23 KJV).

Every single human being on the earth has experienced defeat and will experience many more. How wise to put our hands into the hand of the One who alone can turn defeat into victory.

> Dear LORD, how heartbreaking it must have been for these bloody yet unbowed Southern soldiers to surrender their dear flag. Yet, You are so gracious to bless us in our victories and comfort us in our losses. And thank You that ultimately we are more than conquerors in Christ; at the end we will have victory that is without end.

OCTOBER 18

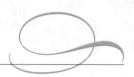

In the Confederate Cemetery in Fredericksburg, Virginia, among the many graves and tombstones stand three headstones that command attention. The inscription of the one on the left reads, "J. R. Gunliffe; who bravely volunteered in the Confederate Army in the Spring of 1862 and had fought at Gettysburg and other memorable battlefields in the 18th Mississippi Regiment. Was instantly killed by a sharpshooter on the 6th of May 1864 at the Wilderness having a short time before advanced on the enemy and driven him back." The one on the right reads, "W. E. Gunliffe; who espoused ardently the cause of Southern Rights at the commencement of the war in 1861 and had fought gallantly as a volunteer in the 18th Mississippi Regiment at Manassas, Leesburg, Fredericksburg and other battlefields, received his mortal wound at Chancelorsville May 2 1863 by the same volley that struck the immortal Jackson and survived only thirty hours breathing while life lasted an earnest prayer for the salvation of his beloved country." The one in the center reads, "This monument is erected in the memory of Richard and William Gunliffe by their fond afflicted mother who is now left childless."

"The Lord preserveth the simple; I was brought low and he helped me" (Psalm 116:6 KJV).

If our perspective is only on the temporal view, the loss of a dear one is pain beyond comfort. But when our perspective is of the hope of eternal life in Jesus Christ, there is abundant comfort.

> Father, sadly it was not uncommon in this war for all the male members of a family to die by combat or disease. Praise the God of all comfort who comforts us and raises us up when we are brought low. Help me to be a comforter to the wounded and to the families of the slain.

OCTOBER 19

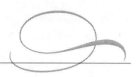

From 1861 to 1865 these major battles were fought in the State of Virginia alone: Harper's Ferry (before it became part of the State of West Virginia), Aldie, Kelly's Ford, Frayser's Farm, White Oak Swamp, I Mannassas, Ball's Bluff, 1st, 2nd, and 3rd Winchester, Williamsburg, Front Royal, Seven Pines, Kernstown, Cross Keys, Port Republic, Oak Grove, Savage Station, Gaines Mill, Malvern Hill, Mechanicsville, Cedar Mountain, II Manassas, Chantilly, Fredericksburg, Chancellorsville, Brandy Station, Wilderness, Spotsylvania Courthouse, Cloyd's Mountain, Drewry's Bluff, New Market, Bermuda Hundred, North Anna River, Cold Harbor, Piedmont, Yellow Tavern, Trevillian's Station, Petersburg, Lynchburg, Wilson's Raid, Mine Run, Cedar Creek, Ream's Station, New Market Heights, High Bridge, Five Forks, Kilpatrick's Raid on Richmond, and Appomattox, forty-nine in all. This doesn't count the many skirmishes between Blue and Gray. There is no difference between a skirmish and a battle when men are wounded or killed. One can imagine the tremendous devastation for the people of the land.

"Behold, the eye of the Lord is upon them that fear Him; upon them that hope in His mercy" (Psalm 33:18 KJV).

Some devastation is unavoidable, such as that described above. Some we bring on ourselves by unwise choices.

> Father, someone once said, "We have met the enemy, and he is us." We bring devastation on ourselves by choices to ignore or violate the principles of life found in Your Word. Help us to consider Your wisdom not as an option, not as a trifle, but as our life. And thank You that Your tender mercies comfort us when we fail.

OCTOBER 20

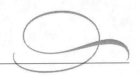

In February, 1865 Union General William Sherman's superior force drove Confederate General Joseph Johnson's troops up through Georgia and South Carolina to the border of North Carolina. Meanwhile U. S. Grant extended his lines around Petersburg, Virginia, thus forcing Robert E. Lee to stretch his rapidly diminishing army almost to the breaking point. General Lee wrote to his wife: "Generals Sherman and Schofield are both advancing and seem to have everything their own way. But trusting in a merciful God, who does not always give the battle to the strong, I pray we may not be overwhelmed. I shall however endeavor to do my duty and fight to the last." As the siege tightened around Petersburg and the Federal successes continued farther south, General Lee's resolve to do his duty did not wane.

"And whatever ye do, do it heartily, as to the Lord, and not unto men" (Colossians 3:23 KJV).

Sometimes our duty seems insignificant, yet in God's economy faithfulness in small things leads to bigger responsibilities of greater significance. And even the things we thought were small may have been much bigger than we knew.

> "Father, General Lee served his country, but his higher calling was to serve You by doing his duty. Help me to be a witness for Christ and a warrior for Christ, doing my duty and bringing glory to You.

OCTOBER 21

Richmond, Virginia, the capital of the Confederacy, fell to Union forces shortly before the end of the war. At that time United States Vice President Andrew Johnson gave this rousing speech in Washington, DC concerning Confederate President Jefferson Davis and others like him: "Hang him! Hang him! Yes, I say hang him twenty times. He and others like him are infamous in character, diabolical in motive. Confiscate their property. When you ask me what I would do, my reply is—I would arrest them, I would try them, I would convict them and I would hang them. Treason must be made odious. Traitors must be punished and impoverished." Fortunately, after Lincoln's death Johnson adopted Lincoln's plan for the South "to let them up easy." Unfortunately the U. S. Congress did not agree, and they initiated the Reconstruction.

"Neither shouldest thou have rejoiced over the children of Judah in the day of their destruction. Neither shouldest thou have spoken proudly in the day of distress. Thou shouldest not have entered into the gate of My people in the day of their calamity. Yea thou shouldest not have looked on their affliction in the day of their calamity nor have laid hands on their substance in the day of their calamity" (Obadiah 12b,13 KJV).

After World War II the United States was more kind to Germany and Japan than the North was to the South after the War Between the States.

> Father, though I am a soldier help me never to be prideful in victory nor to rejoice over another's defeat, nor to take vengeance.

October 22

Mary Smiley wrote this in a letter to her brother, Thomas Smiley, about politics in Virginia: "Dear Brother, this is election day. It has been beautiful so far. Even the morning appears to favor the election for ratifying what the Convention has done. I think a great majority of the people will go for secession, revolution, or whatever it is called. The greatest numbers of the papers urge the people to ratify the acts of the Convention to present a bold and united front to the North against its tyranny. Even the Spectator which you know was as strong a Union paper as could be found." Very few could have known the full ramifications that would result from each of the eleven Southern states voting to secede from the United States. To give birth to the Confederate States of America would involve much more than dropping a vote in the ballot box.

"Trust in the Lord with all thine heart, and lean not unto thine own understanding. In all thy ways acknowledge Him, and He shall direct thy paths" (Proverbs 3:5,6 KJV).

Hindsight is better than foresight. But God has foresight, and if He guides, and we listen, then we do not necessarily avoid opposition, but the final end is good.

> Father, help me to consider all the facts in a matter,
> yield to Your guidance, and go ahead.

OCTOBER 23

Martha White Read wrote to her husband, Thomas Griffin Read, serving in the 33rd Virginia Infantry Regiment of the Confederate Army: "My dear husband, in the quiet of the Sabbath evening (and you remember its quiet here) my heart turns to thee more than ever; tis thee I miss the most. And I know that unless you are in the confusion of a battle, or on a toilsome march, your thoughts linger more than usual on the loved ones at home. I feel assured, dear husband, that you try 'to remember the Sabbath day, to keep it holy.' Even amid the 'turmoil' of the camp you can sometimes withdraw your thoughts from things around you and fix them on sacred subjects, if but for a short time at once, it will serve to feed the flames of devotion in your heart. I do not think that God ever placed a man in circumstances in which he could say with truth, 'I can not serve God here.' I believe that the Christian intent on the service of God can serve Him anywhere."

"Choose this day whom you will serve, but as for me and my house, we will serve the Lord" (Joshua 24:15 KJV).

A better understanding of God's sovereignty takes away much anxiety. Maybe we are not yet where we want to be, but we are where He has placed us right now.

> Father, You have put me where I am; from here, with all that I have and all that I can do, I will serve You.

October 24

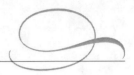

Kentucky Confederate soldier James Blackburn wrote this in a letter home: "My Dear Wife, I have left you and our children in the land of the despot, but God grant that I may soon be able to make the Union men of Kentucky feel the edge of my knife. From this day I hold every Union traitor as my enemy, and from him I scorn to receive quarter and to him I will never grant my soul in death; for they are cowards and villains enough. Brother Henry and I arrived here without hindrance. I have had chills all the way, but I hope to kill forty Yankees for every chill that I ever had." Blackburn never explained the reason for the hatred that boiled up in his life.

"Ye have heard that it hath been said, Thou shalt love thy neighbor and hate thine enemy. But I say unto you, love your enemies" (Matthew 5:43, 44a KJV).

In war it is helpful to distinguish between causes and people. The enemy has a family just as I do. I must defend my country and my cause even to the point of leveling a rifle at the enemy's heart. But I must not hate him or mistreat him when he is prisoner or do spiteful damage to his homeland.

> Father, may I not hate what my enemy stands for
> without hating him personally? Let any hatred I
> have in me be toward evil and not toward people.
> Otherwise it may take bitter root in my heart.

One of the reasons for the military successes enjoyed by Confederate General Stonewall Jackson was the staff of ten officers he had around him. They were: Major W. Hawks, in charge of ordinance for Jackson's army. After being wounded and in delirium, Jackson was heard saying, "Have Major Hawks come up;" Captain J. Hotchkiss, who had no equal as a map maker and to whom Jackson credited the victories of the 1862 Valley Campaign; Major Hunter McGuire, chief medical officer and the surgeon who removed Jackson's shattered left arm when he was wounded at Chancelorsville, Virginia; Captain J.B. Smith; Major H. K. Douglas who, besides serving on Jackson's staff, also served as an aide to Edward Johnson, John Gordon, and Jubal Early. Wounded six times during the war, he survived and wrote a lively account of it titled, "I Rode with Stonewall;" Major D. B. Bridgeford; Captain J. G. Morrison; Lieutenant Colonel A. S. "Sandie" Pendleton who was like a son to Stonewall and indensible to him. Pendleton dressed Jackson's body for burial and was himself mortally wounded at the battle of Winchester, Virginia in 1864; Lieutenant Colonel W. Allen; Major R. L. Dabney, a Presbyterian minister, the main chaplain for Jackson's army, and later the author of "Life and Campaigns of Lieutenant General Thomas J. Jackson."

"Where no counsel is, the people fall, but in the multitude of counselors there is safety" (Proverbs 11:14 KJV).

One sign of wisdom is to seek wise friends and wise counsel.

> Father, keep me in the company of wise and godly
> people so that I might make right choices.

OCTOBER 26

The Confederate government hoped to raise morale and recognize their soldiers. They authorized medals and badges for officers who were "conspicuous for courage and good conduct on the field of battle." For enlisted men there was to be one soldier recognized per regiment after each victory, a man chosen by vote of the regiment members. When the appropriate medals could not be supplied, the Confederate Congress authorized the Roll of Honor in 1862. The Roll of Honor covered all ranks. It was to be preserved in the office of the adjutant and the office of the inspector general. It was to be read at the head of every regiment during the first dress parade after its receipt and to be published in at least one newspaper from every state. Medals were not issued to individual soldiers since the purpose was to emphasize the joint effort. Being on the Roll of Honor was the greatest acclaim the Southern soldier could expect.

"And there shall in no wise enter into it any thing that defileth, neither whatsoever worketh abomination, or maketh a lie, but they which are written in the Lamb's Book of Life" (Revelation 22:27 KJV).

Having been on the honor roll in high school for good grades may not seem to have been such an important thing to a man of fifty. It may seem huge to a lad of sixteen. But the honors given by God will never diminish.

> Father, the Congressional Medal of Honor is the highest award that can be given to a member of the military. The Medal of Freedom is the highest award that a civilian can obtain. Being on the Roll of Honor was the highest honor a Confederate soldier could get. But all these seem microscopic when compared to the honor of having one's name written in the Lamb's Book of Life.

OCTOBER 27

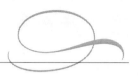

Much has been written about the battle of Franklin, Tennessee fought on November 30, 1864. Six Confederate general officers were killed; there were seven thousand other Southern casualties. This along with the battle of Nashville ended the Confederate Army in the west as a fighting force. There were nine thousand casualties from both sides in just five hours of fighting at Nashville. After the battle of Franklin the son of the owner of the property where the battle was exceedingly intense said this: "In this yard and in that garden I could walk from fence to fence on dead bodies, mostly those of Confederates. In trying to clean up I scraped together a half bushel of brains right around the house and the whole place was dyed with blood." Confederate General and corps commander Frank Cheatham said this: "The dead were stacked like wheat and scattered like sheaves of grain. You could walk on the field on the bodies without touching the ground. I never saw a field like that, and I never want to see a field like that again."

"When thou art in tribulation, and all these things are come upon thee, even in the latter days, if thou turn to the Lord thy God and shalt be obedient unto His voice, He will not forsake thee neither destroy thee" (Deuteronomy 4:30, 31a KJV).

We may die in battle or we may see comrades die. We have been promised tribulation in this life.

> Father, until You end all war there will be war because we live in a corrupt world. Bless, equip, and protect Your people as they battle militarily, spiritually, and morally. Help us to be obedient warriors knowing that You will be victorious.

OCTOBER 28

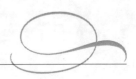

Lieutenant Alonzo Wolverton of the 20th Ohio light artillery, who survived the battle of Franklin, Tennessee, wrote home, "The rebs came on to us in full force and there ensued one of the hardest fought battles since this war commenced. The rebs, determined to conquer or die, made thirteen desperate charges. Several times, they planted their colors within ten feet of our cannon, and our men would knock them down with their muskets or the artillerymen with their sponge staffs and handspikes. I never dreamed men would fight with such desperation. I never expected to come out alive."

"Greater love hath no man than this, that a man lay down his life for his friends" (John 15:13 KJV).

Perhaps recruits don't really expect to be killed or wounded during their tour of duty, but they know it could happen. And when it does, that man or woman has died for the people back home.

> Father, life is precious, and no one is more aware
> of this than the warrior who is willing to lay his
> down. May our cause be just. May the day come
> soon when wars will be done forever.

OCTOBER 29

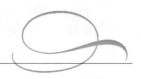

Union Captain Sexton of the 72nd Illinois Infantry Regiment fought in the Carter Garden in the battle of Franklin, Tennessee where the fighting was particularly fierce. He described it like this: "I discharged my own weapon nine times and the most distant man I shot at was no more than twenty feet away. A Rebel colonel mounted our breastworks and demanded our immediate surrender. Private Arbridge thrust his musket against the stomach of the rash colonel and said, 'I guess not,' and discharged his weapon. The effect of the shot was horrible and actually let daylight through the victim." Another soldier said, "The dead were piled up in the trenches almost to the top of the earthworks." Another said, "At the gap in the works where the pike road went through (Carter Garden) were lying a Confederate and a Federal soldier, both with bayonets sent through their bodies. It was plain to see that they were each other's victims."

"Thy men shall fall by the sword, and thy mighty in the war" (Isaiah 3:25 KJV).

The spiritual conflict that rages all around us is just as fierce as war, and the stakes are even higher because what is at risk is the immortal soul. Should we not be as earnest as two men who face each other with bayonets?

> Father, we war against evil and corrupt forces that seek to kill and destroy. Grant us courage in whatever battle we fight, and sustain us until the final victory. Grant Your peace and rest to those who have given their last full measure of devotion.

October 30

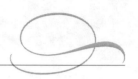

Author David Hinze writes: "The Carter Garden at the battle of Franklin, Tennessee is one of the most critical pieces of ground in the War Between the States. It is when men became living demons brutally fighting at an insanely close range, and yet it represents the dogged persistence of both armies, who refused to yield to their foe. The Carter Garden is as close as we humans will get to the vortex of hell on this earth."

"Beat your plowshares into swords and your pruning hooks into spears. Let the weak say I am strong" (Joel 3:10 KJV).

"And they shall beat their swords into plowshares, and their spears into pruning hooks. Nation shall not lift up sword against nation, neither shall they learn war any more." (Isaiah 2:4b KJV)

If we could but see the eternal perspective, what fervor we would have to fight in a just war and to pursue a peace that is not a selfdeluding fiction.

> Father, You have ordained a time for war and a time for peace. Help us to persevere in war until the victory is won; then help us to pursue peace with equal fervor.

OCTOBER 31

The War for Southern Independence, also known as the Civil War, was the costliest and bloodiest in American history. Forty percent of the combined armies of the Union and Confederacy were casualties. The Union armies suffered six hundred thousand casualties with more than half dying of disease or in combat. The Confederates sustained four hundred thousand casualties with more than two hundred fifty thousand deaths. In comparison to the white Southern population, if the North had suffered commensurately, their death count would have been one million instead of three hundred sixty thousand. In our War of Independence against England twelve thousand died. It would have been ninety four thousand if it had been commensurate to the fraction of Southerners who died in the Civil War. In World War II, with the same comparison, The United States would have had six million dead instead of three hundred thousand. One scholar said, "The Confederacy rendered the heaviest sacrifices in lives ever made by Americans."

Graves of unknown Union dead, Gettysburg National Cemetery.

"For He knoweth our frame; He remembereth that we are dust. As for man, his days are as grass; as a flower of the field, so he flourisheth. For the wind passeth over it, and it is gone, and the place thereof shall know it no more" (Psalm 103:14-16 KJV).

Even in times of peace our span is brief. Wisdom would direct us to be prepared for the inevitable. We can be prepared only in Christ.

> Father, our earthly life is so brief, but we take comfort
> in this promise: "But the mercy of the Lord is from
> everlasting to everlasting upon them that fear Him,
> and His righteousness unto children's children."

NOVEMBER 1

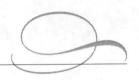

When the last Confederate army surrendered and the war came to an end, the Federal Government took upon itself extraordinary powers. All but one of the first twelve amendments to the United States Constitution limited the powers of the Federal Government. The next six increased Federal power at the expense of the states. The jurisdiction of Federal courts was greatly expanded. In the first seventy-two years of our nation, Southerners had been in the office of president for forty-eight years. After the war a full century passed before a man from a former Confederate state was elected president. Noted Southern history Grady McWhiney has said, "The War for Southern Independence destroyed the South's America as well as the America of the Founding Fathers."

"God is not a man that He should lie, neither the son of man that He should repent. Hath He said and shall He not do it, or hath He spoken and shall He not make it good?" (Numbers 23:19 KJV).

One of God's awesome attributes is that He never changes.

> Father, I thank You that You are immutable. You never change even though the sons of men are given to change. I am so grateful that You are constant and faithful.

NOVEMBER 2

After the War Between the States political power shifted from South to North. In the three-fourths century since the founding of our nation until 1861, twenty-one of the Senate's presidents pro tem had been Southerners. Of the thirty-six speakers of the U. S. House of Representatives, twenty-three were from the South. For fifty years after the war, none of the presidents pro tem or speakers of the house were Southerners. During this same period only five of the twenty-six appointees to the Supreme Court were from the South. The war to begin a new nation and retain a way of life was very costly to the South. A whole generation, two hundred fifty thousand, were dead. But much worse was to come: for twelve years during Reconstruction the Southern states were looked upon as occupied colonies. President Lincoln's desire for a united nation was delayed by bitterness, hatred, and mistrust for many, many years.

"Holy Father, keep through Thine own Name those whom Thou hast given Me, that they may be one as We are" (John 17:11b KJV).

To look backward to past offenses and to hold on to bitterness is to fail to be what we can and should be in Christ.

> Father, unify Your church. Help me to focus on
> You and perform my duty. Help me to reconcile
> men to each other and to You.

NOVEMBER 3

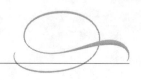

At Appomattox, Virginia, on April 9, 1865, General Lee's army was surrounded by Federal forces and outnumbered ten to one in armed troops. As Lee realized that surrender was his only option, he said, "How easily I could get rid of this and be at rest! I have only to ride along the lines and all will be over! But it is our duty to live, for what will become of the women and children of the South if we are not here to support and protect them?" A British military observer had this to say of General Lee, "In strategy mighty, in battle terrible, in adversity as in prosperity a hero indeed, with the simple devotion to duty and the rare purity of the ideal Christian knight, he joined all the kingly qualities of a leader of men."

"And take not the word of truth utterly out of my mouth, for I have hope in Thy judgments" (Psalm 119:43 KJV).

How much more important is it to do my duty as a husband, a son, a father, a citizen, or a warrior than to gratify my own selfish desires?

> Father, General Lee lived his life according to what he believed. He focused on the assured hope that in Your time You would make things right and all will be well. Help me to do likewise.

NOVEMBER 4

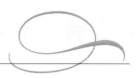

As the State of Virginia debated the proposition of secession from the United States, a Virginia Military Institute professor wrote to his nephew: "I am in favor of making a thorough trial for peace, and if we fail in this, and the State is invaded, to defend it with a terrible resistance." And after Virginia voted to secede, Jackson spoke these words to an assembly of faculty and V. M. I. Cadets: "The time for war has not come, but it will come, and when it does come, my advice is to draw the sword and throw away the scabbard." The pious Jackson lived a life of charity and love as he believed the Scriptures commanded. But when war came, the people saw a different man. The piety remained stronger than ever, but with it came a stern fervor. Efforts for peace had failed. Jackson then fully committed himself to ending the war by victories on the battlefield. He hoped to exact such an enormous cost to Northern men and their resources that they would never invade his beloved Virginia again.

"Whatsoever thy hand findeth to do, do it with thy might" (Ecclesiastes 9:10a KJV).

Whether we realize it or not, we are in a spiritual battle that is as fierce and dangerous as the War Between the States. We need some of Jackson's stern fervor.

> Father, Stonewall Jackson held nothing back in trying to preserve peace, to wage war, or to serve and glorify You. May I be transformed by the renewing of my mind that I may carry out the good, acceptable, and perfect will of God.

NOVEMBER 5

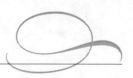

After Virginia seceded from the Union, Colonel Thomas Jackson took five Virginia regiments of raw recruits and forged them into a brigade unmatched by any other unit on either side. These five regiments turned the tide of battle at I Manassas, Virginia and snatched victory from what appeared to be a certain defeat. They would be forever known as the Stonewall Brigade. Jackson was promoted to Major General and ordered to the Shenandoah Valley, leaving his brigade behind with a new commander. In his farewell address to them he said, "You are the First Brigade in the affections of your General, and I hope by your deeds and bearing you will be handed down to posterity as the First Brigade in our Second War of Independence."

"The children of Judah that bare shield and spear were sixty-eight hundred, ready armed to war" (II Chronicles 13:24 KJV).

One of the best metaphors for the Christian life is that of war. The difference is that the violence is primarily at the spiritual level. Those on the front lines see the violence. We in the rear see the casualties. How we ought to pray for those at the front, and be ready to serve there ourselves.

> Father, help me to be a warrior, equipped and ready to fight any foe that comes against Christ and His Gospel. What an honor and privilege to be a warrior in the army of the living God.

NOVEMBER 6

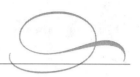

One of the Confederacy's greatest fighting units was John Bell Hood's Texas Brigade. These "Sons of the Alamo" had the distinction of fighting in both the east and west theaters of war. On September 17, 1862 at the battle of Sharpsburg, Maryland, the brigade was called upon to save the Confederate left flank as wave after wave of Union forces crashed against it. The Texans began their fierce fighting in the famous cornfield with eight hundred fifty-four men. After three hours they were reduced to less than three hundred. This brigade fought at Gettysburg, Pennsylvania in July, 1863 and was the only Confederate unit to capture Union cannon in that battle. Two months later in the west, in Alabama, the brigade fought in the battle of Chickamauga where it lost five hundred seventy killed or wounded. The next spring they were back in Virginia, fighting at the battle of the Wilderness. There they came to the front just as the Confederate line was being thrown back by overwhelming Union forces. Upon seeing them, General Lee said, "I'm glad to see you. When you go in, I wish you would give those people the cold steel." They did go in with eight hundred men, and stopped the Union breakthrough, but fewer than two hundred fifty returned.

"Of Zebulon, such as went forth to battle, expert in war, with all instruments of war, fifty thousand which could keep rank. They were not of double heart" (I Chronicles 13:33 KJV).

It requires single-minded commitment to enter battle with the intention of winning or dying.

> Father, grant me courage in the daily battles of
> life; help me not to be doubleminded.

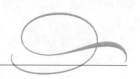

Terrible battlefield losses caused many Confederate units to be consolidated in 1864. The Texas Brigade protested the reorganization so strongly that President Jefferson Davis, not wanting to destroy the brigade's morale, left it intact. Of the five thousand three hundred men who served in the Texas Brigade during the four years of the war, only six hundred twelve were left when General Robert E. Lee surrendered his army at Appomattox, Virginia, April 9, 1865.

"All these men of war, that could keep rank, came with a perfect heart to Hebron, to make David king over all Israel" (I Chronicles 13:38a KJV).

We all go through the terrible battles of life, but at the end we will emerge with transformed hearts.

> Father, thank You that in Christ my heart, which is desperately wicked and deceitful, is being transformed into a perfect heart, the very heart of Christ.

NOVEMBER 8

In October of 1861 Union Colonel William Hoffman was appointed to the post of commissary general of Confederate prisoners of war for the Union. At Johnson Island Prison there were accommodations for a thousand prisoners of war. After Confederate Forts Henry and Donelson fell, the prison held fifteen thousand. Hoffman made cuts in prison rations until Southern inmates were literally starving. The weakened prisoners in Hoffman's crowded, freezing camps suffered all manner of deadly diseases that spread rapidly. He had heard the rumor of starvation and terrible conditions in Southern prisons. So he explained his cruel treatment as "retaliation for innumerable outrages which have been committed on our people." But the South actually lacked provisions for either Northern prisoners or their own soldiers. Hoffman had more resources at his disposal. While thousands of men suffered from scurvy in the Fort Delaware and Elmira prisons, $23,000 sat in a relief fund that he could have used to cure the stricken soldiers. It is possible that Hoffman's orders, given well behind the battle lines, killed more Confederates than the orders of Union commanders in the field.

"Deliver me, O my God, out of the hand of the wicked, out of the hand of the cruel and unrighteous man" (Psalm 71:4 KJV).

God does not always deliver us from acute suffering in one form or another. However, in the end, he will have delivered us forever from every harm.

> Father, thank You for delivering me out of the hand
> of the Devil, the most cruel being of all. Help me to
> tell others of Your mighty power and love that they
> too may be delivered.

NOVEMBER 9

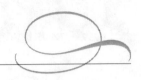

When Southern sympathizers sent clothes to the freezing Confederate prisoners of war at the Elmira, New York, prison, Colonel William Hoffman, commissary general of prisoners for the Union, ordered that only the gray clothes be issued, and the rest burned. When Captain Henry Wirz, commandant of the infamous Andersonville, Georgia prison was hanged after the war, Hoffman was awarded the brevet rank of major general for his supervision of Southern prisoners. Late in the war Hoffman returned to the Federal treasury almost two million dollars—money he saved by forcing his prisoners to live and die in desperate conditions.

"His mischief shall return upon his own head, and his violent dealing shall come down upon his own pate" (Psalm 7:16 KJV).

Ultimately those who show no mercy receive none.

> Father, as the cliche says, "What goes around comes around." May justice and righteous living flow out from my life that I might have a conscience void of offense toward God and man.

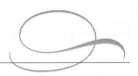

There were not many reverses or setbacks for the strong Union force as they moved down through Georgia toward Atlanta in June of 1864. Under the command of General William T. Sherman, who neither gave nor asked for any quarter, The Federal army attacked an almost impregnable Confederate defensive line at Kennesaw Mountain, Georgia on June 27. One Confederate defender described it this way, "They seemed to walk up and take death as coolly as if they were automatic or wooden men." Another said, "The sun beaming down on our uncovered heads, the thermometer being one hundred ten degrees in the shade, and a blazing fire right from the muzzles of the Yankees guns being poured right into our very faces, singeing our hair and clothes, the hot blood of our dead and wounded spurting on us. I am satisfied that on this memorable day, every man in our regiment killed from twenty to one hundred each. All that was necessary was to load and shoot. In fact, I will ever think that the reason they did not capture our works was the impossibility of their living men passing over the bodies of their dead. The ground was piled up with one solid mass of dead and wounded Yankees."

"What is man that Thou art mindful of him? And the Son of man that Thou visitest him?" (Psalm 8:4 KJV).

One of the great mysteries of existence in this fallen world is the suffering and death of people juxtaposed to the revelation of the utter goodness and mercy of God. Evil's existence perplexes many. The child of God is also perplexed, but he knows that God is at work to redeem men and women from every generation, and when the time is right, He will put an end to evil forever.

> Father, thank You that You consider each life precious and that You are concerned with preserving life. Help me to value each person as You do. Being a true warrior does not negate this; it rather enhances it.

NOVEMBER 11

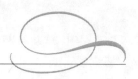

The battle of Kennesaw Mountain, Georgia was an utter and dismal defeat for the Union. Out of an attacking force of twelve thousand they suffered three thousand casualties. The 17,733 Confederate defenders lost about five hundred fifty. In his memoirs after the war, Sherman wrote: "About 9:00 a.m. of the day appointed, the troops moved to the assault, and all along our lines for ten miles a furious fire of artillery and musketry was kept up. At all points the enemy met us with determined courage and in great force. By 11:30 a.m. the assault was over and had failed. Our loss was small compared to some of those in the east." Later Sherman wrote his wife: "I begin to regard the death and mangling of a couple of thousand men as a small affair, a kind of morning dash."

"For Thou hast made man a little lower than the angels, and hast crowned him with glory and honor" (Psalm 8:5 KJV).

God and Sherman had differing scales to weigh the value of human life.

> Father, thank You that you have placed great value
> on each person. The price Christ paid for us on
> the cross was exceedingly precious, and yet You
> view us as worth that price.

NOVEMBER 12

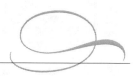

The lives, spoken words, and correspondence of the combatants bear witness that in this terrible war both sides prayed for victory. God chose to give victory to the North. This does not mean that their cause was any more just or that the people were any more righteous. People on both sides were Godfearing, living their lives as best they could and trusting God to bless them and give them victory. But God does what pleases Him and gives Him glory. It is for us to find God's will for us and abide in the center of it. It is for God to bring about the outcome.

"And we know that all things work together for good to them that love God, to them who are called according to His purpose. For whom He did foreknow, He also did predestinate to be conformed to the image of His Son" (Romans 8:28,29a KJV).

God has promised us blessing and tribulation in this world. He has also promised to use both for a blessed end.

> Father, You have promised to work good for those who love You. It is good that You will use victory or defeat, all things, to conform me to the image of Christ. This means that I can be thankful for whatever You choose to bring into my life.

NOVEMBER 13

At the battle of II Manassas, Virginia, on August 29, 1862 the left wing of General Lee's Confederate army under General Stonewall Jackson had withstood repeated attacks from the entire Union Army of Virginia under General John Pope. Entrenched along an abandoned railroad cut, the Southerners were running dangerously low on ammunition. Some were actually throwing rocks at their attackers. One Confederate said, "It was a fearfully long day. For the first time in my life I understood what was meant by Joshua's sun standing still on Gideon, for it, (the sun) would not go down. No one knows how much time can be crowded into an hour unless he has been under the fire of a desperate battle, praying that the great red sun, blazing and motionless, would go down."

"We are troubled on every side, yet not distressed. We are perplexed, but not in despair" (II Corinthians 4:8 KJV).

It is because of Christ that we are not in despair. Not everything depends on me.

> Father, there are so many things in life that are stronger than I, but they are not stronger than You. You are sovereign and in control of all things according to Your will and pleasure. I take great comfort in that.

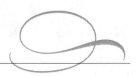

At the battle of II Manassas, Virginia, on the first day of the battle, General Maxcey Gregg's South Carolina Brigade had beaten back five Federal attacks. Asked if he could hold out until reinforcements and more ammunition arrived, he said, "I think I can. My ammunition is about gone, but I still have the bayonet." Division commander A. P. Hill reported to Corps commander Stonewall Jackson that if things continued as they were, there was little hope for success. With a stern look Jackson answered, "General, your men have done nobly; if you are attacked again you will beat the enemy back." As musket fire erupted signaling the next Union attack and Hill rushed back to his men, Jackson called out, "I'll expect you to beat them." After another successful defense of their position, and Hill had reported the news to Jackson, he received this reply: "My compliments, General Hill. I knew you would."

"The horse is prepared for the day of battle, but safety is of the Lord" (Proverbs 21:31 KJV).

Perhaps we are out of ammunition; perhaps we have nothing left but bayonets, but the Lord can put steel in our souls.

> Father, the warrior who is wise places his life in Your hands daily. Gird me for battle, and strengthen me that I may be victorious and defeat the evil that comes against me today.

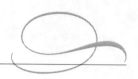

Asked to describe the battle that he had experienced and survived, a Southern soldier said, "It is these hand to hand fights that make war devil's work; for it is they which excite all the bloodthirsty passions and utterly silence every sentiment of humanity. One may fight at long range as a patriot and a Christian, but I believe that no man can engage in one of those close struggles, where he can look into the eyes of his adversary and see his blood, but he becomes for the time at least, a mere beast of prey."

"So God created man in His own image, in the image of God created He him, male and female created He them" (Genesis 1:27 KJV).

The image of God in us has been deeply marred by sin, yet its vestiges give us the semblance of nobility. We who seek Him will one day have the full restoration of His image in us.

> Father, You have created mankind in Your image.
> You made us "a little lower than the angels," and
> we have at times behaved like beasts. Help us to
> live as those who bear the image of God.

NOVEMBER 16

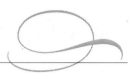

At the battle of Chancellorsville, Virginia, May 3, 1863, a Union soldier said this about the relentless Confederate attacks: "The crash of the musketry was deafening. We loaded and fired as fast as possible, but still they came on." As Southern cannon rained shells down on the Federals from higher ground, a Union officer said, "The shells from the Confederate batteries seemed to fill the air, tearing up the ground, rending the men and the horses limb from limb, blowing up the caissons, exploding and bursting everywhere." At the Chancellor House where Union commanding general Joe Hooker's headquarters were located, a shell from a Confederate battery struck a pillar close to where Hooker was standing, rendering him unconscious. When he came to, he did not relinquish command and gave no orders to guide his army from the catastrophe that was rapidly overtaking it. Finally, an hour later, at 10:00 a.m., much to the disgust of his generals, he gave the order to retreat. The Federals fled the field, withdrawing in the face of a force less than half the size of its own.

"I will send a faintness into their hearts in the lands of their enemies, and the sound of a shaken leaf shall chase them and they shall flee, as fleeing from a sword, and they shall fear when none pursueth" (Leviticus 26:36 KJV).

The outcome, win or lose, is always in God's hands.

> Father, General Hooker had boasted about victory before the battle was fought. Help me to save my comments until after the battles, and to give the glory to You alone.

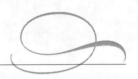

Two hours after the Union army retreated from the Chancellorsville, Virginia battlefield, Confederate Commanding General Robert E. Lee rode through the clearing where the Chancellor House (the erstwhile headquarters of Union commander Joe Hooker) stood. An aide to General Lee described the scene: "The fierce soldiers with their faces blackened by the smoke of battle, the wounded, crawling with feeble limbs from the fury of the devouring flames, all seemed possessed of a common impulse. The long unbroken cheer, in which the feeble cry of those who lay helpless on the earth blended with the strong voices of those who fought, hailed the presence of the victorious chief. As I looked upon him in the complete fruition of the success which his genius, courage, and confidence in his army had won, I thought that it must have been from such a scene that men in ancient times rose to the dignity of gods."

"And after these things I heard a great voice of much people in heaven saying, Alleluia, salvation and glory and honor and power unto the Lord our God" (Revelation 19:11 KJV).

Our dignity lies in belonging to Jesus Christ. That we know Him is the one thing we have to boast about.

> Father, General Lee would have been the first to acknowledge that You alone are God, King of Kings and Lord of Lords. Alleluia, Amen!

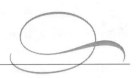

Confederate General Daniel H. Hill was one of the best division commanders in General Robert E. Lee's Army of Northern Virginia. He was very popular with the men he led and admired for his military talents. One of his men called him "a born fighter—as aggressive, pugnacious and tenacious as a bulldog, or as any soldier in the service, and he had a sort of monomania on the subject of personal courage." General Hill's bravery was based on his strong Christian faith. In a letter to his wife he wrote, "If my work is done, I will fall. If not, all the bullets on earth cannot harm me." One biographer wrote of Hill: "During the Civil War, no other general—not even Stonewall Jackson—went into combat with a firmer faith in God." It had been said of him that during the fiercest battle he sat astride his horse viewing the combat and planning his next tactic, totally oblivious of the shells crashing around him and the bullets whining over his head. He was a close friend and brother-in-law to Stonewall Jackson. They shared the Christian faith, and they made war with the fervor of Old Testament warriors.

"And they helped David against the band of rovers, for they were all mighty men of valor, and were captains in the host" (I Chronicles 13:21 KJV).

Is there any reason we should not face the foe with unusual courage, seeing that God really is sovereign and is for us? If God is for us, who can successfully oppose us?

> Father, You appoint those who lead us in the government and in the military. May they be people who fear and obey You, seeking Your wisdom and guidance.

NOVEMBER 19

Before the War Between the States Robert E. Lee found that his service in the U.S. Army kept him away from his family for prolonged periods of time. He cherished time with his family whenever it was possible. Lee's young son, Robert, wrote that when the children were small, "Our greatest treat was for all seven children to get into bed in the morning and lie close to him, listening while he talked to us in his bright entertaining way. The custom we kept up until I was ten years old and over. Although he was so joyous and familiar with us, he was very firm on all proper occasions, never indulged us in anything that was not good for us, and exacted the most implicit obedience."

"Train up a child in the way he should go, and when he is old, he will not depart from it" (Proverbs 22:6 KJV).

Someone has said that good values are caught more than taught. "Do as I say, not as I do" doesn't stick in the hearts of our children.

> Father, help me to give the good counsel and precious gifts of wisdom that I have received to my children and to all those who look to me for leadership. Help me to be a role model of what I teach.

After the War for Southern Independence ended in defeat for the Confederacy, the soldiers of the South came home. Many were sick, and many had lost limbs. They received far less medical and financial help than their Northern counterparts. Many had no home to which to return. The former Confederates had a sad and difficult task of rebuilding their wartorn, devastated land and of caring for widows and orphans. As the Southerners struggled to rebuild their shattered lives, they found themselves fighting a different enemy—starvation. In the North the history books were labeling the war as "The War of Rebellion" and branding all Southerners as "treacherous traitors." One former Confederate said, "The historians tell our children, the children of all America and all the world, that the War Between the States was not only a rebellion, but a rebellion caused by the Southern States' desire to perpetuate the institution of slavery. If this be true, then we as a nation, as a race, must plead guilty to the most horrible indictment which could ever be brought against a nation."

"He that handleth a matter wisely shall find good, and whoso trusteth in the Lord, happy is he" (Proverbs 16:20 KJV).

In human conflicts, whether at the level of families or at the level of nations, it is seldom that one side is totally in the right and the other totally wrong. It is not always clear who, if anyone, holds the moral high ground. Nevertheless, both sides usually claim it.

> Father, help me to investigate matters wisely before believing and making a commitment. Help me always to seek Your guidance.

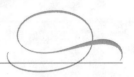

After the war an organization called the United Confederate Veterans (UCV) was formed to provide support for returning Confederate veterans. They helped by providing food and by building and sustaining homes. Also to counter what they considered a legacy of dishonor and a distortion of truth, they appealed to Southerners to tell their version of the war. Without the accounts and publications about the war by returning veterans, the truths that these Sons of the South had sacrificed for might never have been told. One said, "It was not a war for conquest or glory; to call it a rebellion is to speak ignorantly; to call it treason is to add viciousness to stupidity. It was a war of ideas, political conceptions, and of loyalty to ancient ideals of English freedom."

"These were more noble than those in Thessalonica in that they received the Word with all readiness of mind, and searched the Scriptures daily, whether these things were so" (Acts 17:11 KJV).

The child who lies about having his fingers in the cookie jar is engaging in revising history. So does every person who revises history to fit the currently fashionable ideas, e.g. political correctness. Happy is the one who is not deceived by such distortions.

> Father, as the Bereans searched the Scriptures to
> discover ultimate truth, help me to do likewise.
> Also, help me to discover the truth about history
> by broad and diligent study.

NOVEMBER 22

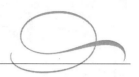

In 1852 Colonel Robert E. Lee was appointed superintendent of the Military Academy at West Point. Lee's oldest son, Custis, had been appointed to the academy two years previously. Lee was determined that his offspring would set a good example. He wrote, "I do not know what the cadets will say if the Superintendent's children do not practice what he demands of them. They will naturally say he had better attend to his own before he corrects other people's children." Lee served as superintendent for thirty-one months and is still recognized as one of the best ever to hold that position. Under his supervision at the Academy there arose cadets who became famous when the war came. For the Union there were Phillip Sheridan, O. O. Howard, James McPherson, and John Schofield. For the Confederacy there were Jeb Stuart, Fitzhugh Lee (Lee's nephew), John Hood, John Pegram, and William Pender.

"But the wisdom that is from above is first pure, then peaceable, gentle, and easy to be entreated, full of mercy and good fruits, without partiality, and without hypocrisy" (James 3:17 KJV).

Wisdom has much to do with wise words matched with equally wise behavior.

> Father, may I be filled with the Holy Spirit so that
> my life may be without even a hint of partiality or
> hypocrisy. May I wisely say what I mean and stead-
> fastly mean what I say.

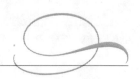

The cold, starving, and miserable Confederate soldiers enduring the Federal siege of Petersburg, Virginia received word that the women of Richmond, Virginia were delivering a "Christmas Feast" to arrive on New Year's Day. A Georgia soldier said, "Our mouths watered till January 1, 1865. On that day all who were able to do so got up very early. The army was to do nothing. The ladies were to do all. They would provide all vehicles, and the goodies would be taken to the half famished men by dainty hands. And we waited. What a long day that seemed to be! Noon came, then two, four, eight, ten, and twelve o'clock, and still no 'goodie wagon.' I became tired and went to sleep with the understanding that those on watch would call me when our dinner arrived. It was after 3:00 a.m. when a comrade called and told me that a detail had just gone out to meet the precious wagon. But O what a disappointment when the squad returned and issued to each man only one small sandwich made up of two tiny slices of bread and a thin slice of ham! A few men ventured to inquire, 'Is this all?' but I think they were ashamed of themselves the next moment. After the 'meal' was finished, a middle aged corporal lit his pipe and said, 'God bless our noble women! It was all they could do; it was all they had.' And every man sat in his tent and had a good cry."

"And they said unto Him, 'We have but five loaves and two fish'" (Matthew 14:17 KJV).

To give out of one's wealth is good. To give out of one's poverty and privation is wonderful.

> Father, You make a lot out of a little, especially when "all" is given. Help me to imitate the boy who gave away his lunch and the widow who gave away her last mite.

November 24

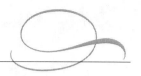

After the loss of Chattanooga, Tennessee and the defeat at Missionary Ridge, the Confederate army was in full retreat toward Dalton, Georgia, some thirty miles southeast. Another complication to their plight was that the artillery and supply wagons were bogged down in mud with Federal forces in hot pursuit. General Patrick Cleburne and his force of four thousand one hundred men were given charge of protecting the Confederate rear. Cleburne's superior, General Braxton Bragg, ordered him to proceed to a narrow railway cut beyond the town of Ringgold, Georgia, and "to hold this position at all hazards and keep back the enemy until the artillery and transportation of the army are secure." Cleburne and his force of four thousand one hundred with only two cannon dug in at Ringgold Gap to await the Union army that outnumbered the Confederates three to one.

"O God, the Lord, the strength of my salvation, Thou hast covered my head in the day of battle" (Psalm 140:7 KJV).

We don't know how each battle of life will end as we go into it. Perhaps we shall die. Perhaps we shall lose. But we know that ultimately, whatever the strength arrayed against us, we have victory in Jesus Christ.

> O LORD, even though the enemy is strong and is greater than I, I commit myself to the One who directs the battle, trusting Him to do what is best for His glory and his Kingdom.

NOVEMBER 25

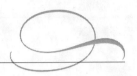

On November 25, 1863 at Ringgold Gap, Georgia a strong Union force approached the smaller Confederate number who were well entrenched. General Patrick Cleburne and his men held their fire until the Federals were almost upon them and then opened up with everything from pistol to cannon. The Federals reeled back and tried to flank the Confederates, first to the right, then to the left. They were beaten back at great loss. One Southern soldier noted, "It was the doggonedest fight in the war. The ground was piled with dead Yankees; they were piled in heaps. From the foot to the top of the hill was covered with the slain, all lying on their faces. It had the appearance of the roof of a house shingled with dead Yankees." Upon hearing that the artillery and wagons were out of the mud, Cleburne stayed a while longer to make sure before retreating. The Confederates suffered two hundred twenty-one casualties while the Union commander admitted to four hundred forty-two. But everyone was assured that the number was much higher. After their defeats at Chattanooga and Missionary Ridge, the Confederates could claim victory at Ringgold Gap.

"When they were but a few men in number, yea, very few, and the Lord wrought a great victory" (Psalm 105:12a and II Samuel 23:12b KJV).

The Confederates were well entrenched. Battles are coming for us too. Shall we not entrench ourselves in God's truth, hearing it preached, reading it, studying it, memorizing it, and meditating on it?

> Father, the greater the odds against me, the greater
> the glory for You. With You all things are possible,
> even bringing victory from defeat. After the cross
> came the empty tomb.

NOVEMBER 26

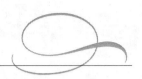

Union General William T. Sherman never explained why, after destroying three textile mills in Roswell, Georgia he ordered the workers, mostly women and young girls, arrested and sent to the North. A reporter wrote that hundreds of terrified women and girls were snatched away from their homes and allowed to take with them only their children and some clothing. Their only crime was "weaving tent cloth and spinning stocking yarn." While at Marietta, Georgia they were joined by one hundred more textile workers. General George H. Thomas reported to Sherman, "I can only order transportation to Nashville, Tennessee where it seems hard to turn them adrift. What had best be done with them?" Sherman answered, "They will be sent to Indiana where they could earn a living there and won't do us any harm." A Federal officer said that most were attractive and it was a "hard job to keep the guards away from them." A newspaper reported, "The refugees from the Sweetwater Factory and from Roswell are going north by train as fast as can be afforded." A Louisville, Kentucky paper reported that they were, "sent here by order of General Sherman, to be transferred north of the Ohio River." No one knows what happened to these people after they reached Louisville or whether they ever returned to their homes and loved ones. One newspaper in Louisville ran this ad: "Families wishing seamstresses or servants can be suited by applying at the refugee quarters on Broadway, between Ninth and Tenth."

"By the rivers of Babylon, there we sat down, yea, we wept when we remembered Zion" (Psalm 137:1 KJV).

Recent events of history reveal that the fact of war does not justify whimsical cruelty. A war crime is a sin against the Almighty.

> Father, in a military war and in the spiritual conflict there are refugees and displaced people. But they are not the enemy. Help us to discern who the enemy is, and to show compassion to the innocent victims of war.

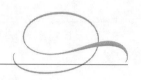

As the sun set on the evening of September 19, 1863, it appeared that the terrible fighting was over at the battle of Chickamauga, Georgia. Some of the bloodiest fighting of the war had taken place with attacks and counterattacks all over the battlefield. Neither line broke, but both suffered terrible casualties. "It seemed as if the fires of earth and hell had been turned loose in one mighty effort to destroy each other." Confederate General Patrick Cleburne's division launched a twilight attack that crashed into the Union line, pushing it back a mile and capturing three cannon and three hundred prisoners. Then darkness halted the fighting.

"A time to love and a time to hate; a time of war and a time of peace" (Ecclesiastes 3:8 KJV).

Fighting a war is terrible. Living under a tyranny is worse.

> Father, the warrior knows how terrible war is. He also knows that peace is won not by pacifism, but by subduing evil. Help us to commit our lives as warriors to that end.

NOVEMBER 28

Because South Carolina was the first to secede from the Union, its lot after the war was especially hard. The cities were in ruin. An observer noted: "The landscape looked for miles like a broad black streak of ruin and desolation—fences all gone; lonesome smokestacks, surrounded by dark heaps of ashes and cinders, marking the spots where human habitations had stood." The U. S. Congress established military rule and a puppet government for twelve years after the war; the former confederate states were powerless to prevent it. Those of the South especially hated two kinds of people: Carpetbaggers—Northerners who came down south with carpetbag suitcases to buy up land, property, and holdings at depressed rates and sell them at higher prices to Northern interests. Scalawags—they were hated worse. These were Southerners who collaborated with the Carpetbaggers or directly with the Northern profiteers to pillage and rob their own people. Their unscrupulous activities prompted one Carpetbagger, "Honest John " Patterson to say, "There are still five more years of good stealing in South Carolina."

"Thou shalt not steal" (Exodus 20:15 KJV).

There are myriad ways of stealing—cheating on income taxes, goofing off at work, shoplifting, robbing a bank, etc. For legislators it can be accomplished by raising taxes unjustifiably. Whether the amount taken is small or great, it is still stealing.

> Father, sometimes (though Your commands are clear) we find reasons to ignore them. Although this is from the Old Testament, we are still responsible to obey it. If our consciences are not clear on this issue, help us to repent of stealing and to make restitution.

NOVEMBER 29

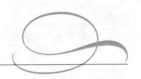

In the winter of 1864–1865 the Confederate army in their trenches around Petersburg, Virginia were literally starving as the Union Army's siege grew longer and tighter around the beleaguered city. One Confederate cavalryman said, "What we had was corn pone cooked three days before and raw Nassau bacon. I was hungry, so hungry that I thanked God that I had a backbone for my stomach to lean against." But compared to the infantrymen in the trenches, this trooper was eating "high on the hog." In addition to being hungry, they were cold, wet, and muddy as they dodged sniper fire. Though the country was picked clean and the little food they did have was hard to distribute, still they carried on. They knew that they were the only substantial Confederate force in the field. They called themselves, "Lee's Miserables," and they let it be known that they would continue the fight.

"Praying always with all prayer and supplication in the Spirit and watching thereunto with all perseverance and supplication for all saints" (Ephesians 6:18 KJV).

Our duty is to persevere in the basics of the Christian walk: Christ the center, obedience to Him, time in the Word, prayer, fellowship, and witnessing.

> Father, as these cold and hungry Rebel soldiers
> persevered in their duty, help me to persevere in
> prayer and the other basics.

NOVEMBER 30

As vast as the differences were between North and South during the War Between the States, the warriors on both sides experienced one thing in common—the savagery of battle and the remembrance of it years later. After the war a Union soldier wrote of the September 19, 1863 battle of Chickamauga, Georgia: "The line in front of us stalks grimly into the smoke. Men cheer, but in that awful roar the voice of a man cannot be heard ten feet away. Men fall to the right and to the left. The line stumbles over corpses as it hurries on. There are flashes in the smoke cloud, terrible explosions in the air, and men are stepped on or leaped over as they throw up their arms and fall upon the grass and scream in the agony of mortal wounds." A Federal cannoneer whose artillery battery fired into a charging Confederate unit said, "The ditch was literally filled of dead and wounded. At this point it actually seemed a pity to kill men so. They fell in heaps, and I had it in my heart to order the firing to cease, to end the awful sight."

"Though I walk in the midst of trouble, Thou wilt revive me" (Psalm 137:7 KJV).

In the awful roar of battle, whether it is an earthly battle or a spiritual battle, God alone can keep us oriented.

> Father, my life is in Your hands. I have given it to
> You not in half measure but the whole to do as
> You will. May I be a warrior filled with the Holy
> Spirit, doing all that duty requires and more.

DECEMBER 1

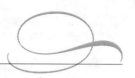

When darkness finally brought the battle of Chickamauga to a halt, soldiers on both sides slept on the ground in freezing temperatures with their weapons by their sides. A Southern infantryman remembered, "All through the night a sharp fire was kept up between the pickets, and the booming of cannon reminded us of the carnage of the past day, and the coming horrors of tomorrow. The cries and moans of the helpless wounded lying between the lines was especially grievous. The plight of these poor fellows was perfectly awful. Friend and foe lying side by side; it was the hardest part of the battle to lie within hearing and not be able to assist them."

"Blessed be the Lord my strength, which teacheth my hands to war, and my fingers to fight" (Psalm 144:1 KJV).

It could be that tomorrow's battle will bring horrors and carnage. We may be perplexed, but we are not in despair. We may be struck down, but we can not be destroyed.

> Father, thank You for my comrades who fight beside me. Give us victory over those who are filled with hate and are bent on doing evil. Help me to heal the wounded and encourage the weak and weary.

DECEMBER 2

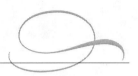

When George B. McClellan took command of the Union Army in June, 1861 in what is now West Virginia, he issued this statement to his men: "Soldiers! I have heard there was danger here. I have come to place myself at your head and share it with you. I fear now but one thing, that you will not find foemen worthy of your steel." Three weeks later he launched an offensive against a much smaller Confederate force in the area and defeated them. He then had this to say: "Soldiers of the Army of the West! I am more than satisfied with you. You have annihilated two armies commanded by educated and experienced soldiers entrenched in mountain fastnesses." McClellan actually had little to do with his army's success, and the Southerners had suffered defeat, not annihilation. But the Northern press, anxious for a hero after I Manassas, dubbed him "Young Napoleon." In a letter to his wife McClellan wrote: "President, Cabinet, General Scott, and all deferring to me, by some strange operation of magic. I seem to have become the power of the land. I almost think that were I to win some small success now I could become a dictator."

"The fear of the Lord is to hate evil. Pride and arrogancy, and the evil way and the froward mouth I hate" (Proverbs 8:13 KJV).

There are some Christian leaders who have seen marvelous success turn into shameful defeat because they began to credit themselves with it.

> Father, in any success that You bring into my life,
> keep pride and arrogance chained and away from
> me where they can do no harm. Only to You be the
> glory, honor, and praise.

December 3

Much has been written about the Union Army under General William Sherman during the infamous "March From Atlanta to the Sea." It left a wake of desolation and destruction. A young mother in Georgia held her two young sons as she watched the Federal soldiers ransack and destroy her home. She said, "Our men will fight you as long as they live, and these boys'll fight you when they grow up." They took food, destroyed what they didn't want and stole valuables. They searched yards for buried items, especially under fresh dirt. In a plantation yard Union soldiers dug up a box and pried it open. Out came the stench of a dead dog. The lady of the house said, "It looks like poor Curly will get no rest. That's the fourth time he's been dug up today."

"Behold, the eye of the Lord is upon them that fear Him, upon them that hope in His mercy" (Psalm 33:18 KJV).

People imagine that they will not be held accountable for harsh deeds. Perhaps not always in this life, but there will be justice in the life to come for the unrepentant.

> Father, I am a soldier. Gird and strengthen me for
> the battle whether it is military or spiritual. But
> help me to show mercy to the weak and helpless
> non-combatants caught up in it.

DECEMBER 4

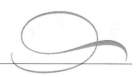

In September of 1864 superior numbers of Union troops captured the Confederate Fort Harrison. After two failed attempts to recapture the fort, Confederate forces dug new earthworks three-and-a-half miles long and closer to the capital of Richmond, Virginia. A Southern soldier who was involved in the work said: "We have been working day and night and scarcely have time to eat what little grub we have to eat." On October 12 General U. S. Grant ordered a "strong reconnaissance to drive the enemy from the work." A Federal officer said, "The reconnaissance was begun with a feeling on the part of nearly every officer and soldier in the command that we were simply marching out to lose several hundred men and be repulsed." The Federals attacked what they thought to be a gap in the Confederate lines only to discover it was a recess and they were taking fire from three sides in a cul-de-sac of death. They had "advanced with a cheer" even though there was "a disturbed look on the face of every officer." The result was predictable: the North withdrew after losing four hundred thirty-seven men; the South lost forty.

"For Thou art my Rock and my fortress. Therefore for Thy name's sake lead me, and guide me" (Psalm 31:3 KJV).

Rudyard Kipling wrote these words about war in Afghanistan: "When your officer's dead and the sergeants look white, remember it's ruin to run from a fight. So take open order, lie down, and sit tight, and wait for supports like a soldier." We can sit tight in God, our fortress.

> Father, You are an impregnable fortress. I am safe
> as long as I abide in You.

DECEMBER 5

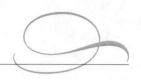

Union forces under General William T. Sherman did not suffer many defeats, but one came in December 27–29, 1862 as the Federals attacked Confederate positions at Chickasaw Bluffs, Mississippi. The Southerners were under the command of General Stephen D. Lee of South Carolina. Lee was the youngest lieutenant general in the Confederacy and one of the most talented. He had made his lines almost impregnable in their defensive position north of Vicksburg. A Union soldier attested to that when he said, "The proposed point of attack upon the bluff proved to be the interior of an arc or semicircle, so as the storming brigade advanced it found itself in the center of a converging fire, a flaming hell of shot shell, shrapnel, canister, and minie balls. Balls came zip-zip into the trees and the ground around us, occasionally, thud, a bullet takes some poor fellow and he is carried to the rear." Before Sherman called off the attacks and retired from the field, the casualty count was 1,776 for the Federals (208 dead, 1005 wounded and 563 missing). For the Confederates, 207 (63 dead, 134 wounded, 10 missing).

"I have set the Lord always before me; because He is at my right hand, I shall not be moved" (Psalm 16:8 KJV).

We have an impregnable defensive position in Christ. However, we must be vigilant to abide in Him.

> Father, in Your power and strength, help me to
> stand fast against the attacks of the enemy until
> he is defeated and You achieve the victory.

DECEMBER 6

Stung with the assertion that he was a "maneuvering general" and not a "fighting general," Union General William T. Sherman decided to attack the Confederate force led by General Joe Johnston at Kennesaw Mountain, Georgia. After an hour-long cannonade by his two hundred artillery pieces, Sherman ordered the attack on what was still a very formidable Confederate defense. A Southern officer described what he saw that hot, steamy morning of June 27, 1864 at 9:00 a.m.: "As if by magic, there sprang from the earth a host of men, and in one long, waving line of blue the infantry advanced." A Confederate infantryman said, "A solid line of blue came up the hill. My pen is unable to describe the scene of carnage that ensued for the next two hours. Column after column of Federal soldiers were crowded upon that line. No sooner would a regiment mount our works than they were shot down or surrendered. Yet still they came." Soon Sherman called off the attack. Later one of General Sherman's staff said that it was necessary to show that Sherman's men could fight as well as Union General U. S. Grant's men in Virginia. This was the reason for the failed attack."

"Only by pride cometh contention, but with the welladvised is wisdom" (Proverbs 13:10 KJV).

In the military the mission comes first, then the men and women. But human life is sacred and should not be sacrificed for anything less just than the defense of the nation. Life must not be sacrificed in order to defend someone's reputation.

> Father, may I never hurt another just to prove a
> point or justify my position.

December 7

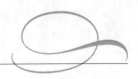

The very worst riot ever to occur in a city in the United States up to the time of the War between the States happened in New York City from July 13 through July 16, 1863. The Federal Government instituted the military draft in order to maintain a fresh supply of troops in the field to fight the rapidly dwindling numbers of Confederates. Many in New York City reacted with hostility; much of the rioters' rage was toward blacks living in the area. Mistakenly, many who rioted blamed the blacks for the war and the necessity of the draft. They hunted down and murdered many black people. Fifteen Union regiments and three batteries of cannon, fresh from the battle of Gettysburg, were ordered to put the riot down. They did at the cost of a thousand casualties, one hundred five dead, and a million and a half dollars in damages.

"And the people shall be oppressed, everyone by another, and everyone by his neighbor" (Isaiah 3:5a KJV).

Participation in mob violence demonstrates ignorance of who God is in His omnipotence and sovereignty.

> Father, the sinful nature of man is so hideous, always seeking to blame others. I'll be greatly relieved to shed the one that plagues me when You come in the twinkling of an eye.

DECEMBER 8

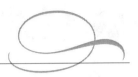

After being checked at the battle of the Wilderness and Spotsylvania Courthouse, Virginia, Union General U. S. Grant again tried to turn the Confederate right flank as he headed south. Confederate General Robert E. Lee, perceiving what Grant would do, sent General Richard Ewell and his force of six thousand to discover the exact position of the Federals and their strength. The Federals and Confederates met between the Alsop and Harris farms. This would be the last part of the battle of Spotsylvania. Next would come North Anna and Cold Harbor before the siege of Petersburg. Union Captain Augustus Brown of the 4th New York Heavy Artillery described the action: "I saw a rebel picket line advancing across an open field in our front. It was a magnificent sight, for the lines moved as steadily as if on parade." As the Federals took cover in the Harris farm house the Confederates opened fire. Captain Brown continues: "The balls came through as if the building were paper." As the Federals pulled back, one survivor said, "The enemy's fire was simply terrible; the ground which was brown and bare when we formed the line, was soon covered with a carpet of leaves and foliage, cut from the limbs of young pine trees."

"Some trust in chariots, and some in horses, but we will remember the name of the Lord our God" (Psalm 20:7 KJV).

To trust our own resources and our own strength is a mistake. Even when we are strong (and especially when we are strong) we must take heed that our reliance is on God alone.

> Father, may our trust be in You as we fight Your battles. May the battles Your warriors fight be always for Your glory.

DECEMBER 9

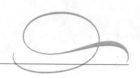

Confederate Commander of the Army of Tennessee, General Braxton Bragg, ordered an attack by his troops on strong, entrenched Federal positions on the last day of the battle of Murfreesboro/Stone's River, Tennessee. All of Bragg's subordinates thought the plan was fool-hardy and suicidal. Division commander, General John Breckinridge told one of his brigadiers, "If I should die, do justice to my memory, and tell the people that I believed the attack to be very unwise, and tried to prevent it." General Roger Hanson called the attack "mur-derous," but he still rode to the front of his brigade, preparing them to make the charge. He called out to them, "The order is to load, fix bayonets and march through this brushwood. Then charge at double quick to within one hundred yards of the enemy, deliver fire, and go at him with the bayonet." Breckinridge noted, "There was noth-ing to prevent the enemy from observing nearly all our movements and preparations." At 4:00 p.m. on January 2, 1863, the signal was given and forty-five hundred Confederates began an attack into what would be a raging inferno. General Breckinridge survived the attack. Thirty-five year old Roger Hanson did not.

"We are troubled on every side, yet not distressed. We are per-plexed, but not in despair" (II Corinthians 4:18 KJV).

Christ is sufficient for us in every situation. For us, even death is noth-ing more than the door into a life more abundant than we can imagine.

> Father, thank You that Christ is greater than the things we fear the most. He has conquered the most desperate enemy mankind has ever had—death.

DECEMBER 10

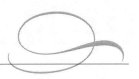

At the battle of Murfreesboro/Stone's River, Tennessee, one Confederate remembered the charge into the Union lines on January 2, 1863: "There were bursting shells that completely drowned out the voice of man, plunging and tearing through our columns." As the Confederates continued the attack, the first Federal line was broken and three brigades were pushed back and were in full retreat. However, the Union artillery raked the Confederates with fire from fifty-seven cannon from across Stone's River as they pushed the Union troops down the slope to the river. That same Southern soldier said, "The very earth trembled as with an exploding mine, and a mass of iron hail was hurled upon us. There were falling timbers, crashing arms, the whirring of missiles in every direction, the bursting of the dreadful shell, the groans of the wounded, the shouts of officers, mingled in one horrid din."

"Yea, though I walk through the valley of the shadow of death, I will fear no evil for Thou art with me. Thy rod and Thy staff, they comfort me" (Psalm 23:4 KJV).

Though the situation was terrifying, God was present with His own in the midst of iron hail and bursting shells.

> Father, how comforting to know that wherever I
> am and in whatever situation, You are there.

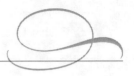

The battle flag became almost a sacred banner to those who fought under it in the War Between the States. Twenty years after the war Confederate battle flags lay rotting in storehouses in the North after being captured or surrendered. Veteran groups in the south requested that the flags be returned. In 1887 President Grover Cleveland, believing that enough reconciliation had taken place, signed the order to return the tattered banners. But he quickly had to rescind the order due to tremendous objections from Union veterans' groups and others. The commander of the Grand Army of the Republic (GAR) said, "May God palsy the hand that wrote that order. May God palsy the brain that conceived it, and may God palsy the tongue that dictated it." Many Northerners insisted that the flags be burned, not returned. It was said that the banners were mementos of as foul a crime as any in human history." Northerners debated the flag issue vigorously; many thought that was why Cleveland lost his bid for reelection. It was 1905 before many of the flags were returned. Sadly that was after many of the men who had fought heroically under them and cherished them had died.

"Lift ye up a banner upon the high mountain" (Isaiah 13:2a KJV).

Symbols are important. A flag is a symbol of a nation. A cross is a symbol of the Gospel of Jesus Christ.

> Father, the battle flag was an inspiration and motivation to the men who carried it into battle. So is the cross of Christ for me.

DECEMBER 12

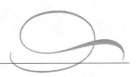

Twenty- year-old Confederate soldier, Robert Alonzo Walden, penned this poem to his sister: "Think of me Sister in dark silent night—when deep blue above us is sprinkled with light—That sweet peaceful hour will soften the heart—and bid all unkindness forever depart—Think of me Sister in moments of joy—When no shadow darkens, no gloom can annoy—Think of me Sister as I think of thee—Fondly and ever, ah think of me." Robert Walden of South Carolina survived the war and was captured at the battle of Five Forks, Virginia just eight days before General Lee surrendered to General Grant at Appomattox, Virginia.

"That ye have good remembrance of us always, desiring greatly to see us, as we also to see you" (I Thessalonians 3:6b KJV).

Shall we not remember and think all the more of Christ who was there for us, taking all the harm and death the enemy could deliver in order that we might live free of blame and escape the wrath of God we so justly deserved?

> Father, thank You for sweet memories of people and events that brought me into a personal, intimate relationship with the Lord Jesus Christ.

DECEMBER 13

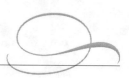

One of the most controversial men of the era of the War Between the States was John Brown. Ardently anti-slavery, Brown and his sons and followers murdered several pro-Confederate men and boys in the period before the war in "Bloody Kansas." Also before the war in 1831 in Virginia, a slave named Nat Turner and as many men as he could gather murdered fifty-five whites. Of those, thirteen were men, eighteen were women, and twenty-four were children. Turner and his gang were caught, tried, and hanged. In 1859 Brown and his followers, financed by wealthy Northern abolitionists, attempted to seize the Federal arsenal at Harper's Ferry, Virginia. His goal was to arm the slaves in the South and bring about a slave insurrection. The raid failed when Colonel Robert E. Lee and a detachment of U. S. Marines defeated the raiders, killing two of Brown's sons and wounding him. Brown was tried in October, 1859, convicted, and hanged on December 2, 1859. Much to the relief of those who financed him, he refused to name them. He was seen as a martyr in the North. Some even called him a saint, and bells rang in Northern churches when he was executed. Southerners who remembered Nat Turner viewed Brown as a cold-blooded murderer.

"Deliver me, O Lord, from the evil man. Preserve me from the violent man" (Psalm 140:1 KJV).

One form of evil is to seek a legitimate end by an illegitimate means.

> Father, before I act, guide me according to Your will and Your Word in all things.

DECEMBER 14

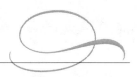

In 1864 Union General William T. Sherman slowed the pace of his march through Georgia from fifteen to ten miles per day so that his men might have more time to forage, pillage, and destroy anything that might benefit the starving Confederacy. A lady in Georgia who had been wealthy but was left destitute had this to say: "But like demons they rushed in! My yards are full. To my smokehouse, my dairy, pantry, kitchen and cellar, like famished wolves they come breaking locks and whatever is in their way. The thousand pounds of meat in my smokehouse is gone in a twinkling; my flour, my meat, my lard, butter, eggs are all gone. My eighteen fat turkeys, my hens, chickens, and fowl, my young pigs are shot down in my yard and hunted as if they were rebels themselves." A Federal soldier said, "This is probably the most gigantic pleasure expedition ever planned."

"I know the Lord will maintain the cause of the afflicted, and the right of the poor" (Psalm 140:12 KJV).

We live in a fallen world, and justice is not always immediate, and relief for the afflicted is not always immediate. Nevertheless, the Lord is the Comforter of the afflicted and the Judge of evildoers. In His time He will bring it to pass.

> Father, in war there are always those who are poor and afflicted. How comforting it is to know the One who sees the sparrow when it falls, who comforts us in our times of need, pain, and grief.

DECEMBER 15

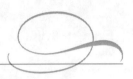

In the late afternoon of August 28, 1862 at Groveton, Virginia, Confederate General Stonewall Jackson gave orders to his officers to align their men for battle and attack the Federal troops who were marching along the road to Centerville, Virginia. Captain William Blackford described what happened next: "Every officer whirled around and scurried back to the woods at full gallop. The men had been watching their officers with as much interest as they had been watching Jackson, and when they wheeled and dashed towards them, they knew what it meant, and from the woods arose a hoarse roar like that from the cages of wild beasts at the scent of blood. Soon long columns of glittering brigades, like huge serpents glided out upon the open field. Then all advanced in as perfect order as if they had been on parade." Six brigades, six thousand Confederates under the command of General Richard Ewell and William Taliaferro attacked the combined Union force under the command of Generals John Gibbon and Abner Doubleday. Gibbon's troops had never been in combat before. During the battle, General Ewell would lose a leg and General Taliaferro would be wounded three times, but remained on the field.

"O God, the Lord, the strength of my salvation, Thou hast covered my head in the day of battle" (Psalm 140:7 KJV).

Jackson's troops displayed a genuine eagerness for battle. Should we not likewise be eager for today's skirmishes, knowing that our General is greater than Stonewall Jackson?

> Father, there is a battle to be fought every day. Christ is my champion. In Him I will be victorious today.

December 16

At the battle of Groveton, Virginia, the opposing lines of Confederates and Federals came within one hundred yards of each other and opened fire. There was no retreating, no tactics, no maneuvering, just loading and firing between the two lines until darkness brought an end to the hostilities. The Federals then withdrew from the field. Union General Gibbon's green troops became veterans in a hurry. In his "black hat" brigade from Wisconsin and Indiana, the casualty count was nine hundred out of twenty-one hundred. Total losses were about thirteen hundred casualties on each side. The next day Confederate Captain William Blackford walked to the battlefield and said, "The bodies lay in so straight a line that they looked like troops lying down to rest. On each front the edge was sharply defined, while toward the rear of each it was less so, showing how men had staggered backward after receiving their death blow."

"As it is appointed unto man, once to die, but after that, the judgment" (Hebrews 9:27 KJV).

Man knows not his time. It is not certain that any of us will live to be a day older. Let us then be ready for death if it comes sooner instead of later.

> Father, death comes to us all, but because of Christ's atoning sacrifice, not all will be condemned in judgment. For the believer, only his works will be judged. For this wonderful truth we praise and give thanks to You, the Lord of Hosts.

DECEMBER 17

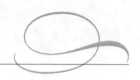

Early in the morning of December 28, 1861, two companies of Federal cavalry were watering their horses in a creek near Sacramento, Kentucky, when over a ridge came a horde of Confederate cavalry screaming the rebel yell and led by a lieutenant colonel. There was fierce, close-range fighting with sabers and pistols until more yelling Southern cavalrymen hit the Union flanks. The Yankee cavalry broke and ran with the Confederates in full pursuit. One Southern horseman said, "We followed them about two and a half miles shooting them at every sight." Every time the Federals stopped to make a stand, on came the lieutenant colonel, slashing and shooting, followed by his men. At the end of the fight the casualty count was amazingly low. Although this battle had no impact in the war, one thing really stood out: this lieutenant colonel with no previous military training had a fierce ability to fight. He would be a force to be reckoned with. This was the first battle for Nathan Bedford Forrest.

"And of Benjamin; Eliada, a mighty man of valor and with him armed men with bow and shield two hundred thousand" (II Chronicles 17:17 KJV).

When a hero comes along, he takes the initiative for what is right and strikes the enemy with all his strength, not concerned for what injuries he might receive.

> Father, Jesus is a mighty man of valor and a force to be reckoned with. The forces of evil have discovered this, and they will be learning much more about it. Praise the Lord!

DECEMBER 18

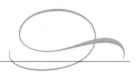

Prior to an amendment to the Constitution banning the right of a state to secede from the Union, it was agreed and understood that states had that right. Senator Henry Cabot Lodge wrote: "It is safe to say that there was not a man in the country from Washington and Hamilton to Clinton and Mason, who did not regard the new system as an experiment from which each and every State had a right to peaceably withdraw." A classroom textbook used at West Point before the war states, "The secession of a State depends on the will of the people of such a State." It was held that a state could choose to leave the Union as it chose to join it. The bloody war took place to destroy that theory. No Confederate leader was brought to trial after the war for treason in the fear that the constitutional legality of secession would be presented as a defense. Jefferson Davis wanted such a trial, but after two years of imprisonment he was released with no trial. All charges were dropped.

"Judges and officers shalt thou make thee in all thy gates which the Lord thy God giveth thee, throughout thy tribes and they shall judge the people with just judgment" (Deuteronomy 16:18 KJV).

One necessity for the security of a nation is to have leaders who are in submission to the rule of law. Once the rule of law is subverted, the one who has the biggest stick becomes the leader and the tyrant.

> Father, please raise up godly people in leadership who govern with just judgment. May this be especially so for our Commander-in-Chief.

DECEMBER 19

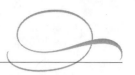

In July, 1864, Union General George Stoneman and four regiments of horsemen raced south through Georgia with the intention of destroying the track of the Macon and Western railroad and then freeing Union prisoners of war held at the Andersonville, Georgia prison camp. Dividing his force, he opted to forego the destruction of the railroad track and just free the prisoners. He rode south toward Macon with twenty-five hundred men. As the Federals drew near, the governor of Georgia issued this plea: "To the citizens of Macon, Headquarters, Macon, July 30, 1864—The enemy is now in sight of your houses. We lack force. I appeal to every man, Citizen or Refugee, who has a gun of any kind, or can get one, to report to the Court House with the least possible delay, that you may be thrown into Companies and aid in the defense of the city. A prompt response is expected from every patriot. Joseph E. Brown—Report to Colonel Cary W. Styles, who will forward an organization as rapidly as possible." The volunteers and local militia put up a stout resistance until the Southern cavalry arrived. After a six-hour battle General Stoneman and seven hundred of his troopers were captured and made prisoners.

"Be ye steadfast, unmoveable, always abounding in the work of the Lord, forasmuch as ye know that your labor is not in vain in the Lord" (I Corinthians 15:58 KJV).

There is much value in maintaining composure in times of crisis and of holding one's ground.

> Father, thank you that sometimes the smaller force may win when the cause is just and the warriors steadfast.

DECEMBER 20

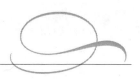

Trying to stem the advance of the Union army as it threatened Atlanta, Georgia, Confederate General John B. Hood ordered three separate attacks on the firmly entrenched Federal lines at Ezra Church, Georgia on July 28, 1864. The first two failed with terrible Southern losses. Then at 3:00 p.m. General Edward C. Walthall's division launched the third attack. A Union officer reported: "Three times he led that grand veteran column into the jaws of death, to charge upon our works, and three times they were repulsed. It seemed as if half the army were firing at the General. I took seven shots at him myself as fast as a musket could be loaded for me. I have seen many mounted officers under fire and in battle, but never saw any man bear himself with more heroic daring in the face of death on every side than he did on that day." As with the first two attacks the third also failed with great sacrifice of life before General Walthall called it off and withdrew to Atlanta. In ten days of fighting the Confederates sustained eighteen thousand casualties. On the night of the battle a Union picket called out to his Southern counterpart: "Well, Johnny, how many of you are left?" The reply was, "Oh about enough for another killing."

"The beauty of Israel is slain upon Thy high places. How are the mighty fallen" (II Samuel 1:19 KJV).

We respect the military because they willingly surrender their lives for the welfare of others. In so doing they faintly resemble our Savior who willingly sacrificed His life for our eternal salvation.

> Father, how costly the battle is where often the
> best and most promising fall. Please receive them
> into Your Kingdom.

December 21

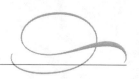

The purposes of the cavalry in the war were many. Not only were they to fight, but also to gather intelligence about the strengths and weakness of the opposition and to screen the movements of their own army from the enemy. One of the reasons for the Union defeat at the battle of Chancellorsville, Virginia in May of 1863 was that the Federal commander, Joe Hooker, had sent his cavalry force of ten thousand troopers, twenty-two cannons, and two hundred seventy-five wagons south on a raid and away from the battle. This deprived him of his eyes and ears. Without the intelligence the cavalry could have provided, Hooker was caught off guard when Confederate General Stonewall Jackson struck the undefended right flank of the Federal army. The three day battle sent the Federals back across the Rappahannock River in full retreat. It was the Confederate cavalry under the command of J.E.B. Stuart who reported to General Robert E. Lee the weakness of the Union right flank. Lee then planned the successful attack. The Confederate cavalry had been in place when needed; the Federal cavalry had not been. To make matters worse, the Union cavalry raid did little damage and had no effect on the war.

"For the Lord giveth wisdom. Out of His mouth cometh knowledge and understanding" (Proverbs 2:6 KJV).

Intelligence is vital in earthly wars and in the spiritual warfare. Our intelligence about the enemy and his wicked devices comes only from Jesus Christ and His Word, the Bible. Have you received today's report? Or is your flank vulnerable?

> Father, help me to seek Your counsel before I make any decision.

DECEMBER 22

In May of 1863 Union General Joe Hooker sent his cavalry force under the command of George Stoneman south to raid with these instructions: "Turn the enemy's position on his left, throwing the cavalry between him and Richmond, isolating him from his supplies, checking his retreat, and inflicting on him every possible injury which will tend to his discomfort and defeat. If you cannot cut off from his column large slices, the General desires that you will not fail to take small ones. Let your watchword be fight, fight, fight, bearing in mind that time is as valuable to the General as rebel carcasses." Hooker then wired President Lincoln: "My plans are perfect, and when I start to carry them out, may God have mercy on Bobbie Lee; for I shall have none." Lincoln replied: "The hen is the wisest of all creatures. She cackles after she lays the eggs." The raid had to be deemed a failure. One Federal trooper noted : "Our only accomplishments were the burning of a few canal boats on the upper James River, some bridges, hen roosts, and tobacco houses." No large engagements were fought but the Federals lost one thousand horses, eighty-two men killed or wounded and three hundred seven missing. The worst was that the Union cavalry was absent from the battle of Chancelorsville.

"The lot is cast into the lap, but the whole disposing thereof is of the Lord" (Proverbs 16:33 KJV).

We need not lament our defeats if we have been faithful. We must not cackle before the egg of victory is laid.

> Father, You direct all things. I will be grateful for Your disposition of all events because You are sovereign. You do what You please and no one can stay Your hand.

DECEMBER 23

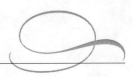

At the battle of Chickamauga, Georgia, on September 19, 1863, a northern reporter had this to say about Confederate attacks against the Union division under the command of General John M. Brannan: "The enemy bore down upon Brannan like a mountain torrent, sweeping away a brigade as if it had been driftwood." The fighting raged back and forth as the Federals were gradually pushed back. A Confederate officer described the battle: "Neighing horses, wild and frightened, were running in every direction; whistling, seething, cracking bullets, the piercing, screaming fragments of shells, the whining sound of shrapnel and the savage shower of cannister all united in one horrible sound. The Chickamauga ran red with blood. The ghastly, mangled dead and horribly wounded strewed the earth for over half a mile. The dead were piled upon each other in ricks, like cordwood, to make passage for advancing columns."

"Whereas ye know not what shall be on the morrow, for what is your life? It is even a vapour, that appeareth for a little time, and then vanisheth away" (James 4:14 KJV).

It is not just in war that men's lives vanish. Seize the day!

> Father, life on earth is so short. Help me to live
> each day, especially today as I should.

DECEMBER 24

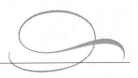

Probably the most feared artillery round in the war was cannister. Used against attacking infantry at short range of four hundred yards or less, cannister had no equal as a cause of devastation and death. A round of cannister was a thin metal cylinder much like a tomato can filled with musket, lead, or iron balls. Some rounds contained nails or some other scrap metal. When the powder ignited, the can would spew out the balls like a giant shotgun from the cannon's muzzle. Cannister rounds killed more men in the war than all other artillery rounds combined. The artillerymen often loaded double or triple charges of cannister when the attacking infantry were within two hundred yards or less. Union General Alpheus Williams described the effect of firing cannister into advancing Confederate ranks: "The Rebels followed with a yell but three or four of our batteries being in position they were received with a tornado of cannister. Each cannister contains several hundred balls. They fell in the very front of the lines stirring up dust like a thick cloud. When the dust blew away no regiment and not a living man was to be seen."

"He shall flee from the iron weapon and the bow of steel shall strike him through" (Job 20:24 KJV).

Tomorrow is the day on which we celebrate the most important birth of all history—the birthday of the Prince of Peace.

> Father, I confess it is easier to devise terrible weapons
> of war than to bring about peace and reconciliation.
> Please hasten the day of the Prince of Peace who will
> surely come again.

DECEMBER 25

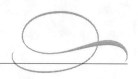

Private Edward Cooper from North Carolina deserted from his post and was caught. At his court martial he produced this letter from his wife: "My dear Edward, I have always been proud of you, and since connection with the Confederate army, I have been prouder of you than ever before. I would not have you do anything wrong for the world, but before God, Edward, unless you come home we must die. Last night I was aroused by little Eddie's crying. I called and said, 'What is the matter, Eddie?' and he said, 'O Mamma, I am so hungry.' And Lucy, Edward, your darling Lucy, she never complains but she is getting thinner and thinner every day. And before God, Edward, unless you come home, we must die." Private Cooper received no punishment for his desertion but was returned to duty. Fourteen other deserters from Tennessee were not so fortunate. They were executed by firing squad. Their chaplain wrote, "I think they were objects of pity. They were ignorant, poor, and had families dependent upon them. War is a cruel thing; it heeds not a widow's tears, the orphan's moan, or the lover's anguish."

"For these things I weep; mine eye, mine eye runneth down with water, because the Comforter that should relieve my soul is far from me. My children are desolate, because the enemy prevailed" (Lamentations 1:16 KJV).

Today we celebrate the birthday of the Prince of Peace. When He comes again, "He shall judge the poor of the people, he shall save the children of the needy, and He shall break in pieces the oppressor" (Psalm 72:4 KJV).

> Father, thank You that when You appear very distant, the truth is that You are then closer than ever. Please draw near to us today, and help us to recognize Your presence.

DECEMBER 26

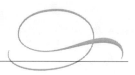

During the war a great Christian revival started in the Confederate Army of Northern Virginia and spread to the Southern armies in the west. In the winter and spring of 1863 one hundred fifty thousand Confederate soldiers trusted Christ as Savior and Lord. Reverend T. J. Stokes, chaplain of the 10th Texas Regiment, wrote this in a letter home: "I have never seen such a spirit as there is now in the army. Religion is the theme. Everywhere, you hear around the campfires the sweet song of Zion. This spirit pervades the whole army. God is doing a glorious work, and I believe it is but the beautiful prelude to peace. I feel confident that if the enemy should attempt to advance, that God will fight our battles for us, and the boastful foe be scattered and severely rebuked." Although Chaplain Stokes was mistaken about the outcome of the war, he was correct about God doing a glorious work. Two hundred men from the 10th Texas Regiment were baptized in one day on April 18, 1864.

"Though I walk in the midst of trouble, Thou wilt revive me" (Psalm 138:7a KJV).

Perhaps God will do a glorious work now, in my time. Perhaps I am here for such a time as this.

> Father, please bring renewal and revival. Begin
> with me.

As a great Christian renewal and revival swept through the Southern armies during the war, Private Benjamin W. Jones of the 3rd Virginia Infantry regiment wrote: "Old professors that had become lukewarm in their zeal, are arousing to a sense of their duty, and many of the openly sinful are growing more temperate and reverent in their regard for religious things. Many ministers have gone out as evangelists to the armies, and some have gone into the ranks as private soldiers, or have become regular chaplains in some command."

"So then because thou art lukewarm, and neither cold nor hot, I will spue thee out of my mouth" (Revelation 3:16 KJV).

A fresh awareness of God's holiness and of the great truths about spiritual reality will keep us from getting lukewarm.

> Father, never allow me to lose my zeal for Christ
> in the sharing of the Gospel.

DECEMBER 28

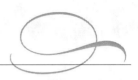

The State of Kentucky remained in the Union and did not join the Southern Confederacy. The 1st Kentucky Brigade of four thousand men was formed in 1861 and were trained in Tennessee. They were committed to the South and served with the Confederate Army of Tennessee. The Confederate Army was forced out of Kentucky in 1862, and so the 1st Kentucky never entered their home state during the war. Consequently they were called "The Orphan Brigade." This brigade participated in many major battles including Shiloh, Corinth, Vicksburg, Baton Rouge, Jackson, Chickamauga, and Missionary Ridge. One thousand two hundred of them took part in the charge at Stone's River, and only eight hundred returned. As the survivors stumbled back their commander was crying out, "My poor Orphans! My poor Orphans!" The Orphan's Brigade was one of the last of the Confederate units to surrender. When they lay down their arms in May of 1865, only five hundred of the original four thousand remained.

"We are orphans and fatherless. Our mothers are as widows" (Lamentations 5:3 KJV).

All of us who are Christians were once orphans in the spiritual sense. We were lost and without hope in the world, and the Father adopted us into His family.

> Father, regardless of our earthly family situation, when we trust Christ He adopts us into the family of God forever. He gives us the warmth of an eternal home and makes us a part of something glorious.

DECEMBER 29

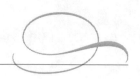

As if combat, disease, hunger, and the elements were not enough for the soldier in the War Between the States to deal with, another enemy raised its head: insects! The worst had to be body lice, burrowing through bedding and clothing, making life miserable. One Confederate wrote: "Months and months we were without a change of underclothing, or a chance to wash what we had worn so long, hence it became actually coated with grease and dust, moistened with daily perspiration under the boiling sun. Pestiferous vermin swarmed in every camp, and on the march, an indescribable annoyance to every well-raised man, yet seemingly ineradicable. Nothing would destroy the little pests but hours of steady boiling and, of course, we had neither kettles nor the time to boil them, if we had been provided with ample means." Another soldier wrote of his first acquaintance with body lice: "Up to this time we had maintained our self-respect and decency. I well remember the feeling of humiliation with which we made the discovery we were inhabited. We were inhabited! What could violate one's autonomy more than losing control of one's flesh?" They washed their clothes in a creek or stream if available and hung them from trees to dry, or from rifles when they were marching. They discarded or burned clothes that were beyond mending.

"Surely He will deliver thee from the snare of the fowler, and from the noisome pestilence" (Psalm 91:3 KJV).

If God notices when the sparrow falls, will He not have concern for even the small things that annoy us?

> Father, thank You that You deliver us from small pests that plague us as well as from the large ones.

DECEMBER 30

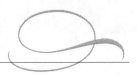

After the war Union Commanding General U. S. Grant said this about Confederate Major John Mosby (called the Gray Ghost by his Federal opponents): There were probably but few men in the South who could have commanded successfully a separate detachment in the rear of an opposing army and so near the border of hostilities as long as he (Mosby) did without losing his entire command." In March of 1863 Mosby led a raid behind Union lines and captured thirty-three Federals, including Brigadier General Edwin Stoughton, and fifty-eight horses. Upon hearing of the raid, President Abraham Lincoln remarked, "I am sorry, for I can make brigadier generals, but I can't make horses." Mosby survived the war though he suffered many battle wounds. His command was disbanded in April, 1865.

"And after him was Shamgar, the son of Anath which slew of the Philistines six hundred men with an ox goad, and he also delivered Israel" (Judges 3:31 KJV).

Perhaps God will help us to see what we can do for His glory though we hold a humble ox goad instead of a sword.

> Father, there is no limit to what a man can do
> when You call him and equip him.

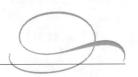

On April 9, 1865 at Appomattox, Virginia, surrounded by men and resources that outnumbered his own ten to one, Confederate General Robert E. Lee agonized over the decision he had to make. "There is nothing left for me but to go and see General Grant, and I had rather die a thousand deaths." As he looked over the mass of Union infantry in battle array against him, he was tempted: "How easily I could be rid of this, and be at rest! I have only to ride along the line and all will be over! But it is our duty to live. What will become of the women and children of the South if we are not there to protect them?" Then putting on his best uniform, he told an aide, "I have probably to be General Grant's prisoner and I thought I must make my best appearance." Then he mounted Traveller, and with Colonel Marshall and Sergeant Butler rode off to meet with General Grant and surrender the remnant of the

Army of Northern Virginia, putting an end to fighting and bloodshed. It was also an end to a country, a country that Lee and those who wore the gray had so heroically tried to establish. The Confederate States of America was no more.

Wilbur McLean home where Lee surrendered to Grant, Appomatox, Virginia, 1865.

"His troops come together and raise up their way against me and encamp round about my tabernacle" (Job 19:12 KJV).

Even in defeat if we are in Christ, we are more than conquerors.

> Father, though all seemed lost to General Lee, he held tightly to Your promises, and You sustained him. Sustain me too, and enable me to hold to duty when I encounter defeat and reverses in the battles of life.

BIBLIOGRAPHY/SOURCES

E. Porter Alexander, *Fighting for the Confederacy*, (Chapel Hill, North Carolina, University of North Carolina Press, 1989).

Dee Brown, *Bury My Heart at Wounded Knee*, (New York, Bantam Books, 1971).

Shelby Foote, *The Civil War, A Narrative, Volumes I-III*, (New York, Vintage, 1958, 1986).

John J. Dwyer, *The War Between the States, America's Uncivil War*, (Denton, Texas, Bluebonnet Press, 2005).

Thomas H. Flaherty, Editor, *The Civil War*, (Alexandria, Virginia, Time-Life Books, 1986).

Gary W. Gallagher, Editor, *Lee the Soldier*, (Lincoln, Nebraska, University of Nebraska Press, 1996).

Robert Selph Henry, *First with the Most—Forrest*, (Wilmington, North Carolina, Broadfoot Publishing Company, 1987).

Jed Hotchkiss, *The Confederate Military History of Virginia*, (USA, Blue and Gray Press).

Clint Johnson, *The Politically Incorrect Guide to the South (And Why It Will Rise Again)*, (Washington, DC, Regency Publishing Company, 2006).

Randolph H. McKim, *The Soul of Lee,* (Virginia, Virginia Gentleman Books, Stuart's Draft, 1918–2002).

Jack McLaughlin, *Gettysburg, the Long Encampment,* (New York, Bonanza Books, 1943).

Louisa H. A. Minor, *The Meriwethers and Their Connections,* (Joel Munsell's Sons, 1892).

Rodel H. Rumburg, *John Pelham of Alabama, the Gallant Chief of J. E. B. Stuart's Horse Artillery,* (Spout Springs, Virginia, Society for Biblical and Southern Studies, 2005).

Stewart Sifakis, *Who Was Who in the Civil War,* (New York, Facts on File Publications, 1988).

Philip Van Dorn Stern, *Robert E. Lee: the Man and the Soldier,* (New York, Bonanza Books, 1963).

Grady McWhiney, *The Civil War,* (Abilene, Texas, McWhiney Foundation, 2005).

Emory M. Thomas, *Bold Dragoon—The Life of J.E. B. Stuart,* (New York, Vintage Books, 1988).

Thomas E. Woods, *The Politically Incorrect Guide to American History,* (Washington, D C, Regency Publishing Company, 2004).

J. Steven Wilkens, *All Things for Good, the Steadfast Fidelity of Stonewall Jackson,* (Nashville, Tennessee, Cumberland House, 2004).

J. Steven Wilkens, *Call of Duty, the Sterling Nobility of Robert E. Lee,* (Elkdon, Maryland, Highland Books, 1997).

Civil War Historical Cards, Atlas Editions, 1994.

Civil War Preservation Trust Letter.